Media & Public Affairs
Robert Mann, Series Editor

REWIRING

Politics

Presidential Nominating Conventions
in the Media Age

EDITED BY COSTAS PANAGOPOULOS

LOUISIANA STATE UNIVERSITY PRESS
BATON ROUGE

Published in cooperation with the Kevin P. Reilly Center for Media and Public Affairs

Published by Louisiana State University Press
Manufactured in the United States of America
First printing

DESIGNER: Michelle A. Garrod
TYPEFACE: Adobe Caslon Pro, Univers
TYPESETTER: G&S Typesetters, Inc.
PRINTER AND BINDER: Edwards Brothers, Inc.

Library of Congress Cataloging-in-Publication Data
    Rewiring politics : presidential nominating conventions in the media age / edited by Costas
Panagopoulos.
        p.   cm. — (media and public affairs)
    "Published in cooperation with the Kevin P. Reilly Center for Media and Public Affairs."
    Includes bibliographical references and index.
    ISBN-13: 978-0-8071-3206-7 (cloth : alk. paper)
    ISBN-10: 0-8071-3206-3 (cloth : alk. paper)
        1. Political conventions—United States.   2. Nominations for office—United States.
3. Presidents—United States—Election.   4. Mass media—Political aspects—United States.
1. Panagopoulos, Costas.   11. Series.
    JK2255.P33 2007
    324.273′0156—dc22

                                                                            2006014073

The paper in this book meets the guidelines for permanence and durability of the Committee on
Production Guidelines for Book Longevity of the Council on Library Resources. ∞

To my parents—George and Vasiliki Panagopoulos

CONTENTS

REWIRING POLITICS

1

INTRODUCTION

Presidential Nominating Conventions in the Media Age

Costas Panagopoulos

Viewed as deliberative bodies, the national party conventions are an abomination—huge and disorderly assemblies of often inexperienced strangers faced with difficult and important decisions to make in a few days. But usually national conventions are not called upon to make decisions; most of the time they meet to legitimize and celebrate a decision that has already been made.

DONALD MATTHEWS, *Presidential Nominations: Process and Outcomes* (1974)

IT WAS ABOUT 6 A.M. on September 1, 2004, and I was on the tenth floor of Madison Square Garden in New York City—the epicenter of the American media universe for the week—waiting to begin an interview with a morning network news program about the Republican National Convention (RNC) that had convened its proceedings there the previous evening. The glass booth, one of dozens similarly transformed into mini television broadcast studios for the occasion, overlooked thousands of empty red, white, and blue chairs neatly arranged before a stage draped in patriotic colors. Outside, groggy—but still angry—anti-Bush protesters had started to assemble for what turned out to be another full day of anticlimactic demonstrations, while denizens of the 15,000-member press legion gathered inside to reflect on the convention activities. The usual suspects, experts and talking heads besides academic observers, were all there ready to do their part of the spin. (I passed former New York City mayor Rudy Giuliani, the previous evening's highly anticipated and highly energizing convention kick-off speaker, as I entered the booth.)

The reporter came in as I gazed at the ceiling where thousands of red, white, and blue balloons were being held captive by netting until their scheduled release on the final night of the convention following President Bush's acceptance speech. "You know they raised the whole floor of Madison Square Garden by six inches to make the hall look more intimate on TV," the reporter told me. "No, I didn't know," I answered, wondering how great the difference in viewers' perceptions must need to be to offset the expense incurred by the

RNC to create a more familial setting. "Yup, well, these little details seem to be all that counts at these things these days," he continued. Surely, he couldn't be right, I hoped, but I said, "It does seem that way, doesn't it?" The social scientist in me wondered how much truth there was in his statement. But when he asked me on the air whether conventions still matter, I emphatically, almost impulsively, rattled off a half dozen reasons why I believed conventions remain an important part of the process of presidential selection in America.

To argue convincingly that national conventions matter in American politics today and to understand fully their relationship to contemporary presidential campaigns, it is necessary to trace the evolution of these quadrennial events and to dissect the developments that have essentially transformed the nature and role of conventions in modern campaigns. To be sure, national nominating conventions have undergone significant changes over the past few decades, developments influenced in large part by the growth in mass media. In a sense, changes in mass media created an impetus—or a stimulus—to which convention organizers have responded. Some of these changes have provided parties unprecedented opportunities to capitalize on conventions while others have presented considerable challenges. Faced with both opportunities and challenges over the past few decades, political parties have adapted conventions in an effort to maximize their goals, indicating at the very least that conventions must serve some meaningful purpose and offer parties even modest benefits. Perhaps the best evidence that conventions continue to matter is that they continue to exist, even in altered form. After all, why would rational political parties invest so heavily in events that are entirely useless and ineffectual? Nevertheless, the manner in which conventions have evolved within the context of new (and sometimes hostile) media environments, has generated important questions for political observers. The selections included in this volume describe and analyze many of these developments and aim to provide readers with a comprehensive understanding of the complexities, realities, and implications associated with national nominating conventions in the media age. The discussion we advance is rooted in the following broad themes (or claims).

Developments in mass media have provided powerful stimuli for convention change. Not unlike the effects of the proliferation of newspapers and radio, the growth of television (and more recently, the Internet) has altered the environment in which conventions operate. On the one hand, parties benefit from the promise of widespread access to convention proceedings facilitated by television. On the other hand, broad access to conventions means parties must adjust convention content to balance appealing to moderate voters without turning off partisans. Moreover, competition for ratings in a climate of declining interest in politics has presented parties with new challenges to broaden the appeal of convention content. These conditions have altered party leaders' considerations in planning and executing conventions.

Conventions have changed in response to stimuli exerted by changes in mass media. Presidential nominating conventions have undergone significant change over the past five decades, and major adaptations have occurred largely in response to changes in the media. Television has probably influenced party leaders to adapt conventions more directly than any other singular cause, but more recent developments in media—cable and the Internet—have also had an effect on the way conventions are organized and executed. This is especially true of major party conventions, which attract the lion's share of media attention. Changes to minor party conventions, however, which are traditionally ignored by the media, have been modest at best.

Conventions still matter. Despite many of the changes we observe, conventions continue to contribute meaningfully to the presidential selection process and to the dynamics of presidential campaigns. Conventions influence levels of support for candidates, for example, and affect the amount of political information available to the electorate. Indeed, sizable segments of the electorate report making up their minds about which candidate to vote for during conventions.

Conventions continue to evolve but not necessarily towards irrelevance. Television was the driving force behind many of the developments in conventions that we observed over the post–World War II period. Stimuli created by new developments in mass media exert powerful influence over conventions, and conventions will continue to evolve in response to these new stimuli, including cable television and the Internet. Even as aspects of conventions continue to evolve, conventions are likely to serve useful purposes in the future and to remain institutionalized features of presidential politics. The role of conventions in the process of presidential selection may have changed over the past few decades, but new and important roles for conventions continue to surface.

CONVENTIONS IN HISTORICAL CONTEXT

Every four years, at least since September 1831 when the Anti-Masonic Party held the first presidential nominating convention, Democrats and Republicans from each state formally convene to nominate a presidential candidate to represent the party in the general election race that follows. The establishment

3

of national conventions for the purpose of nominating presidential candidates marked the formalization of political parties in the United States, enabling parties to gather partisans from all geographic areas and to weld them together as a cohesive unit in pursuit of the quadrennial effort to elect a president.

For over a century, nominating conventions were typically lively and animated events, settings for intense candidate and policy debates that frequently erupted in volatility and excitement. At the 1912 Democratic national convention in Baltimore, Maryland, for example, it took forty-six ballots for Woodrow Wilson's supporters to break a deadlock and to wrestle the nomination away from fellow contenders U.S. House Speaker Champ Clarke of Missouri, Representative Oscar Underwood of Alabama, and Governor Judson Harmon of Ohio. Twelve years later, after nine days of stalemate, delegates at the Democratic convention in New York voted 103 times before Wall Street lawyer John W. Davis clinched the nomination as a compromise candidate between New York governor Alfred E. Smith and Wilson's Treasury secretary William G. McAdoo. That was back in the heyday of nominating conventions, when fat cats in smoke-filled rooms did battle over contenders and the nomination was not a foregone conclusion before the convention even began.

THE GROWTH OF TELEVISION AND THE RISE OF STAGED CONVENTIONS

For over a century, national conventions remained the purview of the select few who attended the meetings and reveled in the enthusiasm. With the growth of mass media technologies, political conventions became important national events. Indeed a special relationship exists between conventions and media technology. David Shedden writes, "Every four years, journalists experiment with new inventions at presidential conventions. Some historical periods offer more innovation than others do, but the conventions serve as interesting markers about the evolution of news technology." In 1844, news of convention proceedings was transmitted by telegraph for the first time. By 1880, convention reporters used a "new gadget," the telephone, and, on June 10, 1924, the Republican National Convention in Cleveland, Ohio, was the first to be broadcast on radio. Indeed, radio coverage of conventions was so desirable initially that manufacturers used conventions to boost radio sales. RCA ran print ads to promote its Radiola product:

> Cheer with the galleries when the delegates march in! No "influence" needed this year for a gallery seat at the big political conventions! Get it all with a Radiola Super-Heterodyne. When the delegates march in—

4

their banners screaming; when the bands play and the galleries cheer—
be there with a "Super-Het." Hear the pros and cons as they fight their
way to a "platform" for you. Hear the speeches for the "favorite son."
The sudden stillness when the voice of a great speaker rings out. The
stamps and whistles and shrill of competitive cheering. Hear the actual
nomination of a president. It used to be all for the delegates' wives and
the "big" folks of politics. Now it's for everybody. Listen in. Get it all!
With the newest Radiola.[1]

Television coverage of conventions quickly followed. In June 1940, NBC's
experimental station W2XBS became the first television station to broadcast
from a presidential convention when it aired reports from the Republican
convention in Philadelphia, and the first live convention reports arrived on
June 21, 1948, during the Republican convention.[2] Television promised unprecedented access to convention proceedings, and networks initially provided
Americans with nearly gavel-to-gavel coverage. The public tuned in to watch.
As recently as 1976, the typical household watched eleven hours of convention coverage on television.[3] Conventions were exciting—and newsworthy—
because nominations were undecided and convention proceedings were consequential and, relatively speaking, interesting. Few states held primaries to
bind delegate decisions, and conventions were gatherings of party chieftains
and activists from across the nation who had no legal obligations or commitments to designated candidates. In the heyday of nominating conventions,
freewheeling and dealing delegates routinely offered and withdrew their support in exchange for concessions on platform planks or promises of future
political payoffs, appointments, and patronage.

Television almost instantly revolutionized conventions. After watching
the first fully televised Republican convention in 1952, Democratic Party officials made changes in the appearance and layout of their own conventions to
better suit their new audiences.[4] By 1956, both parties further amended their
convention programs to better fit the demands of television coverage. Officials altered the length of the conventions, dropped daytime sessions, created
uniform campaign themes for each party, limited welcoming speeches and
parliamentary organization procedures, scheduled sessions for prime time so
as to reach a maximum audience, and worked hard to conceal any intraparty
battling.[5]

Contemporary conventions are staged primarily as mega–media events designed to electrify the party faithful and to woo undecided voters by dazzling

them. Scholars have demonstrated that support for the party's nominee is boosted immediately after the convention, and the prevailing nostrum seems to be: the bigger and better the convention, the bigger the boost. Party leaders now spend elaborate effort and resources to orchestrate, anticipate, plan, schedule, rehearse, time, and script every detail of every minute of conventions—especially those proceedings that will air during primetime television coverage.

The design and execution of conventions as massive media events has required party organizations to solicit the expertise of media and communications professionals and specialists. Increasingly, parties turn to political consultants, image specialists, strategists, and television production experts to put on the best show possible to reinforce key party messages. "It's very simple," claims Republican convention veteran Bill Greener (who has worked on every convention since 1984). "If it's good TV, people will watch it. If not, they won't." Greener suggests the sea change occurred in 1972 when RNC manager Bill Timmons organized with extraordinary precision the convention to renominate incumbent Richard Nixon. "We hadn't seen anything like it before. Since then, the move toward planning conventions as TV events continues. There is a greater need for specialists," Greener claims. Don Fowler, CEO of the 1998 Democratic National Convention and Democratic National Committee chairman in 1995–1996, describes how critical he felt it was to find talent with expertise in producing live events for television. "Politicians are good at many things," says Fowler, "but not necessarily TV production . . . In 1988," he recalls, "I went to Hollywood and hired Gary Smith and Dwight Hemion to help produce the convention. They understood the techniques of live TV production. This had never been done before." Smith and Hemion went on to help orchestrate the Democratic conventions in 1992, 1996, and 2000.[6]

Tom C. Korologos, a Republican operative who was involved in planning every convention between 1972 and 2000, agrees. "There is more and more consultation with public affairs professionals," he claims. "We are increasingly preoccupied with the overarching question: 'How's this going to look on television?' We turn to the media and entertainment guys more and more," he adds.[7] Strategists work closely with media and communications consultants to present the right messages in the most compelling ways. Professional convention managers are careful to prevent boring lulls in the action and to keep potentially divisive rules or platform fights out of primetime viewing hours. They orchestrate "spontaneous" demonstrations and telegenic events such as the release of hundreds of colorful balloons on the convention floor.

Consultants coach speakers on makeup, wardrobe, and how to read the Tele-PrompTer. Eric Lieber, a television consultant for the Democrats in 1976, said that gavel banging was a sign of disorder and use of the gavel was restricted to three times a session, regardless of what was happening on the floor.[8] The layout of the convention hall is designed with television, not the comfort of the delegates, as the first priority.[9] In fact, the average reporter has greater access to important convention actors than does the average delegate, and prominent reporters have more influence on the conduct of conventions than do the delegates.[10] Delegates are treated as extras, handed the appropriate signs and banners to wave and given instructions on when to cheer. Almost all words spoken are scripted. Republicans in 1992 required each of the more than one hundred podium speakers to submit their speeches to a small team of speechwriters charged with keeping the talk from the podium tuned to a particular theme, whether that meant just some small edits or drafting a new speech from scratch.[11] Speeches are fed into TelePrompTers and timed so that signs and chants can be coordinated with key moments and suggested responses are given to likely interview targets. Very little is left to chance, and the parties coordinate their schedule with network broadcast plans. Everything must be presented as going according to schedule and according to plan, momentum must be preserved at all costs, and anything that highlights the inevitability of the frontrunner's majority is encouraged and cultivated.[12]

Anxious convention managers concerned that coverage of the event should be smooth and entertaining to viewers have encouraged shorter keynote and nominating speeches and have virtually eliminated secondary speeches.[13] Popular speakers, often celebrities, military heroes, and prominent women are chosen to deliver the key addresses, and individuals chosen to give the nominating speech are strategically selected to appeal to target audiences. In 1972, New York governor Nelson Rockefeller was chosen to nominate Richard Nixon despite that Rockefeller was a longtime foe of the candidate. In 1988, George H. W. Bush was nominated by his daughter-in-law as part of a Republican effort to stress the importance of family. And in 2004, outgoing Democrat senator Zel Miller broke party ranks to nominate George W. Bush for a second term.

NO NEWS HERE: TUNING OUT TO MUNDANE CONVENTIONS

Critics argue that choreographed conventions have become less interesting and mostly ceremonial. They are perceived to be simply gatherings held to ratify the choice of the primary voters in the states rather than bargaining conventions.[14]

Since 1952, nomination front runners have had to hold on to the coalition they built before the convention rather than continue to search for support at the convention. The nomination is typically assured on the first ballot, so candidates now use the conventions as a form of extended advertising, introducing themselves to the electorate in a favorable light and projecting the party's desired image to the viewing audience in a relatively uncontested format.

The nature of coverage of proceedings has also changed. Television networks anxious about high ratings assign their most important anchors to cover conventions from overhead booths, and they are assisted by scores of reporters roaming the floor in search of fast-breaking stories and potentially interesting interviews. Researchers stand by ready to explain what is happening on the podium or the floor, and a number of people are assigned to flip through books or make telephone calls to find needed information so that the anchor can talk intelligently about the proceedings.

Television cultivates an illusion of action, maintaining viewer interest by switching back and forth between events that are taking place at the same time in various locations, which can create a false sense of confusion or disorder at the conventions. John S. Jackson argues that the place and deference afforded to the media at the conventions recognizes the surrogate role they play as the eyes and ears of the public at large, and the parties recognize that the images and impressions the media transmit, the themes they develop, and the events and personalities they decide to cover become the public's major window onto the convention.[15] Images and issues developed or solidified during the convention are crucial because they tend to carry over into the fall campaign. To be fair, the media has an agenda dedicated to enhancing its own success, maximizing viewer appeal, and building its reputation during the conventions. They look for conflict, controversial decisions, and power brokering. They race to be the first to learn and announce important decisions such as the name of the vice-presidential candidate or the new national party chair and to project their opinions about what it all means for the general election.

These developments have engaged parties and television networks in an interesting dance over the past five decades. As parties have controlled convention dynamics more and more, networks have increasingly ignored the events and withdrawn coverage. As several of the subsequent chapters discuss in detail, network coverage of conventions has dropped precipitously since the 1960s. Networks blame the parties and believe their drastic scaling down on coverage reflects the vast majority's lack of interest in conventions that have ceased to be a compelling centerpiece of presidential drama.[16] In 2004, David

Westin, president of ABC News, wrote in the *Washington Post:* "If we broadcast extended convention coverage when most Americans would rather be watching something else, our audiences will flock to the alternative programming. If the conventions themselves were as interesting as they were in 1948 or 1956—or even 1968—then we wouldn't have this problem. But as we all know too well, they aren't. As much as we might like to coerce people into watching what we think to be good for them, we simply don't have that power."[17]

Scholars echo these notions. Jackson contends, "In turn, the networks' declining coverage has required parties to script conventions even more in order to maximize favorable coverage within the constraints of severely limited exposure."[18] The 1996 Republican convention, for example, was so highly scripted because most networks carried only five hours of coverage, leaving convention managers with little choice but to carefully stage events. Most speakers were limited to ten-minute speeches, and the Republicans made heavy use of infomercial videos. ABC anchor Ted Koppel left early, telling viewers that there was "no more news here."

THE IMPACT OF INSTITUTIONAL REFORMS

Other key reforms over the second half of the twentieth century have affected the way conventions are executed. The McGovern-Fraser Commission, appointed by the Democratic Party after the tumultuous 1968 Democratic convention to address unfair and exclusionary practices in the delegate selection process, recommended a series of measures including the elimination of restrictive fees and petition requirements for delegate candidates, and restrictions on voter registration, the unit rule, and proxy voting. The commission also recommended limiting the influence of party committees in the selection of delegates, required written rules for governing the process, demanded adequate public notice of all meetings pertaining to delegate selection, and called for standardized apportionment. Scholars find that the guidelines have substantially democratized the system by opening avenues for citizen participation and greatly reducing the power of party leaders.[19] The Republicans also made some reforms to their conventions during the 1970s, but they were not as extensive or as well implemented as the Democratic changes.

Both parties today follow complicated formulas for selecting delegates. Since 1972, Republicans have followed a complex procedure that includes six at-large delegates, three delegates for each congressional district, and bonus delegates for elected officials and state party leaders, and considers turnout in the last presidential election. That year the Democrats instituted a system of apportionment based half on the voting strength of the state's Democratic vote in the last three presidential elections and half on the state's Electoral College votes. The number of delegates attending conventions has increased greatly since the 1950s.[20] The number of Democratic delegates increased from 1,642 in 1952 to 2,477 in 1956. In 1980 that number rose to 3,331 and then climbed to 4,290 in 1996. The Republicans also increased the number of delegates at their convention from 1,348 in 1972 to 2,277 in 1988.

In recent years, delegates have been pledged in state primaries and caucuses and thus have had little flexibility in the choice of the party's nominee, although they still play a role in platform debates and in establishing the image the party projects on television.[21] If the delegates move to ideological extremes, they often nominate candidates who go on to lose badly in the general election. Republicans learned this lesson when they nominated Senator Barry Goldwater, and Democrats realized the same thing in 1972 when they nominated Senator George McGovern. Nevertheless, growing ideological polarization on both sides has resulted in pressure to select nominees who share the more extremist preferences of the party elite rather than positions favored by the majority of voters.[22] Growing polarization along ideological lines also creates additional challenges for parties striving to present a moderate image on television in an effort to attract uncommitted voters.

The Mikulski Commission in 1973, which advanced the goals of the McGovern-Fraser Commission and required delegates to state their presidential preference in order to ensure that voter preferences would be accurately reflected, helped to change the way people wheel and deal at the conventions. Nelson Polsby and Aaron Wildavsky show that the candidates at the convention try to perfect their organizations and maintain communication with as many of their delegates as they can.[23] In the old days, pledged delegations actively supported their candidates while bossed delegates negotiated for the disposal of their votes. The role of the negotiators has sharply diminished since most delegates come to the convention pledged to one presidential candidate, thus requiring little bargaining.

The reforms enacted by both parties have helped to transform national conventions into mere ratifying assemblies. Gone are the days when delegates wielded any real power at conventions and when candidates and parties worked tirelessly to woo their support. The 1960 Kennedy campaign, for example, started a card file containing information on people who might be delegates and who might influence delegates more than a year before the convention. Individual coordinators were assigned to each state at the convention to keep an hourly watch on developments within the delegations. During contemporary conventions, party leaders monitor state delegations but primarily in order to assure that choreographed moments occur without glitches.

THE FUTURE OF PRESIDENTIAL NOMINATING CONVENTIONS

It remains to be seen what role conventions will play in upcoming elections. Many critics contend that conventions have outlived their usefulness, are largely ineffectual, no longer control their central function, and are hopelessly bogged down with problems.[24] Others contend that the national conventions persist because they are important for the parties and produce nominees and platforms that are viewed as legitimate, despite that conventions are complicated and flawed.[25] Herbert Waltzer has praised television coverage for reforming conventions and politics.[26] He credits television for "initiating improvements in convention procedure, purging politics of the phony and charlatan, slaying the wild orator and one-speech politician, ending the reign of cabals in smoke-filled rooms, creating a better informed electorate and transforming the national convention into a national town meeting." Old-style conventions where party bosses choose the nominee behind closed doors are all but impossible with today's media scrutiny. Steamroller tactics such as blatantly unfair rulings by the convention chair or forced recesses during roll calls to deflate enthusiasm for a candidate and mobilize opposition support are largely things of the past.

This book investigates many of these related questions and offers an indepth view of how national nominating conventions have changed in the media age. In the end, the assembled chapters are generally optimistic about the importance of national conventions and suggest that these events do matter to the presidential selection process in meaningful ways despite the changes we can observe and critique. The contributing authors probe a wide range of topics and offer insights about nearly every major aspect of national conventions. Each chapter presents detailed accounts and analyses intended to balance theory and empirics. Overall, the book helps readers to assess the changing role of conventions in contemporary politics, the forces driving these developments, and the implications for parties, politics and society.

In chapter 2, I discuss the "bounce" (or "bump") in support that a candidate typically receives during his party's convention. I present a detailed historical account of the magnitude of the convention bounce over five decades and reflect on conditions that affect the size of the convention bump.

In chapter 3, Michael Hagen and Richard Johnston trace the impact of conventions on campaign dynamics. Drawing upon data from the 2000 National Annenberg Election Survey, they track the views of the national electorate through rolling cross-sections throughout the 2000 campaign. Their extensive analyses shed light on conventions' impact on public preferences, information and attention to politics during the campaign, and news and political advertising. The authors conclude that "the party conventions remain among the most important events of presidential campaigns."

Convention delegates are the public face of the party during these national affairs. Scholars have observed that political conventions tend to attract delegates who are more extreme in their viewpoints than the average party member. As such, parties struggle to portray a moderate face during conventions, even as their delegates espouse viewpoints that are less mainstream. In chapter 4, John Green and John Jackson present the findings of a survey of convention delegates conducted at the 2004 national conventions. Green and Jackson investigate the attributes, activities, and attitudes of convention delegates, drawing contrasts to delegates of previous conventions and to the public at large. The authors present evidence of sharp ideological cleavages between party elites and find that ideology plays an increasingly dominant role at conventions. They explain that changes in the mass media account partly account for the shifts they observe.

In chapter 5, J. Mark Wrighton discusses changes to the presidential nominating process which occurred during the media age and considers how these developments have influenced the national conventions. He also investigates the dwindling interest in and coverage of conventions and assesses the effects of campaign finance reform and regulation on convention financing. Wrighton concludes that, despite several concerns, national conventions continue to serve important purposes in the American political system and occupy a special place in the presidential selection process. In chapter 6, I discuss conventions' role in generating information about presidential campaigns. Despite declining coverage and viewership, conventions continue to increase overall media attention to the campaign, thereby providing the electorate with useful information they may use to reach a voting decision.

While major party conventions may have changed significantly during the media age, minor party presidential nominating conventions seem to have changed less dramatically. In chapter 7, John Berg argues that these conventions continue to serve important functions, even as some observers feel contemporary major party conventions fail to do so. Berg's insights present a unique perspective from which to consider developments in conventions. His analysis suggests that the low level of media attention which minor party conventions typically receive has allowed them to remain functional rather than to become ceremonial.

The eyes of the nation are on a party and its candidates during conventions, and the party operatives are fully aware of it. They strive to make sure everything seems perfect for the audience. Yet things do not always go as planned, and sometimes things go wrong. In the media age, convention crises can be crippling. In chapter 8, Sam Garrett discusses convention problems and presents case-study accounts of select crises over the past few decades. Garrett presents elite interviews to expand his case-study approach and develops a key theoretical framework within which to consider developments in convention crises during the media age. He also considers how conventions are organized to limit and manage crises.

A study of developments in the media age and their impact on conventions would be incomplete without some discussion of the Internet. In chapter 9, Michael Cornfield shows us how the Internet is influencing communications at and about the conventions. His analysis, based on reflections from the 2000 and 2004 campaigns, reveals how the parties are shifting gears to accommodate the Internet at conventions, as they had once done for television. Cornfield argues that the real-time, interactive nature of this new medium has the potential to radically transform convention coverage and deliberation. In addition to the Internet, and partly as a result of declining coverage by the networks, cable television has been stepping in to fill voids in coverage. Jonathan Morris and Peter Francia describe in chapter 10 the evolution of cable coverage of conventions in recent years and argue that it differs qualitatively from network coverage in systematic and meaningful ways. They discuss these differences and reflect on the implications for both viewers and parties.

In chapter 11, Terri Fine argues that the deliberative nature of presidential nominating conventions has declined and attributes this decline to political parties and the mass media. As a consequence, Fine believes that the role that party conventions play in serving democratic goals has gone unmet in the media age. She also claims that the parties and the media can help to recast the role of conventions as deliberative and meaningful. Her thoughtful analysis is grounded in democratic theory and driven by the optimism of her problem-solution framework.

The concluding chapter by preeminent campaigns and elections scholar Gerald Pomper offers a powerful (and witty) critique, reflects on the future of presidential nominating conventions in America, and recommends a series of practical reforms intended to help parties to reconcile their conventions with key developments in the mass media. Pomper suggests that, even if only as political rituals, conventions will endure.

The analyses presented in this volume by established scholars and experts offer a wide range of perspectives from which to evaluate developments in national conventions. Overall, the authors suggest that the fundamental changes that have taken place over the past few decades have been fueled, at least partly, by the mass media. In the end, however, the basic consensus is that conventions *do* matter in meaningful ways, even in the media age.

NOTES

1. David Shedden, "The First Convention Broadcast: Radio at the 1924 Conventions," December 22, 2004, www.poynter.org/content/content_view.asp?id=70880 (accessed October 5, 2005).

2. B. Shafer, *Bifurcated Politics: Evolution and Reform in the National Party Convention,* (Cambridge: Harvard University Press, 1988).

3. Thomas Patterson, "Election Interest Is Up Sharply, But Convention Interest Is Not," Vanishing Voter Project: Harvard University, press release, July 21, 2004.

4. B. Shafer, *Bifurcated Politics.*

5. S. Jarvis, Presidential Nominating Conventions and Television, www.museum.tv/archives/etv/P/htmlP/presidential/presidential.htm (accessed June 22, 2004).

6. Costas Panagopoulos, "Behind the Balloons: National Conventions and Political Consultants," *Campaigns and Elections* (July 2004).

7. Ibid.

8. Charles C. Euchner and John Anthony Maltese, *Selecting the President: From 1789 to 1996* (Washington, DC: Congressional Quarterly, 1997).

9. N. W. Polsby and A. Wildavsky, *Presidential Elections: Strategies and Structures of American Politics,* 10th ed. (New York: Chatham House, 1999).

10. John S. Jackson, *The Politics of Presidential Selection* (New York: Longman, 2001).

11. Polsby and Wildavsky, *Presidential Elections.*

12. Jackson, *The Politics of Presidential Selection.*

13. Euchner and Maltese, *Selecting the President.*

14. Ibid.

15. Jackson, *The Politics of Presidential Selection.*

16. Ibid.

17. David Westin, Don't Blame the Networks," *Washington Post,* July 30, 2004, p. A19.

18. Jackson, *The Politics of Presidential Selection.*

19. Euchner and Maltese, *Selecting the President.*

20. Ibid.

21. Polsby and Wildavsky, *Presidential Elections.*

22. Anne N. Costain, "Changes in the Role of Ideology in American National Nominating Conventions and Among Party Identifiers," *Western Political Quarterly* 33, no. 1 (1980): 73–86.

23. Polsby and Wildavsky, *Presidential Elections.*

24. Morris Fiorina and Paul Peterson, *The New American Democracy,* alternate 3d ed. (New York: Addison Wesley Longman, 2003).

25. Jackson, *The Politics of Presidential Selection.*

26. H. Waltzer, "In the Magic Lantern: Television Coverage of the 1964 National Conventions," *Public Opinion Quarterly* 30, no. 1 (1966): 33–53.

2

FOLLOW THE BOUNCING BALL
Assessing Convention Bumps, 1964–2004
Costas Panagopoulos

FEW FEATURES OF THE process of presidential selection in the United States
have changed as dramatically as the national presidential nominating conventions. Once the setting for passionate candidate and policy contests between party factions, critics assert that contemporary conventions are primarily ceremonial: giant, quadrennial pep rallies or intricately orchestrated
partisan productions that offer little guidance by way of useful information
for the electorate.[1] Others describe conventions as "nonevents," representing a
significant break from the past when conventions were deliberative meetings
that featured genuine debate and negotiation among party leaders. Indeed,
between the mid-nineteenth and mid-twentieth centuries, at least two ballots
were necessary to select a nominee at twenty-six conventions (ten Republican
and sixteen Democratic); the last time more than one ballot was necessary in
modern times was 1952.[2]

These developments in the nature of nominating conventions may be
partly accountable for the patterns we observe in the timing of the voting
decision. Data presented in Figure 2.1 demonstrates a sizable decline in the
proportion of voters who reach a decision about their presidential vote during
the conventions from about one-quarter of voters in the 1960s to about one-
tenth in recent election cycles. In fact, an analysis of the data suggests that the
proportion of voters who reach a voting decision during the period of the conventions has declined by over one percentage point per election cycle between
1964 and 2004 (regressed on time and a constant, the coefficient equals -1.04
with standard error $= 0.42$; $p < .05$; $N = 11$ Adj. R-squared $= 0.34$).

Despite these realities, nominating conventions remain crucial elements
of presidential campaigns. Thomas Patterson argues that "conventions retain a
purpose for which they were invented in the 1830s—the rallying of the party
faithful. But they also serve a modern purpose. They boost interest in the cam-

FIG. 2.1. Time of voting decision, 1964–2004

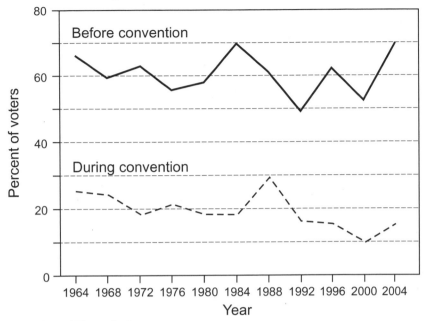

Source: National Election Studies.

paign and heighten citizens' understanding of the candidates. In an age of 10-second soundbites and 30-second ads, the conventions stand alone as an opportunity for the public to hear at length why each party and its nominee should be entrusted with the presidency."[3]

A feature—or byproduct—of national nominating conventions that has attracted considerable attention from scholars and politicians alike is the convention "bump" (or bounce) that tends to follow each convention. Simply stated, the bump is the increase in support (relative to preconvention support in opinion surveys) that a candidate typically receives at the conclusion of the party's convention.

The theoretical intuition behind the convention bump is rather straight-forward. Conventions offer the political parties the opportunity to present their candidates and images to voters in a positive and relatively uncontested format. Parties dominate the flow of information during conventions, exert notable control over the message disseminated through media outlets, and generally attract favorable coverage during the convention period. Thomas

Holbrook explains that "as voters learn more about the candidate and are exposed to campaign rhetoric on behalf of the candidate, they are more likely to support the candidate."[4]

The resulting spike in support that typically follows nominating conventions can be consequential for presidential contenders. James Campbell, Lynna Cherry, and Kenneth Wink have shown that while part of the bump is temporary, there is also evidence that the increase in support can have lasting implications.[5] Campbell estimates that, "a healthy portion," about half of the net convention bump, carries through to Election Day.[6]

CONVENTION BUMPS: MEASUREMENT AND DATA

Scholarly approaches to measuring convention bumps have varied despite the relative simplicity of the concept. The method commonly used to calculate convention bumps was developed initially by Campbell, Cherry, and Wink.[7] The preconvention level of support is based on trial-heat polls taken between six days and two weeks prior to the opening of the convention. Postconvention support is based on surveys conducted during the week following the last day. The percentages are based on the share of respondents who expressed support for one of the two major party candidates for president, and the bump is the difference between the two preference measures.[8]

Reliable survey results are unavailable prior to 1964; thus, most analyses of convention bumps start there. Even so, other methodological considerations must be taken into account. First, most scholars determine preferences using data from Gallup surveys. While Gallup poll data on presidential preference is widely and consistently available, recent scholarship suggests the data may be susceptible to short-term fluctuations that skew the results, especially when samples are classified by estimates of respondents' likelihood of voting in the election.[9] Second, other sample-based differences may also be consequential, and decisions about whether to use samples of registered voters or likely voters may influence measurement significantly. A third issue revolves around the appropriate number of pre- and postconvention surveys to be included. Some scholars advocate including multiple surveys conducted over several days by various organizations and using mean levels of support averaged over a set of surveys. Others espouse looking at single surveys that either immediately precede or follow conventions. Finally, there is substantial debate over how to allocate preferences for non–major party candidates even as most studies simply exclude these and limit the analysis to preferences for major-party candidates only.

My aim in this study is to maximize the precision of the data by incorporating several considerations described above. I estimate pre- and postconvention support using available Gallup data for the period 1964–1988 and ABC/*Washington Post* data for elections 1992–2004. Preferences are measured from surveys of registered voters taken immediately prior and immediately following each party's national nominating convention.[10] Preferences indicate the share of two-party support for major-party candidates only.

CONVENTION BUMPS OVER TIME: 1964–2004

The magnitude of convention bumps over the period 1964 to 2004 are displayed in Figure 2.2. The data demonstrate that the size (and, in the case of the chaotic Democratic convention of 1972, the direction) of convention bumps is considerably variable across election cycles but not necessarily across parties. On average, Democratic and Republican candidates extracted an equal twelve-point increase in support following their nominating conventions.[11] This estimate is substantially larger than previous estimates of convention bumps.[12] Interestingly, the lowest increase registered for a Republican candidate was the bump of only four percentage points earned by President George W. Bush following the 2004 convention. The highest bump for a Republican candidate (twenty points) was afforded to Richard Nixon in 1968. Postconvention bumps for Democratic candidates in this period range from a reverse, two-point *drop* in support for McGovern in 1972 to the highest increase ever recorded (thirty-six points) for Bill Clinton in 1992. An analysis of the data reveals that postconvention bumps for Democratic candidates have been much more variable than those for Republican candidates (standard deviations of 10.8 and 5.2 percentage points, respectively), but few other party-based differences emerge in the initial analysis. The data reveal no trends in the size of convention bumps over time for either party's candidates. While the magnitude of convention bumps has fluctuated across specific election cycles, it has remained relatively stable over time for candidates of both major parties, and I observe no general patterns of surge or decline in the size of convention bumps between 1964 and 2004. The overall stability we observe over time in the magnitude of convention bumps is puzzling, especially given developments in related aspects of national conventions.

EXPLAINING PATTERNS IN CONVENTION BUMPS

Previous studies have provided numerous explanations for the variation we observe in the magnitude of convention bumps. Scholars have demonstrated

FIG. 2.2. Convention bump, 1964–2004

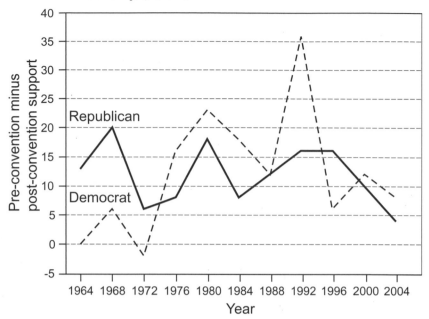

Source: Calculated by author from Gallup (1964–88); ABC/*Washington Post* (1992–2004).

that postconvention increases in support tend to be higher for the party that hosts the first convention, typically the nonincumbent party. Campbell, Cherry, and Wink explain that this finding is reasonable for three reasons.[13] The first convention occurs earlier in the campaign season when a larger segment of the electorate is either undecided or not committed strongly to a specific candidate. Second, information is more scarce earlier in the campaign. Finally, voters are generally less knowledgeable about the challenging party which typically that holds the first convention.[14] This finding has remained robust across other similar analyses. Convention bumps have also been shown to be larger for candidates who are trailing as they enter their conventions, most likely for informational reasons similar to those described above. Campbell finds that trailing candidates gain about eight percentage points on average after their conventions, while frontrunners gain only above five points over their preconvention support.[15]

The theoretical underpinnings of the hypotheses tested by these analyses are driven by an information-based model of convention effects rooted in press coverage of convention proceedings. Despite the critical connection between

FIG. 2.3. Network coverage of conventions, 1964–2004

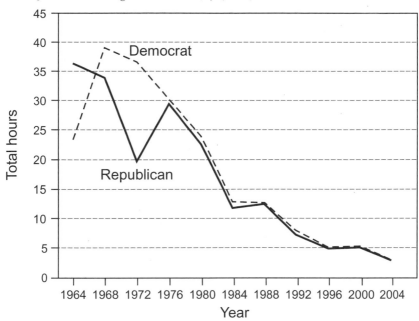

Source: Vital Statistics on American Politics.

the level of information about candidates generated by the convention and transmitted by the media, few empirical analyses explicitly incorporate measures of convention coverage and exposure in an effort to establish such links. The following model explaining the variation in convention bumps includes such measures.

The omission of measures of media coverage of conventions (and exposure to such coverage) potentially leaves much of the story untold. In fact, a key development over the study period is the sharp drop in the media's coverage of conventions. Even as conventions tend to increase the overall amount of front-page newspaper attention devoted to the presidential campaigns,[16] television coverage of actual, unfiltered convention proceedings has plummeted over the past four decades.[17] Data on the total number of hours of network coverage of each party's convention proceedings between 1964 and 2004 is presented in Figure 2.3. The general pattern of decline applies to both parties. Whereas television networks routinely devoted between thirty to forty hours of coverage to conventions during the 1960s, network coverage dropped tenfold to its lowest level ever (three hours for each convention) in 2004. Analysis

FIG. 2.4. Convention viewership, 1964–2004

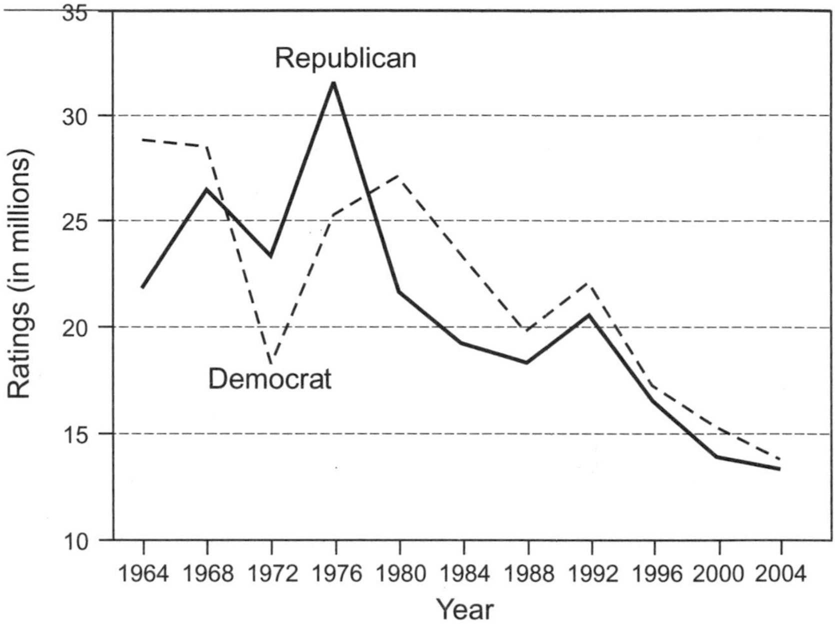

Source: Vital Statistics on American Politics.

indicates that the total number of hours devoted to both parties' conventions by the networks has fallen steadily by an average of more than seven hours per election cycle (regressed on time and a constant, coefficient = −7.01; standard error = 0.75; p<.01; N = 11; Adj. R-squared = 0.90).

Figure 2.4 presents similar, although not identical, data on convention audiences in terms of ratings for convention viewership between 1964 and 2004. The data reveal a similar pattern of decline. Whereas over 25 percent of households with televisions routinely watched convention coverage in the 1960s, ratings had dropped to about 15 percent of households for the three most recent convention cycles.

The decline in media coverage may be partly accountable for the decline in the proportion of voters who make up their minds during conventions. Table 2.1 presents the findings of regression analyses that support the hypothesis that declining coverage time and audience sizes help explain the dwindling rate of vote decisions arrived at during the conventions. The analyses show that higher ratings and audience sizes are associated with higher rates of decision making during conventions. The simultaneous decline in ratings, coverage, and

TABLE 2.1. Vote choice decision-making during conventions

INDEPENDENT VARIABLES	MODEL 1	MODEL 2
Coverage (networks total hours)	0.24***	—
	(.08)	
Audience (ratings)	—	0.54***
		(.19)
Constant	14.79***	7.63*
	(1.68)	(4.16)
N	22	22
Adj. R-Squared	0.28	0.25

Note: Dependent variable: Proportion of voters who made up their minds about which candidate to vote for during national conventions (NES). Ordinary least squares. Standard errors are given in parentheses.
*$p<.10$ **$p<.05$ ***$p<.01$

decision making at conventions over the period of this study suggests a linked phenomenon.

It is reasonable to expect a relationship between media coverage of and attention to convention proceedings and the magnitude of convention bumps. Specifically, we may expect a negative relationship to exist between these media coverage and attention variables and the size of convention bumps. If this is the case, then the developments we observe over this period—the declines in network coverage and viewership—should be depressing the overall size of convention bumps over time. Yet there is no evidence that the overall size of postconvention increases in support has been dragged down by the declining coverage and attention phenomenon. The empirical model I develop and test below examines these questions further.

Two other factors that may influence the size of the convention bump are the portion of the electorate that is undecided before the conventions and the level of interest in the presidential campaign. More undecided voters signify greater opportunities for conventions to earn their support. Persuading voters who have already decided which candidate to support on Election Day is clearly a taller task. Undecided voters are not only more likely to be influenced by what they learn during conventions but they are also more likely to be interested in acquiring information that may help them to reach a decision and, to that end, may turn to the conventions for help. Thus, we can expect a positive relationship between the overall proportion of undecided voters and the size of the convention bump.

According to the data presented in Figure 2.1, on average, 59 percent of voters were undecided by the time conventions convened between 1964 and 2000. The data also suggest, however, that the segment of the electorate that has been undecided at the start of the conventions is declining over time, even though the decline is not statistically significant at conventional levels (regressed on time and a constant, coefficient = −0.85; standard error = 0.72; p<0.27; N = 11; Adj. R-squared = 0.04).

The level of interest in the presidential campaign is also likely to affect the size of the convention bump. Patterson suggests that the level of interest in the presidential election affects the number of "inadvertent" convention viewers.[18] Unlike "deliberate viewers," who Patterson claims turn on the television set intending to watch the conventions, inadvertent viewers come across the convention coverage while watching television and decide to stay tuned. The level of election interest affects the number of inadvertent viewers, and greater interest will act to generate attention to conventions and consequently boost convention bumps.

Interest in the outcome of the 2004 presidential election was higher than it had ever been over the period of the study. Fully 85 percent of National Election Studies respondents reported that they "care[d] a good deal" about which party won the presidential election. In fact, despite the overall sense of political disengagement many studies have recently reported, Figure 2.5 presents evidence that interest in the outcome of presidential campaigns has climbed steadily between 1964 and 2004.[19] In fact, an analysis of the data (regressed on time and a constant) reveals that the proportion of the electorate that "cares a good deal" about which party wins the presidential election (compared to the percentage who indicate they "don't care") has increased by over 2 percentage points in each election cycle over this period (coefficient = 2.17; standard error = 0.62; p<.01; N = 11; Adj. R-squared = 0.53).

Here I test an empirical model to explain the variation we observe in the magnitude of convention bumps over the period 1964 to 2004. I propose that the size of convention bumps will be a function of the following factors: *audience size* (measured in ratings points), *coverage* (measured as the total number of hours of coverage by television networks), *campaign interest* (measured as the proportion of NES respondents who report caring "a good deal" about which party wins the presidency), and *undecided voters* (measured as the proportion of NES respondents who indicate they had not decided which candi-

FIG. 2.5. Presidential campaign interest, 1964–2004

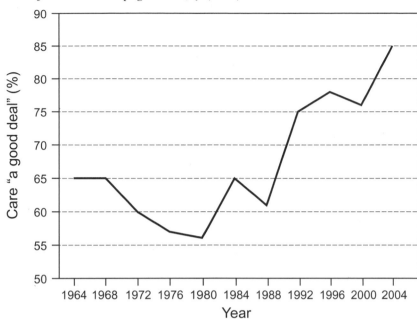

Source: National Election Studies.

date to support before the conventions started). I also include a time variable and a dummy variable for the party that hosted the *first convention.* I expect positive relationships between each of these variables and the dependent variable (*convention bump*).

Table 2.2 presents the results of the multivariate regression analysis. The findings reveal support for several hypotheses. Confirming the results of previous studies, hosting the first convention in the cycle significantly boosts the magnitude of the convention bump.[20] All else being equal, the party that hosts the first convention earns a postconvention boost that is 8.69 points higher on average than the bump afforded to the party that hosts the second. Of course, as I discussed above, it is difficult to disentangle this "first convention" effect from an "incumbency effect," since the incumbent party typically holds its convention last. Nevertheless, the findings remain robust that the first convention bump is significantly higher than the second.

There is no evidence that campaign interest affects the size of the bump. The coefficient for this variable does not achieve conventional levels of signifi-

TABLE 2.2. Explaining convention bumps

INDEPENDENT VARIABLES	COEFFICIENT
Audience size	1.13^{**}
	(0.54)
Coverage	-0.33
	(0.31)
Campaign interest	$-.04$
	(0.26)
Undecided voters	0.37
	(0.24)
First convention	8.69^{***}
	(3.12)
Time	1.02
	(1.37)
Constant	-35.20
	(28.86)
N	22
Adjusted R-squared	0.34

Note: Dependent variable: Convention bump (post-convention minus pre-convention support [%]). Ordinary least squares. Standard errors are given in parentheses.
$^{*}p<.10$ $^{**}p<.05$ $^{***}p<.01$

cance. One possibility is that campaign interest is expressed as larger audience size, but no independent effect emerges from the results.

The proportion of undecided voters at the start of the conventions appears to exert a positive effect on the magnitude of bumps, as expected, but the coefficient is only significant at the $p<.12$ level. Nevertheless, the results suggest that for each percentage point increase in the proportion of the electorate that is undecided, the size of the convention bump is likely to increase by 0.37 percentage points.

The results of the analysis with respect to the media coverage and audience size variables suggest that higher ratings are associated with larger bumps once we control for total hours of network coverage. All else being equal, for each additional percentage point increase in audience ratings, the convention bump increase is expected to rise by 1.13 percentage points.

I have shown that several factors help explain the variation in the bump, including the timing of each party's convention, the proportion of undecided voters in the electorate, and the size of the television audience. One remaining task is to speculate about why the magnitude of the convention bump, which has varied over the study period, shows few signs of surge or decline for either party. After all, a reasonable expectation, given the steep decline in audience size (ratings) between 1964 and 2004 (especially in conjunction with the simultaneous slight decline in the segment of the electorate that is undecided by the time of the conventions), would be that the magnitude of bumps overall should have declined during this period. One limitation is that the relatively small number of observations available limits the conclusions we can draw from the analysis. Conceivably, a more satisfying explanation could be that despite the decline in network ratings and coverage over this period, increases in the volume of news generated from conventions and transmitted in filtered format through other media channels during convention periods (see chapters 3 and 6) provide Americans with enough new information to influence their views about candidates even if they did not directly watch convention proceedings. Another possible explanation is that increase in attention and coverage devoted to conventions by cable television networks (discussed in detail in chapter 10) is mitigating the depressing effect of dwindling network ratings. As data about these factors becomes available over time, future analyses could investigate the effects of each more systematically.

NOTES

1. Costas Panagopoulos, "Behind the Balloons: Political Consultants and National Nominating Conventions," *Campaigns & Elections* (July 2004).

2. Thomas M. Holbrook, *Do Campaigns Matter?* (Thousand Oaks, CA: Sage, 1996).

3. Thomas Patterson, "Election Interest Is Up Sharply, But Convention Interest Is Not," Vanishing Voter Project, Harvard University, press release, July 21, 2004.

4. Holbrook, *Do Campaigns Matter?*

5. James E. Campbell, Lynna Cherry, and Kenneth Wink, "The Convention Bump," *American Politics Quarterly* 20 (1992): 287–307.

6. James E. Campbell, *The American Campaign* (College Station: Texas A&M University Press, 2000).

7. Campbell, Cherry, and Wink, "The Convention Bump."

8. Holbrook, *Do Campaigns Matter?*

9. Robert S. Erikson, Costas Panagopoulos, and Christopher Wlezien, "Likely (and Unlikely) Voters and the Measurement of Campaign Dynamics," *Public Opinion Quarterly* 68 (winter 2004): 588–601.

While overanalyzing small differences in polls is a common hazard, 2004 data do underscore how bounce measurements can differ. The Gallup Organization's final poll before the July 26–29 Democratic convention was completed July 21, five days before the convention began; it had John Kerry and George W. Bush at 47–43 percent support. Gallup's postconvention poll, completed August 1, had a 47–48 percent Kerry-Bush race—a net loss of five points for Kerry on the margin, the only negative bounce in Gallup data since George McGovern's in 1972.

By contrast, the 2004 ABC News/*Washington Post* pre-Democratic convention poll was completed July 25, four days later than Gallup's and the very night before the convention began; it found a 46–48 percent Kerry-Bush race (i.e., six points better for Bush on the margin). The postconvention ABC/*Post* poll, completed the same date as Gallup's, had a 50–44 percent race—a positive bounce of eight points for Kerry, which is nearer the long-term average.

10. Note that while there are some differences between the approach I adopt and Campbell, *The American Campaign,* our respective estimates of convention bumps for corresponding periods correlate at the 0.84 (Pearson's R p<.01) level.

11. Excluding Bill Clinton's unusually high bump of thirty-six points in 1992, Democratic candidates averaged ten-point bumps over this period.

12. Campbell, Cherry, and Wink, "The Convention Bump"; Campbell, *The American Campaign;* Holbrook, *Do Campaigns Matter?*

13. Campbell, Cherry, and Wink, "The Convention Bump."

14. Holbrook, *Do Campaigns Matter?*

15. Campbell, *The American Campaign.*

16. Only the *New York Times* was included in this study.

17. Holbrook, *Do Campaigns Matter?*

18. Patterson, "Election Interest."

19. Robert Putnam, *Bowling Alone: The Collapse and Revival of American Community* (New York: Simon and Schuster, 2000).

20. Holbrook, *Do Campaigns Matter?;* Campbell, Cherry, and Wink, "The Convention Bump."

3

CONVENTIONS AND CAMPAIGN DYNAMICS

Michael G. Hagen
Richard Johnston

THE PARTY CONVENTIONS REMAIN among the most important events of presidential campaigns. Though their function in some respects has changed dramatically, the conventions continue to provide an occasion for launching a party's general-election campaign and for introducing—or reintroducing—the party's candidates to the electorate. Parties invest millions of dollars and enormous planning effort in the conventions every four years. Some of those resources are devoted to making those attending feel welcome, of course. But much is spent on developing the message, accommodating the press, and making sure the party looks its best on television. One measure of their success is a phenomenon the political lexicon has given a colloquial term, the *bump*. The bump is the favorable change in a candidate's standing in the polls which can be attributed to the party's convention. Political observers make predictions about the bump, watch the bump carefully as it develops, and read into the bump afterward a great deal about the convention, the candidate, and the party's prospects in the November election. While much is made of bumps, however, less is understood. This chapter surveys the 2000 convention bumps and explores their underlying factors.

The analysis reported here draws upon data from the 2000 National Annenberg Election Survey and from content analyses of campaign news and advertising. The Annenberg Survey features a "rolling cross-section," a continuous tracking of the views of the national electorate that permits the study of factors operating in real time.[1] In addition, the survey included panel studies bracketing each of the party conventions. A sample of the respondents interviewed for the rolling cross-section just prior to the Republican convention were reinterviewed between the conventions, and a sample of those interviewed for the rolling cross-section during this period between conventions were reinterviewed immediately after the Democratic convention.[2] News data come from detailed coding of the three networks' early evening broadcasts.[3] And advertising data, including ads sponsored by groups independent of the candidates, originate with the Campaign Media Analysis Group (CMAG). These data locate the airing of ads precisely in time and place, where "place" means a Designated Market Area (DMA).[4]

THE 2000 BUMPS

In the summer of 2000, following the custom, the challenging party held its convention before the party of the president held its own. The Republicans convened in Philadelphia on July 31, 2000. The Democrats assembled in Los Angeles on August 14. Both conventions lasted four days. Figure 3.1 shows the magnitude and timing of shifts in the electorate's general-election vote intentions over the span from the Fourth of July through Labor Day, September 4. The period was a dynamic one—and a critical one in the campaign.

The Bush tracking is nearly the mirror image of the Gore tracking. The percentages of the electorate supporting other candidates or lacking a preference altogether did not change much over these two months—declining by only

FIG. 3.1. Presidential vote intentions in the 2000 convention period

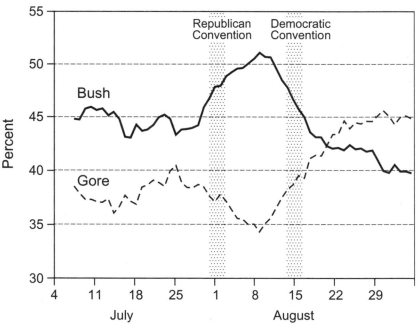

about two percentage points, all told. It does not necessarily follow that any changes in the major-party candidates' vote shares represent shifts in preference between the two; the Annenberg panel data show substantial movement of individuals between the camps of both candidates and the third category. The stability in the category that includes individuals without a preference starkly contrasts with the 22 percent who typically respond in a postelection survey that they decided their presidential vote during the conventions (see Table 3.2).[5] If 22 percent made up their minds during the 2000 convention period, another 20 percent must have become undecided. A more plausible interpretation is that the postelection question is not very reliable.

Each party's convention bumped up its candidate's share of the intended vote. The race was not entirely static prior to the conventions. Through the first three weeks of July, George W. Bush held a substantial lead, but the lead shrank slightly, from about nine points early in the month to about three points one week before the Republican convention began. From that point until one week after the Republican convention closed, however, Bush's share of vote intentions grew steadily, from 43 percent to 51 percent, while Al Gore's share fell from 41 percent to 34 percent. The benefit to Bush from the Republican convention thus amounted to as much as seven or eight percentage points—slightly larger than the average convention bump over the past thirty years.[6]

The bump from the Democratic convention was even larger. The candidates' fortunes were reversed on August 10. For the rest of the month, Gore's stock rose. By the day after the Democratic convention, Bush's seventeen-point lead had shrunk back to three points, and Gore's share continued to rise. Within days Gore had taken the lead, a lead that grew to about six percentage points and held steady through the first week of September. All told, Gore picked up eleven or twelve percentage points around the Democratic convention—nearly twice the size of the thirty-year average. The bump for Gore was sufficiently large to propel the race from one Bush led on the Fourth July to one Gore led on Labor Day.

In historical perspective the 2000 pattern is unusual. James Campbell's analysis of presidential campaigns from 1964 though 1996 yields two main generalizations about variation in the magnitude of convention bumps. One is that the first convention of a presidential campaign typically produces a bump more than twice as large as the bump produced by the second. The other is that the bump from the convention nominating the candidate who trails in the race tends to exceed the bump from the front-runner's convention.[7]

The two generalizations are related, of course. The convention of the incumbent president's party always comes second, and that party's nominee-to-be—especially when he is the incumbent himself—usually leads in the polls before the conventions. The first convention is that of the challenger, who usually trails. What made 2000 unusual is that George W. Bush led Al Gore in the polls during the early summer, before the conventions. Following the historical pattern, the frontrunner's convention generated the smaller bump in vote intentions; counter to the historical pattern, that convention was the first.[8]

INFORMATION AND ATTENTION

Only a handful of Americans, of course, experience the party conventions firsthand. A substantial number watch at least some live convention coverage on television, but even that group constitutes only a small fraction of the electorate. According to Nielsen Media Research, the audience for the 2000 Republican convention on cable and broadcast news outlets averaged about 14 million homes; the Democratic convention was watched in about 15.4 million homes.[9] Questions asked in the course of a telephone survey about politics seem likely to elicit an exaggerated estimate of the audience for conventions. Even so, nearly 60 percent of those interviewed for the 2000 Annenberg Survey said they had watched no more than a few minutes of a convention. During the convention period, as throughout the rest of the campaign, most Americans get information about politics indirectly, through the news media.

Every four years, it seems, the broadcast television networks reduce their live coverage of the conventions. The fact remains, however, that the conventions fuel relatively heavy news coverage of the campaign.[10] Figure 3.2 shows changes in the volume of coverage devoted to the 2000 presidential campaign by the evening news programs of the three major broadcast networks from July 4 through Election Day.[11] The nightly newscasts gave a great deal coverage to the conventions in 2000. In fact, the volume of news about the campaign was greater in early August than at any other time prior to the last week of the campaign. In terms of sheer volume, the convention period offered one of the most extensive and sustained opportunities of the year for a citizen to be exposed to news about the campaign.

The surges in coverage are worth noting in detail. The volume of campaign news, fairly constant over the first two weeks of July, began to rise on July 20, more than a week and a half before the Republican convention began. During the third week of July the volume of coverage was double the volume early in the month, and the following week—still prior to the opening of the con-

FIG. 3.2. Campaign news volume, advertising volume, and attention to campaign

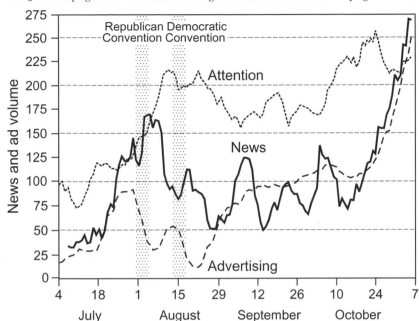

vention—it doubled again. The peak of news coverage during the convention period came on the last evening of the Republican convention—just hours before, that is, George W. Bush's speech to accept the party's nomination. The volume of news remained heavy, though somewhat reduced, over the four succeeding days, then dropped off sharply. Roughly speaking, coverage around the Democratic convention followed a similar path. The volume of news rose again just before the start of the Democratic convention and, as with the Republicans, peaked on the last evening of the convention and remained heavy for a time afterward. In both cases, in short, heavy coverage was not confined to the four days of the convention itself but preceded and followed it.

While the time paths of coverage coinciding with the two conventions were in these respects similar, coverage of the two differed in another significant respect. Coverage before, during, and after the Republican convention was much heavier than coverage around the Democratic convention. Coverage on the evening of Gore's acceptance speech was only half as heavy as on the evening of Bush's.[12] Coverage in the preceding week was likewise heavier for the Republican convention than for the Democratic one. This disparity between the parties sheds some light on an ambiguity in previous analysis of convention news coverage. Thomas Holbrook found that in 1984, 1988, and 1992 the *New York Times* covered the Democratic conventions a bit more heavily than the Republican conventions. Because the Republicans held the White House in all three of those election years, it was unclear whether the Democrats were advantaged in the volume of news because their candidates were less well known than the incumbent president or vice president they opposed, or because Democratic conventions, as Holbrook put it, "are usually more spirited."[13] The Republican news advantage in 2000 suggests that it is more likely the challenger status of the party holding the first convention, not the party's reputation for holding spirited conventions, that accounts for the typical pattern of coverage.[14] Whatever the explanation, the difference in the sheer volume of news about the two conventions cannot obviously explain the difference in the magnitude of the two convention bumps. The more heavily covered convention in 2000 produced the smaller aggregate change in vote intentions.[15]

News was not the only source of information about the campaign and potential influence on the electorate during this period in 2000. Both campaigns and their allies paid for extensive advertising broadcast on local stations in strategically important television markets during July and August. Figure 3.2 traces the number of ads aired over a seven-day period on a station in an average market in a state that could reasonably have been expected to be competitive.[16] At its peak, the volume of campaign advertising in July nearly equaled the volume in September. Even in early July, viewers in a target market might have seen as many as two ads per day about the presidential campaign. Then, the campaigns began to increase the volume of advertising on July 17, just two days before the increase in news coverage began, and it peaked on July 30, the day before the Republican convention opened. The seven-day sums in Figure 3.2 understate the instantaneous decline in advertising volume as the convention began. Additional ads were aired in the week preceding the Democratic convention, after which advertising slacked off again. During the last week of August, the volume of advertising began a rise that would not end until Election Day. In many ways, then, the trajectory of advertising volume roughly parallels the trajectory of news volume, rising in advance of the first convention, falling back afterward, then rising again—to a lower level—before the second convention, and falling back again.

The combination of heavy campaign news and heavy campaign advertising might be expected to signal to the electorate that important events in the presidential campaign are at hand and that the time has come to devote more attention than usual to politics. As Figure 3.2 shows, the electorate's level of attention to politics did in fact rise from mid-July through mid-August, increasing nearly 30 percent.[17] The sharpest increase came during the first two weeks of August, lagging somewhat behind the heaviest volumes of news and ads.

It is possible to distinguish the particular contribution of advertising to the increase in the electorate's attention to the campaign by taking advantage of the wide geographic variation in the distribution of television advertising in 2000. Throughout the summer and fall, the presidential campaigns focused their resources narrowly on the states that were most competitive, where, because of the unit rule most states follow to allocate votes in the Electoral College, a small shift in the popular vote would have a large impact on the election's outcome.[18] The campaign amounted in some respects to a natural experiment, in which one large fraction of the electorate was exposed to campaign advertising and the other was not. Network television news about the campaign, of course, was equally available to both fractions. Dividing the Annenberg samples into those to whom advertising was and was not available, however, provides an opportunity to appraise the independent effect of advertising on attention.

Advertising by itself appears to do little to alert the electorate to attend to the campaign. Figure 3.3 tracks attention to the campaign over the convention period separately in those television markets that saw heavy campaign advertising during this period and those that did not. There are some hints that residents of high-volume markets were more attentive to the campaign at times, and in a couple of cases those times coincided with heavy advertising. In mid-July, when the volume of advertising first began to rise sharply, attention to the campaign in the high-volume markets increased a bit more rapidly than in the low-volume markets. The gap between the two groups lasted only ten days, however. From just before the Democratic convention until at least Labor Day, the high-volume group was more attentive than the low-volume group. But the differences, on the whole, were slight, averaging less than .02 on the scale from zero to one. The convention period saw a substantial increase in the electorate's attention to the campaign, but campaign advertising appears not to have been the catalyst for much of the increase.

INTRODUCING THE VICE-PRESIDENTIAL CANDIDATES

Comparing the ebbs and flows in the coverage the two campaigns received over the entire length of the race underscores the unique character of news during the convention periods. Figure 3.4 traces separately the volume of news statements about the Bush campaign and the Gore campaign. Generally, the volumes of news devoted to the two candidates were similar. Only during

FIG. 3.3. Attention to campaign, by advertising volume

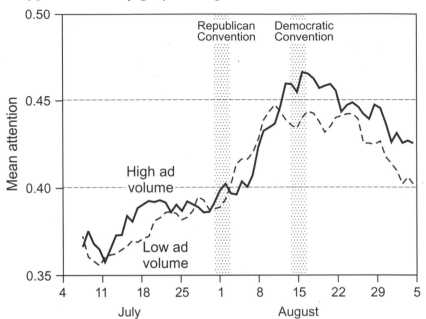

the convention periods did one candidate dominate the news for an extended time. The sharp increase in campaign news prior to and during the Republican convention was exclusively about the Republican campaign. Coverage of the Democratic campaign was flat until the last day of the Republican convention, then increased immediately, while coverage of the Republican campaign plummeted. In each case the convening party dominated the news from a week before their convention through their convention's last day.

The separate tracks for the two campaigns demonstrate that the disparity apparent in the total volume of coverage surrounding the Republican and Democratic conventions translated into a disparity in coverage of the two parties' overall campaigns. The coverage of the Democrats during the period of Republican dominance and the coverage of the Republicans during the period of Democratic dominance were almost equal in volume. But the volume of coverage devoted to the Republicans around their convention was more than fifty percent greater than the volume devoted to the Democrats around their convention.

The coverage devoted to a campaign while it dominated the news was overwhelmingly positive. Over the entire campaign from July 4 until Election

FIG. 3.4. Campaign news volume, by candidate

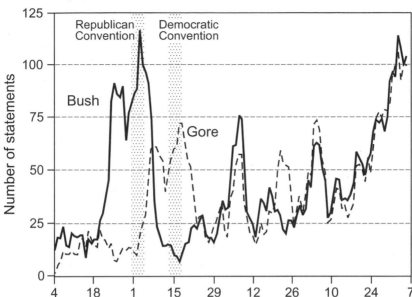

Day, 26 percent of the news about Bush and 28 percent of the news about Gore was negative. During the period when the Democratic convention dominated the news, in contrast, just 14 percent of the coverage devoted to the Democrats was negative; the parallel figure for the Republican convention is 15 percent. Both conventions, in short, produced for the meeting party remarkably heavy, one-sided, favorable news coverage.

The increased volume of campaign news prior to each convention to some degree simply anticipates the convention as an important marker in the presidential campaign. During the 2000 campaign the increase in each case also coincided more precisely with a specific newsworthy event: the announcement of the party's vice-presidential candidate. The biggest one-day jump of the campaign in the volume of coverage of the Republicans came on July 24, when George W. Bush announced Dick Cheney as his running mate. The first day following the Republican convention on which the Democrats received more coverage than the Republicans was August 6, the day before Al Gore named Joe Lieberman to be his vice-presidential candidate. In each case the vice-presidential announcement marked the start of the period during which the party dominated the news.

Each nominee's choice of running mate was the focus of a major portion of convention news coverage. Neither Richard Cheney nor Joseph Lieberman was well known nationwide, at least by comparison with the presidential candidates, before being named to their respective tickets. Asked in early July to rate each candidate on a scale from 0 (very unfavorable) to 100 (very favorable), just 4 percent of the electorate declined to rate Al Gore and 5 percent declined to rate George Bush. In contrast, 40 percent of those interviewed over the first two days after Bush named him to be his running mate were unable to rate Dick Cheney, and 46 percent of those interviewed during Joe Lieberman's first two days in the national spotlight were unable to rate him. The flood of news about the campaign raised the profile of each vice-presidential candidate. One week after the close of the Republican convention, the percentage declining to rate Cheney had fallen 13 points, and one week after the Democratic convention the percentage unable to rate Lieberman had fallen 16 points.

The conventions also made the electorate evaluate the vice-presidential candidates, like the presidential candidates, more favorably—especially on the Democratic side. Figure 3.5 tracks the ratings of all four. The average rating

FIG. 3.5. Favorability, by candidate

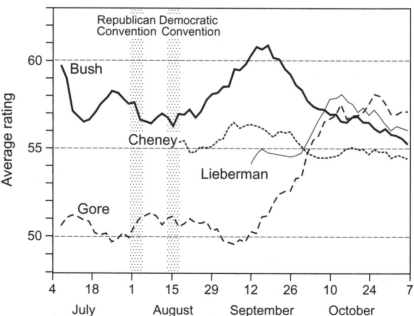

given Cheney by those who could rate him on the scale from 0 to 100 rose slightly, from 55 to 56. Two weeks later, Lieberman's average rating rose from 55 to 58. To the extent that evaluations of the vice-presidential candidates influenced vote intentions, both conventions in this sense indirectly benefited their tickets through those evaluations.

From another angle, however, the potential effects of the two vice-presidential candidates were very different. The shifts in evaluations of Bush and Gore track closely the shifts in vote intentions. The comparison between the two candidates on each ticket is instructive. Throughout this period Cheney was viewed less favorably than Bush, and the Republican convention improved Bush's standing much more than Cheney's. To the degree that potential voters' views of Cheney influenced them, those views on average tended to diminish the surge in vote intentions Bush enjoyed as a result of the Republican convention. Lieberman, on the other hand, was in a position to help Gore, because the electorate thought more highly of the Democratic vice-presidential candidate than of the presidential candidate. This was particularly true when Lieberman was named to the ticket between the conventions, when evaluations of Gore were at their nadir. In terms of the overall evaluations of the electorate as a whole, at a critical juncture Cheney was a liability to the Republican ticket and Lieberman was a boon to the Democrats.

THE EFFECTS OF NEWS AND ADVERTISING

During the 2000 convention period the two campaigns employed quite different strategies for spending on advertising. Figure 3.6 distinguishes the volumes of advertising aired by the two presidential campaigns, their parties' national committees, and other allied groups. As in Figure 3.2, the lines track the average number of ads aired over the previous seven days on one station in a television market in a competitive state. The Democrats aired ads at close to a constant rate through July and early August, about seventeen ads per station per week. The Democrats doubled the number of their ads on the air during the two weeks between conventions, then cut off advertising during the week following their convention. The Republicans, on the other hand, aired little advertising in early July. During the two weeks preceding their convention, however, the volume of pro-Bush advertising was nearly four times that of pro-Gore advertising. Between conventions the Republicans again cut back almost to zero, and they did so again following the Democratic convention. While the Democrats were in session, however, the volume of Republican advertising was about two thirds of the Democratic volume. Beginning in the

FIG. 3.6. Advertising volume, by candidate

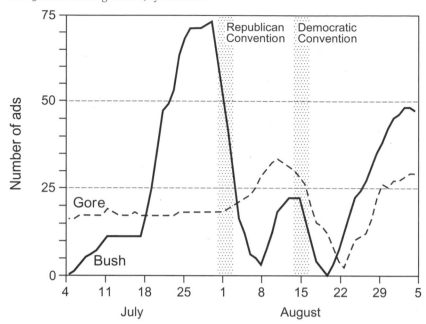

last week of August, both campaigns resumed advertising, with the Republican volume substantially exceeding the Democratic volume.

Taken together, the two campaigns' strategies produced a mix of advertising very similar to the mix of news. Figure 3.7 displays the net valence of news and of advertising. The measure of news valence is based on coders' scoring of the positive, neutral, or negative tone of each statement about a candidate identified in the network news.[19] The scores for coverage of the two candidates have been summed, so that values greater than zero represent a period of coverage that was more positive about Gore than about Bush and values less than zero a period that was more positive about Bush than about Gore. The measure of advertising valence is simply the difference between the number of ads favoring Gore and the number favoring Bush aired during the previous week. Positive values indicate that Gore advertised more heavily than Bush; negative values indicate that Bush advertised more heavily than Gore. For comparison, the figure repeats the tracking from Figure 3.1 of Gore's share of vote intentions as measured in the Annenberg survey.

The parallels between the news and the ads are striking. Both heavily favored Bush during the last week of July, and both favored Gore—albeit by only half as much—during the second week of August. To be sure, the dynamics of news and ads differed in some respects. The two are slightly out of phase, with changes in advertising generally leading changes in news by a few days. In early July the ad balance favored Gore while the news balance favored Bush; in late August the two were reversed. Broadly speaking, however, news valence and ad valence tracked one another remarkably closely.

We make no causal claim about this correspondence. While it is certainly possible that journalists were responding in part to the advertising strategies of the campaigns and campaign decision makers were allocating resources partly in response to the news, it seems to us that the two groups probably were responding independently, in the main, to the rhythm of events and of the convention calendar. Whatever the causal association between news and ads during the period, the two do appear to influence the electorate's vote intentions, but only after a substantial lag in time. The shift in news and ads from mildly pro-Gore to strongly pro-Bush began in the middle of July; Gore's share of the vote subsequently fell, but the fall did not begin until ten days later. Bush's wide advantage in news and ads began to subside at the start of the Republican convention; Gore's vote share started to rise about ten days later. Gore's advantage in advertising crested a week before the Democratic convention, and his advantage in news peaked just two days later (although news coverage favored Gore by nearly as much as his convention ended). Gore's share of the vote, however, continued to climb for another two weeks. The electorate's response to the volume and valence of the messages made available during the convention period was not instantaneous but rather sluggish.

The time series in Figure 3.7 offer some suggestions that the influences of campaign news and advertising were not identical. During the first week of July the valence of advertising remained nearly flat, but the valence of news moved in Gore's direction, and the following week Gore's standing in the electorate improved. Over the last two weeks of August the valence of advertising moved in Bush's direction, but the valence of news was constant, and Gore's share of the vote did not decline. In general, however, the close temporal correspondence between news and ads makes it difficult to distinguish their effects over time.

The geographic variation in advertising volume provides much better purchase on the distinction between news and ad effects. In television markets where little or no advertising was aired, changes in vote intentions obviously cannot be attributed to ads. Figure 3.8 tracks the dynamics of vote intentions in the markets that saw little or no television advertising and, for comparison,

FIG. 3.7. News valence, ad valence, and vote intentions

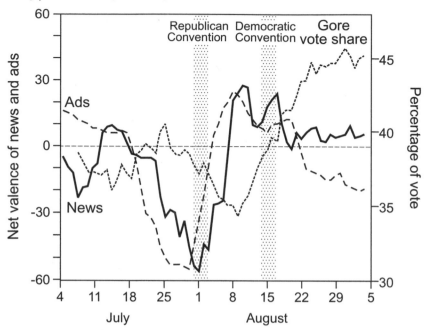

the valence of campaign news. To underscore the observation above about the lag in the electorate's response to information about the campaign, news valence in Figure 3.8 has been lagged ten days.

The convention bumps are clearly evident, even among residents of areas that saw no television advertising.[20] Even where ads were scarce, Gore's share of vote intentions fell eight percentage points during the two weeks bracketing the Republican convention and rose eleven points over the next two weeks. The correspondence between vote intentions and the lagged measure of news valence is quite close, at least until the end of August, when the news turns less decidedly pro-Gore but Gore's share of the vote continues to grow. There is an element of simpleminded curve fitting here, of course; the ten-day lag was chosen not for any theoretical reason but rather to maximize the correspondence between the news and the vote. Even so, the correspondence strikes us as strikingly strong. A substantial portion of the bumps associated with the party conventions in 2000 must be attributed to campaign news coverage.

Advertising mattered as well. Figure 3.9 shows, alongside the same measure of advertising valence that appears in Figure 3.7, the *difference* between

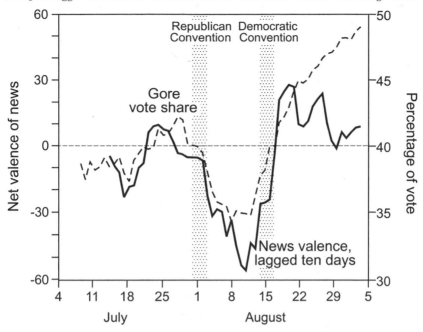

FIG. 3.8. Lagged news valence and vote intentions in markets with low advertising volume

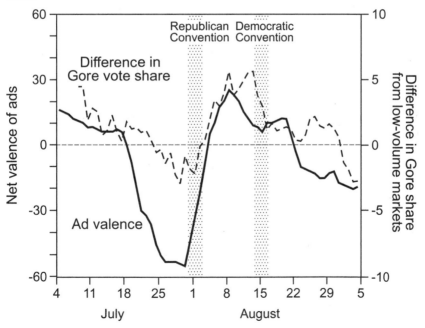

FIG. 3.9. Ad valence and difference in vote intentions in markets with high advertising volume

Gore's vote share in the markets with heavy advertising during this period and Gore's share in the markets that saw little or no advertising.[21] Vote intentions in the areas that saw advertising clearly diverged at times from vote intentions elsewhere, and the divergences correspond for the most part to changes in the balance of advertising. This is clearest in August. Early in the month, when the wide Republican advantage in advertising was reversed, Gore's share of the vote among residents of high-volume areas rose to exceed his share elsewhere by as much as six percentage points. When the advertising advantage Gore held diminished, so did Gore's advantage in the markets seeing ads. By the end of the month, Bush was out-advertising Gore again, and Gore's standing in the areas where ads were aired fell below his standing in the rest of the country. The association between the valence of advertising and the difference in vote intentions is not as close in late July. While the Bush advantage in advertising peaked at twice the level of Gore's later advantage, Gore's share of vote intentions in late July declined by only four to five percentage points. The impact of advertising during this period was not simply a function of the sheer disparity in the numbers of ads aired by the two sides. Then, too, the impact of advertising was certainly small by comparison with the impact of news; the differences between the two groups of television markets are much smaller than the differences over time. But it does seem clear that the dynamics of advertising contributed to the dynamics of vote intentions during the 2000 convention period.

Combining the tone and volume of ads and news, however, does not uncover an explanation for the relative magnitudes of the convention bumps in 2000. The Republican advantage in the valence of news and ads around their convention far outstripped the Democratic advantage around theirs, and yet the Democratic bump was larger than the Republican bump. The difference in the dynamics of vote intentions during the period does not simply reflect differences in the quantities and qualities of the information associated with the conventions.

EXPLAINING THE DIFFERENCE

Scholars have offered two main types of explanations for variation in the magnitude of convention bumps. The first emphasizes the quantity of prior information about the candidates in the hands of the electorate. The impact of new information is greatest when the quantity of prior information is smallest. One reason that first conventions typically produce larger bumps than second conventions, Campbell suggests, is that the candidates of the challenging party tend to be less well known than the incumbents at this point in the campaign.[22] As Holbrook points out, too, the dissemination of information stimulated by the first convention, at least in principle, increases the amount of prior information potential voters possess in advance of the second convention and mutes its impact.[23] Regardless of the pertinence of this explanation for convention bumps in general, however, this perspective cannot explain the pattern in 2000, when the larger bump followed the second convention, the convention that nominated the incumbent vice president.

Holbrook points to another factor to account for variation in the magnitude of convention effects: the difference between each candidate's prior standing in the electorate and the candidate's equilibrium level of support. This equilibrium is the electorate's "natural predisposition" toward the candidate under the prevailing national conditions, and it is susceptible to estimation using models that forecast presidential election outcomes months in advance. The impact of any campaign event, from this point of view, depends upon whether the event works to pull a candidate's support away from its equilibrium level or pushes the candidate's support toward the equilibrium. Other things being equal, an event that would push the electorate out of equilibrium will have a smaller impact than one that would reassert the equilibrium.[24]

The equilibrium in 2000, accepting Holbrook's operationalization, is easy to identify. Political science forecasts of the 2000 election were unanimous (and now infamously so) in their prediction that Al Gore would win.[25] The electorate was at quite some distance from this equilibrium prior to the party conventions, when Bush held a substantial lead. If Holbrook's account is correct, the Gore campaign enjoyed the larger bump in 2000 because the Democratic convention moved the electorate in the aggregate closer to the equilibrium.

The logic of this account also can be tracked, using the Annenberg data, at the individual level, at least in a rudimentary way. An individual's equilibrium might simply be characterized as his or her party identification, and an intention to vote contrary to party identification might be taken as a deviation from equilibrium.[26] Table 3.1 shows vote intentions of the electorate, broken down by party, in early July.[27] Just before the conventions, a larger fraction of Republicans (84 percent) than of Democrats (75 percent) expressed an intention to vote for their party's presidential candidate. In addition, more of those without party affiliation supported Bush than Gore, 41 percent to 31 percent. Before the conventions, in short, independents and Democrats available to get behind the Democratic candidate outnumbered the number of Republicans available to be added as Bush supporters.

TABLE 3.1. Vote intentions prior to conventions

	VOTE INTENTIONS			
Party identification	Gore	Bush	Other	Percent of electorate
Democratic	75	13	12	30
Independent and other	31	41	28	41
Republican	9	84	7	29

Democrats also responded more dramatically to their convention than Republicans did to theirs. Figure 3.10 focuses on changes in vote intentions beginning in mid-July, separately for the partisan groups and the others, by showing deviations from the early July numbers in the percentage of each group expressing an intention to vote for Gore.[28] The Republican convention drew Democrats and Republicans alike into the Bush camp. Gore's vote share among Republicans fell about four percentage points between mid-July and the week following their convention, and his share among Democrats fell three points. Thereafter, the trend in Gore's share turned upward, but much more sharply among Democrats than among Republicans. From a week before the Democratic convention to a week after, Gore's support among Republicans returned to its early-July level, and it held steady through Labor Day. While the Democratic convention improved Gore's standing among Republicans by four percentage points, however, it improved his standing among Democrats by about twelve. The run-up to the Republican convention had the perverse effect of increasing the Democratic candidate's percentage among those not identifying with a party, although that increase was wiped out in the aftermath of the Republican convention. The impact of the Democratic convention among independents and other nonidentifiers, however, was very much like that among Democrats—and again much greater than its impact among Republicans.

This portrayal of partisan differences in the magnitude of reactions to the two conventions might be misleading on two grounds. First, the pool of Republicans who might have switched their allegiance to Bush as a result of their convention was smaller than the pool of Democrats who might have switched to Gore as a result of theirs, which limits the scope for growth in Republican support for Bush. Second, examining changes in the vote intentions of the three groups in time-series data presumes membership in those three groups to be static. This presumption is certainly consistent with some

FIG. 3.10. Changes to intention to vote for Gore, by party identification

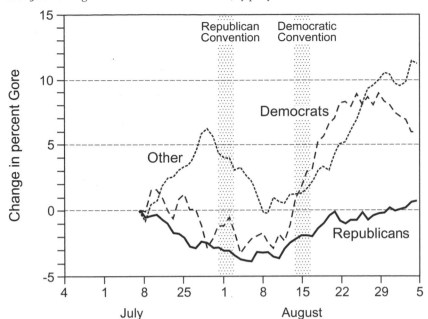

views of the stability of party identification. But in fact, the percentages falling into the three groups in Figure 3.10 were not constant, as Figure 3.11 makes clear.[29] Between the week before the Republican convention and the week after, the percentage of the electorate professing to identify with the Republican party grew by four percentage points. Although it is true Republicans were only a bit more likely to support Bush after their convention than before, it is also true that the ranks of the Republicans swelled during that period. To almost the same degree, however, Democrats became more numerous during the Democratic convention period. Moreover, the increase in Gore's support among Democrats and nonpartisans after the Democratic convention actually understates substantially the impact of the convention, because during that same period the percentage of the electorate identifying themselves as Republicans dropped by six percentage points. Taken together, these patterns confirm rather than contradict the conclusion that the Democratic convention period constituted a stronger stimulus to the electorate than the Republican convention period.

This inference is further buttressed by data from the Annenberg panel studies, which allow examination directly of the postconvention vote inten-

FIG. 3.11. Changes in the distribution of party identification

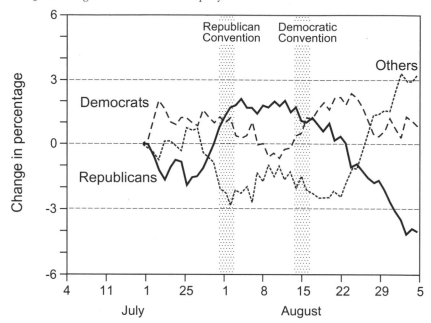

tions of people whose preconvention vote intention and party identification are known. Table 3.2 shows, for each convention and within each partisan grouping (as defined by the interviews conducted *before* each convention), the percentage among those who did not support the named candidate before the convention who had switched their support to the candidate by the time they were reinterviewed after the convention.

This more rigorous test confirms that few partisans were persuaded by the other party's convention to support the candidate nominated there. Substantial numbers were brought into their own party's fold, however, by both conventions. About equal numbers of Democrats (26 percent) and Republicans (24 percent) who did not support their party's candidate before the opposing party's convention were pushed by the convention to support their own party's candidate by the time it was over. But the partisan disparity apparent in the time-series data is evident in the panel data as well. Forty-three percent of Democrats who did not support Al Gore prior to the Democratic convention had been persuaded a week or two later to support him. By comparison, just 27 percent of Republicans who did not support their party's candidate before

TABLE 3.2. Changes in vote intentions during conventions

PARTY IDENTIFICATION	REPUBLICAN CONVENTION	DEMOCRATIC CONVENTION
	Percent switched to Bush	*Percent switched to Gore*
Democratic	5	43
Republican	27	5
Other	14	20
	Percent switched to Gore	*Percent switched to Bush*
Democratic	26	2
Republican	4	24
Others	8	7

the convention did so afterward. Independents and people with other party preferences were drawn to the party's nominee by both conventions. Without a commitment to either party, more among this group than among Democrats shifted their support to Bush during the Republican convention, and more among this group than among Republicans shifted their support to Gore during the Democratic convention. Among those not identified with a party, however, the impact of the Democratic convention appears to have been a bit larger than that of the Republican convention. Twenty percent of those in that group who did not support Gore prior to the Democratic convention did so afterward, compared to 14 percent with regard to Bush and the Republican convention.

CONCLUSIONS

The party conventions in the summer of 2000 produced bigger bumps than usual. By historical standards, the vote intentions of the electorate in the aggregate changed a great deal. Many features of the 2000 convention period pointed to a larger expected bump for the Republicans than for the Democrats. George W. Bush was challenging an incumbent vice president, and his convention was first, conditions that historically have produced the larger changes in vote intentions. News coverage of the Republican's convention was much heavier than coverage of the Democrats', and at least as positive. And the Republicans advertised just prior to their convention much more heavily than the Democrats did prior to theirs. Nevertheless, the clear beneficiary of the bumps, taken together, was Al Gore, who trailed in the race on the Fourth of July but led on Labor Day. That reversal came about because the bump in Gore's favor associated with the Democratic convention was substantially larger than the bump Bush enjoyed from the Republican convention.

These dynamics appear to comport well with the notion that the impact of campaign events in the aggregate depends upon the discrepancy between a candidate's standing in the electorate prior to the event and the candidate's equilibrium level of support. In the summer of 2000, most analysts agreed that conditions favored Gore, but most voters favored Bush. At the individual level, this disequilibrium is evident in the disagreement between party identification and vote intentions. Before the conventions, a markedly larger fraction of Democrats than of Republicans intended to vote for the opposing party's candidate. Even if the two conventions had succeeded in bringing the same proportions of their wayward identifiers back into the fold, the Democratic bump would have been greater than the Republican one. But the Democrats enjoyed an additional advantage because the stimuli surrounding their convention persuaded a larger fraction of Democrats intending to defect to support the party's candidate. One responsible factor appears to be Gore's decision to name Lieberman to be his running mate. But whatever the elements of the convention at play, it was the combination of the conventions' individual-level effects and the state of the electorate before the conventions that yielded the larger bump for Gore and, at the start of the fall campaign, produced a race that looked very much like the one forecast by many earlier in the year on the basis of the prevailing state of the nation.

In its broad outlines, at least, the dynamics of public support during the 2004 convention period resembled those in 2000, with the parties reversed. In 2004 it was the Republican incumbent, George W. Bush, who enjoyed the larger bump, following his party's convention in early September. John Kerry, the Democratic challenger, led the race entering the convention period, but the bump delivered by the Democratic convention, in late July, was limited. In 2004 as in 2000, the candidate leading the race prior to the conventions trailed following the conventions.

The two campaigns differed in an obvious and instructive way, however. In 2004, George Bush was able to hang on to his postconvention lead and win in November; in 2000, Al Gore lost his postconvention lead and, eventually, the White House. A party's convention can provide a boost to a presidential campaign, in both of these cases propelling the trailing candidate into the lead. But even a large convention bump is not sufficient, by itself, to decide the outcome of the presidential campaign.

NOTES

1. All telephone numbers were generated at random and then assigned to "replicates," also at random. Each replicate thus is a representative subsample of the larger, total sample, with enough randomly generated telephone numbers to yield fifty completed interviews over a two-week clearance period. Replicates were then released to field day by day, at least one per day and often more. By clearing each replicate the same way (allowing for seasonal variation in accessibility), the day on which a respondent happens to be interviewed becomes as much a product of random forces as that person's initial selection for the overall sample was. The density of interviewing can vary from period to period without loss of this random character. This paper draws upon the period of highest density, when six replicates, enough to yield 300 completed interviews, were released to field each day. For an explication of the "rolling cross-section" method, see Richard Johnston and Henry E. Brady, "The Rolling Cross-section Design," *Electoral Studies* 21 (2002): 283–95. For more on the Annenberg Survey, see Daniel Roemer, Kate Kenski, Paul Waldman, Christopher Adasiewicz, and Kathleen Hall Jamieson, *Capturing Campaign Dynamics* (New York: Oxford University Press, 2003).

2. Interviews for the preconvention wave of the Republican convention panel were conducted from July 21 through 30. Interviews for the postconvention wave of the Republican panel and the preconvention wave of the Democratic panel were conducted from August 4 through 13. Interviews for the postconvention wave of the Democratic panel were conducted August 18 through 27.

3. The news was coded at the Annenberg School under the direction of Paul Waldman.

4. The Designated Market Area classification was devised by Nielsen Media Research on the basis of research on viewing habits. Nielsen divides the nation into 210 DMAs, each consisting of counties whose residents tend to view the same stations. The boundaries we use here are those Nielsen applied in 2000. A disadvantage of CMAG is that it tracked, in 2000, only the top seventy-five markets. Fortunately for our analysis, these DMAs span the full range of competitiveness and thus of campaign intensity.

5. James E. Campbell, *The American Campaign* (College Station: Texas A&M Press, 2000).

6. Ibid., 148–49.

7. Ibid., 149.

8. The 2000 campaign is not entirely without precedent. In 1988 another incumbent vice president trailed the race entering the convention period but led the race after the conventions.

9. Jim Rutenberg, "The 2000 Campaign—The Television Audience: Democrats' Party Outdrew the G.O.P.'s," *New York Times*, August 19, 2000, A12.

10. The 2000 campaign was typical in this regard. For evidence on earlier campaigns, see Thomas M. Holbrook, *Do Campaigns Matter?* (Thousand Oaks, CA: Sage, 1996), 59–63.

11. The line on the figure represents the total number of "statements" about the campaign made during the three evening newscasts on the date indicated and on the preceding six days. News stories were broken into statements as the first act of coding. For coding purposes a statement was defined operationally as a segment of coverage relying on one source to discuss one candidate and one topic. A statement is typically one sentence in length but is sometimes longer or shorter. On the assumption that few viewers watch more than one network newscast per night, the total number of statements aired by the networks has been divided by three.

Because it does not include the air time given to the conventions themselves but only coverage during the regular newscasts, the figure actually understates the amount of information about the conventions available through the networks.

12. This observation is based on inspection of the daily news volumes, though it is as true of the seven-day sum.

13. Holbrook, *Do Campaigns Matter?*

14. The Republican advantage in 2000 also is inconsistent with the view, appealing in some quarters, that the earlier disparities arose because the news media favor the Democrats. Neither the data presented here nor Holbrook's data can be used to assess yet another explanation: the party holding the first convention may receive more news coverage simply because their convention is first.

15. This is consistent with Holbrook's observation that in the three campaigns he studied, the volume of news and the change in the polls were not strongly related (*Do Campaigns Matter?* 82).

16. For more on the campaign strategy and the measurement strategy with regard to advertising, see Richard Johnston, Michael G. Hagen, and Kathleen Hall Jamieson, *The 2000 Presidential Election and the Foundations of Party Politics* (Cambridge: Cambridge University Press, 2004), chapter 4.

17. The measure of attention combines responses to a survey question about the number of days in the previous week that the respondent followed the campaign on network news and the amount of attention the respondent paid to network news coverage of the campaign. The second item was asked only of those who followed the news about the campaign for at least one day. The combined measure is scaled from zero to one. For more information, see Johnston, Hagen, and Jamieson, *The 2000 Presidential Election*, 94–95.

18. Ibid.

19. For these calculations, explicit references to the candidates' standing in polls were excluded. Smoothing is by five-day prior moving average.

20. Because other kinds of presidential campaign activity—visits from the candidates, radio advertising, direct mail, and so on—tend to occur in the same places that see television advertising, it is reasonable to infer that markets seeing little television advertising saw relatively little of the other sorts of campaigning as well.

21. Smoothing for this figure is by ten-day prior moving average.

22. Campbell, *The American Campaign.*

23. Holbrook, *Do Campaigns Matter?*

24. Ibid.

25. See *PS: Political Science & Politics* 34 (March 2001).

26. For a sophisticated account of the importance of partisanship in conditioning the joint impact of the 2000 conventions, see D. Sunshine Hillygus and Simon Jackman, "Voter Decision Making in Election 2000: Campaign Effects, Partisan Activity, and the Clinton Legacy," *American Journal of Political Science* 47, no. 4 (2003): 583–96.

27. These figures are based on the 2,893 interviews conducted from July 4 through 17.

28. A figure based on the percentage intending to vote for Bush would yield identical conclusions. Because this figure traces the paths of subsamples, the moving average used to smooth the data has been lengthened to ten days.

29. The data in Figure 3.11 have been smoothed using a seven-day prior moving average.

4

National Convention Delegates

John C. Green

John S. Jackson

NATIONAL PARTY CONVENTIONS ARE fast becoming the Rodney Danger-fields of U.S. political institutions: they don't get no respect. After all, these quadrennial national gatherings are no longer deliberative bodies that make independent decisions of obvious importance, such as choosing presidential nominees. The development of the presidential primary system and the resulting candidate-centered and media-focused politics now settles the presidential nominations long before the conventions. The presumptive nominees play a dominant role in writing the party platform and exercise great control over the messages generated by the convention sessions themselves. Indeed, the highlight of contemporary conventions is the presidential nominees' acceptance speeches. As a consequence, journalists, pundits, and not a few political scientists regard the national conventions as colorful anachronisms, mostly symbols with little substance.

This lack of respect does not, however, extend to the party delegates, the men and women who actually make up the convention bodies. Journalists and pundits are fascinated by their attributes, activities, and attitudes, while political scientists have produced a rich literature on them. After all, many delegates are important political decision makers beyond the convention hall,[1] including the nominees' key backers from across the country and followers of rival candidates.[2] Their ranks are filled with the contemporary brokers of electoral resources: office-holders, party executives, interest group leaders, fundraisers, campaign consultants, and grassroots activists.[3]

These elites represent the "party" as manifested on the eve of a particular election, its organizational mechanics and ideological militias.[4] And the profile of convention delegates reveals the raw material from which the general election campaign can be organized. Thus, the national conventions are staging grounds for presidential campaigns, where the parties engage in compromising, coalescing, and introducing the themes and personalities critical for the general election. In this regard, the conventions deserve more respect than they typically receive.[5]

This chapter profiles the Republican and Democratic national convention delegates in 2004. Based on the most recent Party Elite Study (PES), it describes the attributes, activities, and attitudes that made up the raw material for organizing the 2004 presidential campaigns.[6] Unless otherwise noted, longitudinal comparisons made in the text are to previous PES surveys conducted by the authors.[7] On the whole, the PES data are consistent with media surveys of the 2004 national convention delegates, the results of which will be presented where relevant to supplement the PES data.

The 2004 convention delegates closely resembled their recent predecessors, with a few changes. In terms of attributes, the delegates tended to reflect the social characteristics of their party's mass base, but such tendencies were blurred by the delegates' high social and political status. Indeed, the Republican and Democratic delegates resembled each other in their concern with office seeking and party work. The rival party elites did differ on the importance of representing interest groups in party politics, and they tended to be members of the rival organizations central to each party's coalition. The distinctive party profiles were the sharpest on attitudes; the GOP delegates were quite conservative in nearly every respect and Democrats quite liberal. These differences were especially large on policies advanced by President Bush during his first term but extended to longstanding divisions on foreign and domestic policy. Overall, the 2004 party elites were among the most polarized in recent times, fitting well the deeply divided condition of the electorate as a whole.

DELEGATE ATTRIBUTES IN 2004

A good place to begin the national convention delegate profile is with demographics. Table 4.1 looks at gender, race, religion, and age, comparing the Republicans (the incumbent party in the 2004 presidential campaign) to the Democrats (the challenger). Both sets of delegates tended to reflect the demography of their party's mass constituencies on the first three attributes but not the fourth. In fact, these demographic differences were blurred by the high social and political status of these party elites.[8]

The first item in Table 4.1 is Gender. Contemporary voting behavior is characterized by a "gender gap," with women typically voting more Democratic and men more Republican, a pattern both reflected and encouraged by the role of women among party elites.[9] Democrats have institutionalized a de-

TABLE 4.1. National convention delegates and demography, 2004

	REPUBLICAN	DEMOCRAT
Gender		
Female	44	50
Male	56	50
Race		
White	85	68
Black	6	18
Hispanic	4	5
Other	5	9
Age		
35 or under	8	13
36 to 50	25	29
51 to 65	45	41
66 or over	21	17
Religion		
Observant Evangelical Protestant	24	3
Less observant Evangelical	6	5
Observant mainline Protestant	11	4
Less observant mainline	20	15
Black Protestants	5	15
Observant Catholic	12	10
Less observant Catholic	12	19
Jewish	2	6
Other Christians	5	1
Other faiths	1	8
Unaffiliated	3	14

Source: Authors' 2004 survey.
Note: Weighted N = 500 for each party.

gree of gender equality by requiring that one-half of the delegates be women. The Republicans have no such rule and as a consequence had more male delegates in 2004, 56 to 44 percent. This gender difference is smaller than in 2000, when women made up 39 percent of the GOP delegates. This change may reflect the steady increase of women in all aspects of politics now endemic to both parties.

Race is an even more powerful factor in American politics than gender. As Table 4.1 shows, the 2004 Republican delegates were overwhelmingly white (85 percent), with just 6 percent of the GOP delegates African American,

4 percent Hispanic, and 5 percent other or mixed race.[10] These figures are largely unchanged from 2000. The Democrats are more diverse in this regard, reflecting the important role of minorities in the party's coalition: almost one-fifth of the Democratic delegates were African American (18 percent), another 5 percent were Hispanic, and 9 percent other races. The remaining Democratic delegates were white (68 percent).

Another category in Table 4.1 is Religion, where affiliation and worship attendance were combined to produce "observant" (weekly worship attendance) and "less observant" (less than weekly attendance) members of the major religious traditions. A "religion gap" has become an important and controversial aspect of politics in recent times, pitting the most observant religionists against the less so.[11] In 2004 religion was almost as powerful a predictor of presidential voting behavior as party identification for mass voters, so it is not surprising that it would also divide the party elites.

The largest proportion of Republican delegates (24 percent) was Observant Evangelical Protestants. This group is commonly associated with the "religious right," but is actually a good bit more diverse. When combined with Observant Mainline Protestants and Catholics, religious observant Christians made up almost one-half (47 percent) of the GOP delegates. Less Observant Evangelicals, Mainliners, and Catholics accounted for almost two-fifths (38 percent) of the GOP delegates. The remaining one-sixth came from minority faiths and the unaffiliated.

The Democratic delegates were more diverse in this respect. The largest group was Less Observant Catholics (19 percent), followed closely by Black Protestants and Less Observant Mainline Protestants (both 15 percent), and the unaffiliated (14 percent). When taken together, the Less Observant made up almost two-fifths of the Democratic delegates. The Observant groups together accounted for a little more than one-sixth of the Democratic delegates, while Jews and Other Faiths were nearly as numerous (15 percent).

For the most part, the religious profile of the delegates was fairly stable during the 1990s. The most important change was the uneven increase in Observant Evangelicals among the Republicans, with a substantial increase over 2000 and a modest increase over 1996. At the same time, the number of Observant Mainline Protestants declined over the period, so the sum of observant white Christians remained constant at the GOP convention. Meanwhile, according to data we gathered in earlier studies, the proportion of unaffiliated delegates slowly increased from 1996 to 2004.

Age has also mattered in party coalitions, with the "generation gap" mattering in different ways at different times.[12] But as Table 4.1 shows, the 2004 delegates had a very similar age profile in both parties. The modal category was 51 to 65 years, accounting for two-fifths of each party. The Republicans had a few more senior citizens than the Democrats and the Democrats had a slight edge in delegates under 35 years and between 36 and 50 years. This lack of difference may reflect two factors: age is not the divisive factor it once was in party politics, and it typically takes some time to acquire the political status to become a delegate. In any event, the age distribution in 2004 differed little from other conventions in the 1990s.

The party delegates bear less resemblance to their mass constituencies in terms of socioeconomic status, as can be seen with regard to education and occupation in Table 4.2. These patterns reveal that convention delegates were on balance social as well as political elites. This version of the "iron law of oligarchy," whereby party elites had higher status than their co-partisans in the mass public, is a standard finding in the literature.[13] The plain fact is that convention delegates are political elites, and they share the distinctive socioeconomic characteristics of other elites.

Both Republican and Democratic delegates were well educated, with more than three-quarters having a four-year degree or postgraduate education. Very few delegates reported a high school diploma or less (and many of these were senior citizens, reflecting the education standard of previous generations). The Democratic delegates were a little bit better educated than the Republicans, having a few more advanced degrees and graduate training.

This high level of education fit the occupations of convention delegates, which were dominated by various kinds of professionals.[14] One important difference between the parties was the proportion of "New Class" professionals—writers, teachers, social workers, and scientists—whose jobs involve the production and use of information. Such professionals made up 24 percent of the Democratic delegates, almost twice the proportion of the Republican delegates in such fields. But the parties were essentially tied on three other kinds of professionals. For instance, both parties have the same proportion of lawyers (11 percent) and about the same proportion of technical professionals, such as accountants, engineers, and computer programmers (6 and 7 percent, respectively).

In addition, Republican and Democratic delegates had about equal numbers of political professionals (13 and 15 percent, respectively). This category

TABLE 4.2. National convention delegates and education and occupation, 2004

	REPUBLICAN	DEMOCRAT
Education		
High school or less	5	7
Some college, associate degree	19	15
Four-year degree	36	26
Graduate training, degree	35	43
Advanced degree	5	10
Occupation		
New class professionals	14	24
Political professionals	13	15
Lawyers	11	11
Technical professionals	6	7
Small business owners	19	6
Business managers	9	4
Government workers	4	9
Clerical, blue collar	4	7
Homemakers	7	1
Retired, other	13	16
Public office and other occupations		
Current political professionals	13	15
Past office-holder	11	7
Future office-holder	40	42
Professional occupations	12	22
Business occupations	13	5
Other	12	10

Source: Authors' 2004 survey.
Note: Weighted N = 500 for each party.

includes current office-holders, party and interest-group leaders, and a wide variety of professional campaign activists. It is interesting that the parties have rough parity in this regard, given that the Democrats reserve spaces for "super delegates" drawn from elected Democratic officials.[15] In 2004, it appears that Republicans chose nearly as many elected officials to serve as delegates.

As one might expect, the Democrats had an edge over the Republicans with blue collar and clerical workers (7 to 4 percent) and nonpolitical government employees (9 to 4 percent). Similarly, Republicans led among small business owners (19 to 6 percent) and corporate managers (9 to 4 percent) but also among self-described homemakers (7 to 1 percent). Delegates who were retired or had other occupations (such as college students) were found in about equal numbers (13 percent for the GOP, 16 for Democrats). These occupational characteristics appear to confirm the standard stereotypes of which groups make up the core constituencies of the two parties.

The prominence of professionals among Democratic and Republican delegates has been increasingly common over the last thirty years, following changes in the national economy.[16] But the presence of political professionals, especially office-holders, represents a bit of a trend back toward the conventions of the mid-twentieth century.[17] The final entry in Table 4.2 explores this pattern by adding two pieces of information, showing delegates who had served as office-holders previously and those who planned to seek public office in the future. If one adds the past officials in each party (11 percent Republicans, 7 percent Democrats) to the current political professionals, more than one-fifth of each convention was made up of political professionals. But more importantly, better than two-fifths of each set of delegates aspired to public office (40 and 42 percent, respectively). Thus, a grand total of 64 percent of the delegates could be classified as office seekers or office-seeker aides. Clearly, ambition for future office was alive and well among Republican and Democratic delegates alike in 2004 (see Schlesinger on the importance *of ambition and* office seeking in contemporary parties).[18] Interestingly, the Republican business and Democratic New Class professional biases remain among the delegates who reported no connection to office seeking, past, present or future.

As one might surmise from the education and occupation of convention delegates, they were well off financially. Although the PES surveys do not include a measure of income, other evidence reveals that about three-fifths of both sets of delegates reported family incomes of $75,000 or more in 2004. However, Republicans were more affluent overall: more than one-quarter claimed a yearly income of $1 million or more, compared to about one-sixth of the Democrats.[19]

DELEGATE ACTIVITIES IN 2004

Past research has revealed that convention delegates are very active in politics.[20] Table 4.3 reports several kinds of activities in which party elites specialize, beginning with serving as national convention delegates. About two-fifths of both sets of delegates reported serving previous to 2004 and almost three-fifths were first-time delegates. Although the exact figures vary from year to year, these patterns were similar to conventions in the 1990s, revealing a high level of turnover among delegates, with a large influx of new delegates in each election cycle. The national conventions were certainly characterized by a "circulation of party elites."[21] Two-fifths of delegates reported having been active primarily in county party committees. The remaining delegates reported that their activity was primarily at the state or national level. Two-fifths of the Republicans were active at the state party level and the remaining one-sixth at the national level. The Democrats showed a slightly different pattern, with one-third active at the state level and one-quarter at the national levels. The only major difference from the conventions in the 1990s was a higher level of national party service among the Democratic delegates.

The convention delegate literature has made much of the conflict between party-oriented "professionals" (or "pragmatists") versus candidate- and issue-oriented "amateurs" (or "purists").[22] Table 4.3 reports one measure of these orientations among the 2004 delegates: a dichotomous choice between an emphasis on party work versus an emphasis on candidate and issue engagement. In 2004, both conventions were dominated by delegates that reported an emphasis on party work, four-fifths of the Republicans and three-quarters of the Democrats. Looked at another way, the party-oriented "professionals" outnumbered the candidate- and issue-oriented "amateurs" three to one or better. This pattern was quite stable for the Republicans in the 1990s and fluctuated a bit more for the Democrats. Indeed, the candidate and issue orientation of the Democratic delegates was up a bit in 2004, approaching the level of 1992 (31 percent). These findings certainly fit with the greater professionalism of party elites evident since the 1970s.[23] In short, neither convention is numerically dominated by amateurs, although they are a larger proportion of the Democratic delegations than the Republican delegations. This finding may be a function of the Democrats being the out party in 2004.

Table 4.3 does, however, reveal a longstanding difference between the major party delegates.[24] Democratic delegates are much more likely to see themselves as representing a particular group at the convention; more than two-thirds of the Democratic delegates reported this representative role, while more than three-fifths of the Republicans did not. Here, too, the pattern fits with the conventions in the 1990s, although the exact numbers vary a bit from year to year. In 2004, both sets of delegates were more likely to see themselves as representing a group than in the 1990s.

Of course, organized interests were a critical element in the profile of party elites.[25] Table 4.4 reports the proportion of the elites who belonged to a wide variety of interest groups and who were active in or leaders of such organizations. For ease of presentation, Table 4.4 breaks up the groups by those that were more common among Republican delegates, those common in both par-

TABLE 4.3. National convention delegates and political activity, 2004

	REPUBLICAN	DEMOCRAT
Past delegate		
Yes	41	41
No	59	59
Party service		
County	41	41
State	42	34
National	17	25
Motive		
Regularly does party work	82	75
Works for candidate, issue	18	25
Represents a group		
Yes	39	69
No	61	31

Source: Authors' 2004 survey.
Note: Weighted N = 500 for each party.

ties, and those more common among the Democrats. These data reveal the traditional elements of each party's coalition and the elite nature of delegates.

It should come as no surprise that membership in business groups was more common among the Republican delegates, with almost one-half of the delegates belonging to or being active in such associations. While business interests were hardly absent from Democratic ranks, they were about half as numerous in relative terms. These figures have changed little from recent conventions or indeed from past decades. However, the next most important groups, antiabortion and religion-based organizations, are recent additions to the Republican coalition. Membership in right-to-life groups accounted for one-third of the GOP delegates in 2004, while religious group membership were found among more than one-quarter of the delegates.

Membership in right-to-life groups increased over the 1990s, while membership in religious groups varied a good bit. The latter is dominated by Christian right groups that have been the source of considerable conflict within the Republican camp. Members in both groups were rare among Democrats in 2004 (7 and 15, respectively). It is worth noting, however, that supporters of a "Christian left" made up about one-quarter of 2004 Democratic delegates (data not shown). Finally, farm organization members were about twice as

TABLE 4.4. National convention delegates and group membership, 2004

		REPUBLICAN	DEMOCRATIC
More Republican			
Business	Member	31	16
	Activist/leader	16	7
Right to life	Member	21	6
	Activist/leader	12	1
Religious	Member	15	10
	Activist/leader	12	5
Farm	Member	12	5
	Activist/leader	3	3
Veterans	Member	10	7
	Activist/leader	2	4
Common in both parties			
Community service	Member	24	18
	Activist/leader	15	15
Party-affiliated	Member	23	20
	Activist/leader	24	18
Professional	Member	16	18
	Activist/leader	4	5
Hispanic	Member	3	3
	Activist/leader	2	4
Jewish	Member	3	3
	Activist/leader	2	4
More Democratic			
Gay, lesbian	Member	1	6
	Activist/leader	1	5
Party-unaffiliated	Member	1	10
	Activist/leader	1	6
Women's	Member	8	12
	Activist/leader	4	6
Educational	Member	5	12
	Activist/leader	4	10
527 committee	Member	4	14
	Activist/leader	1	2

TABLE 4.4. *(continued)*

		REPUBLICAN	DEMOCRATIC
Reform groups	Member	7	15
	Activist/leader	2	7
Labor	Member	3	15
	Activist/leader	1	13
Feminist	Member	2	19
	Activist/leader	1	9
Environmental	Member	6	22
	Activist/leader	3	8
Pro-choice	Member	5	22
	Activist/leader	2	11
Civil rights	Member	5	26
	Activist/leader	5	12

Source: Authors' 2004 survey.
Note: Weighted N = 500 for each party.

common among Republicans as Democrats but were not especially numerous overall.

Common to both sets of delegates were community-service (such as Kiwanis and Rotary clubs), party-affiliated (such as college Republicans and Democrats), professional (such as medical and legal societies), veteran, Hispanic, and Jewish groups. Participation in the first four types of groups is another marker of the delegates' elite status, since such groups are central to political life in many communities across the country. However, the partisan parity among Hispanic and Jewish groups is a bit of a surprise and differs from the conventions in the 1990s. Given the small number of delegates belonging to such groups, any interpretation must be advanced with caution, but this change may represent a modest broadening of the Republican reach into these traditionally Democratic communities. One way to do so is to include representatives of such groups among those privileged to attend the national conventions. Certainly the Bush campaign in 2004 made a concerted effort to reach out to the Hispanic and Jewish communities and tried to recruit their votes. All of this strategic thinking is a part of making the party "combat ready" for the fall campaign.

The remaining eleven groups were more common among the Democratic delegates than the Republicans in 2004. The largest groups were stalwarts of the Democratic coalition and accounted for more than one-quarter of the delegates: civil rights (38 percent), pro-choice (33 percent), environmental (30 percent), feminist (28 percent), and labor (28 percent) organizations. While such memberships were hardly unheard of in the Republican camp, the Democrats typically outnumbered the GOP in this regard by more than three to one. These patterns were similar at the earlier Democratic conventions and are indicators of the attempts of both parties to mobilize their base through outreach to larger social movements.[26] Three other types of groups, nonpartisan reform groups (such as Common Cause, League of Women Voters), nonfeminist Women's groups (such as American Association of University Women), and education organizations (such as the National Education Association) accounted for about one-fifth of the Democratic delegates, and Republicans were one-third to one-half less common than Democrats. Gay rights groups were the least common of these organizations and had very few Republican adherents, despite the publicity accorded to the Log Cabin Republicans in 2004.

The Democratic delegates were more numerous in two other kinds of organizations, party-unaffiliated groups and 527 committees. Party-unaffiliated groups, such as the Democratic Leadership Council (DLC), played a major role in Democratic Party politics in the 1990s and were roughly the same size in 2004 as in the past, more than one-sixth of the delegates. The 527 committees represent an innovation of the 2004 campaign, and include such prominent organizations as Americans Coming Together (which conducted registration and get out the vote programs in 2004) and the Media Fund (which attacked President Bush's record in office). Created to raise and spend "soft money," which was banned by law in 2002, membership in such groups accounted for one-sixth of the Democratic delegates. Both types of groups also existed in Republican circles, such as Empower America (a counterpart to the DLC), and the Swift Boat Veterans for Truth (a 527 committee that attacked Senator John Kerry's military record). However, in 2004 the Republican delegates were markedly less likely to participate in both kinds of groups.

DELEGATE ATTITUDES IN 2004

What about the political attitudes of convention delegates in 2004? Table 4.5 begins with self-reported ideology, and it reveals a strong division between the two major parties. Nearly four-fifths of the Republicans called themselves

TABLE 4.5. National convention delegates and ideology and issue priorities, 2004

	REPUBLICAN	DEMOCRAT
Ideology		
Very conservative	23	1
Conservative	55	2
Moderate	21	39
Liberal	0	44
Very liberal	0	14
Issue priorities		
Foreign policy	64	24
Social policy	12	5
Political process	5	9
Economic policy	19	62

Source: Authors' 2004 survey.
Note: Weighted N = 500 for each party.

"conservative" and almost three-fifths of the Democrats labeled themselves "liberal." In addition, more Republican delegates chose the "very conservative" designation (23 percent) than Democrats chose the "very liberal" option (14 percent). At the same time, self-described moderates were less common among the Republicans (21 percent) than Democrats (39 percent). There were virtually no liberals at the GOP convention and very few conservatives at the Democratic meeting (3 percent). Simply put, the elite-level cadres of both parties are now quite polarized into two very different ideological camps.

In 2004, both party's delegates were marginally more polarized in terms of ideology than at the 2000 conventions, but these patterns were consistent with the patterns in the 1990s.[27] Party delegates have, however, become more ideological since the 1950s,[28] but even then, Republican delegates had conservative views and Democrats held liberal positions.[29] Indeed, one of the most persistent findings of the literature is that each party's delegates have always held more intense views that the mass public, with Republican delegates holding more conservative positions on most issues than Republican voters, and Democratic delegates holding more liberal positions on most issues than Democratic voters.[30] Although comparable survey data for the mass public are not available at this writing, there is every reason to believe this pattern persisted in 2004.[31]

In part, this difference between party elites and voters' patterns reflects the greater knowledge and political commitment of the party elites compared to the mass public. However, this tendency has expanded over the last three decades as American politics has polarized more broadly. In this sense, the major parties have moved closer to the ideal of party "responsibility," taking clear and distinct positions on issues.[32] But it also suggests that the more moderate positions frequently taken by presidential candidates may more accurately reflect the public's views.

The second entry in Table 4.5 describes the delegates' issue priorities in 2004. Here the differences were larger than ideology. When asked to list the "single most important problem facing this country," more than three-fifths of the Republican delegates chose a foreign policy response, such as the war in Iraq or terrorism. In contrast, more than three-fifths of the Democrats picked an economic issue, such as jobs or welfare programs. Although distinctly secondary priorities, about twice as many Republicans mentioned a social issue, such as abortion or marriage (12 to 5 percent); the Democrats returned the favor on political-process issues, such as campaign-finance reform or a biased news media (5 to 9 percent).

Thus, the major party elites were largely talking past each other in terms of issue priorities in 2004. One reason for this pattern was the sudden rise of foreign policy issues after the terrorist attacks on September 11, 2001. This presented a major change from previous conventions for the Republicans. During the 1990s, both sets of party elites tended to focus on economic issues. For example, in 1996, 56 percent of Republicans and 73 percent of Democrats gave priority to an economic issue, and just 1 percent of each party listed a foreign policy matter. (The GOP did give higher priority to social issues in 1996, 33 to 18 percent.)

Foreign Policy Issues. Table 4.6 looks at the foreign policy views of the party elites. On the controversial issue of the Iraq war, the parties were deeply divided. For example, three-quarters of the Republican delegates said the Iraq war was "completely justified" while seven in ten Democrats said it was "completely unjustified." Just a few delegates (3 percent of both sets) agreed with the dominant views of the other party, and only about one-quarter of the delegates reported doubts about whether the Iraq war was justified.

Such divisions reached beyond the Iraq war to the broader policy positions behind it. For instance, party elites strongly disagreed as to whether the United States should pursue preemptive attacks in the future. Here nearly four-fifths of the Republicans supported the idea of a preemptive attack and the same proportion of Democrats opposed such a policy. In a similar vein, Republican delegates were deeply skeptical of working through the United

TABLE 4.6. National convention delegates and foreign policy, 2004

	REPUBLICAN	DEMOCRAT
Iraq war		
Completely justified	76	0
Probably justified	22	3
Probably unjustified	2	26
Completely unjustified	1	70
*Preemptive attack in the future**		
U.S. should attack	79	20
U.S. should not attack	21	80
*U.S. should work through the United Nations**		
Extremely important	8	79
Somewhat important	45	21
Not so important	47	0
Defense spending		
Greatly increase	24	30
Increase	57	17
Neutral	16	26
Decrease	3	40
Greatly decrease	0	14

Source: Authors' 2004 survey.
Note: Weighted N = 500 for each party.
*CBS / *New York Times* Delegate Polls, 2004.

Nations to maintain world peace, with just 8 percent saying it was "extremely important" and 47 percent saying it was "not so important." In contrast, 79 percent of Democratic delegates said working through the UN was "extremely important" and none thought it was "not so important." To say that the elites of the two parties have quite different world views is almost an understatement; they almost live in two different cognitive worlds.

There were also similar differences on defense spending, an issue that has frequently divided the major parties.[33] Four-fifths of the Republican delegates favored increasing defense spending (with one-quarter strongly in favor). In contrast, more than one-half of the Democratic delegates favored reducing defense spending (with one-sixth strongly in favor). About one-fifth of the Democrats favored more defense spending and almost no Republicans favor less. The 2004 pattern on this issue represents a small shift away from increased defense spending compared to 2000, particularly among Democrats. And the

TABLE 4.7. National convention delegates and economic issues, 2004

	REPUBLICAN	DEMOCRAT
Bush tax cuts		
Strongly approve	56	0
Approve	29	1
Neutral	5	1
Disapprove	8	10
Strongly disapprove	2	88
Health insurance		
Strongly favor private insurance	47	2
Favor	38	5
Neutral	6	9
Oppose	7	40
Strongly favor government insurance	2	44
Special help for minorities		
Strongly oppose special treatment	31	3
Oppose	32	9
Neutral	19	11
Favor	16	50
Strongly favor helping minorities	2	27
Public services		
Strongly support reducing	16	0
Support	46	6
Neutral	21	8
Oppose	13	34
Strongly oppose reducing	4	52

Source: Authors' 2004 survey.
Note: Weighted N = 500 for each party.

pattern was quite different from 1992, when few Republicans favored more defense spending and a very large majority of Democrats favored a decrease.

Economic Issues. Table 4.7 reveals equally deep divisions between the party elites on economic questions. The first entry covers reactions to President Bush's tax cuts. More than four-fifths of the Republican delegates supported the tax cuts and more than one-half supported them strongly. The Democrats were even more adamantly opposed, with nearly 100 percent opposing the tax cuts and almost 90 percent opposing them strongly. As with foreign policy, the signature economic policy of the Bush administration produced intense division between the parties.

The Republicans and Democrats also disagreed on the level of public services provided by the federal government. Almost two-thirds of the GOP delegates favored fewer public services (one-sixth felt strongly about such cuts), while more than four-fifths of the Democrats opposed a reduction in services (and more than one-half felt strongly about it). The disagreement was modestly less intense on another staple of partisanship, national health insurance. Here better than four-fifths of the Republicans favored private insurance (almost one-half strongly), while the Democrats favored government insurance by about the same margin (with more than two-fifths supporting this position strongly). Finally, there was also division over whether minorities should receive special assistance from the government. More than three-fifths of the Republicans opposed such assistance to minorities, while almost four-fifths of the Democrats supported such assistance.

These three economic issues have long differentiated the major parties.[34] The 2004 differences on public services were sharper because the Republican delegates moved sharply to the right; the Democratic delegates had already made a comparable shift to the left in 2000. In contrast, divisions over health insurance were also sharper because the Democrats had moved leftward after 2000. Meanwhile, the division over minority assistance was fairly stable throughout the 1990s. On balance, the delegates were more polarized in 2004 than in the most recent election years, but a high degree of polarization has long been evident on these issues.

Social Issues. Table 4.8 turns to social issues, beginning with another topic new to the political agenda in 2004, the question of defining the legal status of marriage. Almost three-quarters of the Republican delegates favored passage of a law defining traditional marriage (between one man and one woman), about one-quarter preferred some kind of civil union, and very few supported same-sex marriage. Here the Democrats had a more even division: nearly one-half of the Democratic delegates favored same-sex marriage, another two-fifths civil unions, and just one-eighth favored laws that maintained traditional marriage against the alternatives.

The perennial hot button issue of abortion produced similar differences, but here it was the Republicans turn to be more divided. About two-thirds of the GOP delegates favored a pro-life position (banning all abortions or allowing them only under restrictive circumstances). It is notable, however, that only 18 percent of the Republican delegates took the most pure pro-life position. In contrast, more than 90 percent of the Democratic delegates held pro-choice positions, and almost eight in ten saw abortion as strictly a personal

TABLE 4.8. National convention delegates and social issues, 2004

	REPUBLICAN	DEMOCRAT
Marriage		
Traditional marriage	72	12
Civil unions	24	40
Same-sex marriage	4	48
Abortion		
Never permitted	18	1
Only in special cases	51	7
If need established	16	13
As personal choice	15	79
School vouchers		
Strongly favor	50	3
Favor	24	4
Neutral	7	6
Oppose	10	14
Strongly oppose	6	73
Death penalty for murder		
Strongly favor	52	5
Favor	35	23
No opinion	3	4
Oppose	7	34
Strongly oppose	3	34

Source: Authors' 2004 survey.
Note: Weighted N = 500 for each party.

choice, thus taking the most adamant pro-choice position. Although a large minority of Republicans held pro-choice positions, very few Democrats were pro-life.

Not all social issues concern sexual matters. One increasingly divisive issue is school vouchers. About three-quarters of the Republican delegates in 2004 supported school vouchers, with one-half favoring them strongly. Democrats were adamantly opposed, at more than four-fifths, with nearly three-quarters strongly so. Republicans also endorsed the death penalty for convicted murderers by almost 90 percent (with more than one-half having strong opinions), while the Democrats were more divided, with some two-thirds opposing the death penalty (about one-third strongly so). But more than one-quarter of the Democratic delegates supported capital punishment for murder.

Such social issues have become an increasing part of the division between the major parties in the 1990s.[35] Republican delegates have tended toward the pro-life position all along, and the Democrats have been strongly pro-choice. If anything, the 2004 figures appear to represent a modest moderation in abortion attitudes since 2000. School vouchers show even more stability, with a very large majority of Democrats strongly opposing vouchers and roughly a majority of the Republicans favoring them. Opinion on the death penalty also remained consistent in recent times among these party elites.

PARTY PROFILES IN 2004

In 2004, the major party convention delegates had distinctive profiles. There were important differences in delegate attributes, especially on race, religion, and occupation. However, the tendency of Republicans to be white, traditionally religious business professionals and the Democrats to be more racially diverse, less traditionally religious New Class professionals was blurred by the high social and political status of both delegations. Indeed, these rival party elites resembled each other in their focus on office seeking and party work. They did differ on the importance of representing groups in party politics. The delegates were deeply involved in rival interest groups, with the Republicans belonging to business and conservative Christian groups, while the Democrats belonged to labor unions and a host of liberal causes, including civil rights, feminism, and environmentalism. Civil society was clearly well represented inside the halls of the 2004 national conventions.

The signature party profiles were sharpest in terms of delegate attitudes. The Republican party elites were quite conservative, both in terms of self-identified ideology and the range of foreign policy, economic, and social issues. Meanwhile, the Democratic party elites were self-described liberals and held liberal positions on the full range of issues. While there is some nuance on particular topics, the rival delegates were highly polarized, especially on issues closely associated with President Bush. Perhaps because of these special issues in 2004, delegates had sharply divergent issue priorities, with the Republicans most concerned with foreign policy and the Democrats focused on the economy.

However, sharp ideological cleavage between party elites is simply a variation on a theme common in recent times: the national conventions have been the organs of "advocacy parties" for many decades now,[36] the culmination of a gradual shift away from the less ideological parties of the mid-twentieth

century and earlier.[37] It may not be entirely a coincidence that ideology became dominant among the national convention delegates during the same
time period that the mass media came to play a major role in national politics,
including convention coverage. However, the exact nature of this parallel development is far from clear and both may well be the results of deeper shifts in
American society.[38] The polarization among these delegates is certainly related
to the now familiar "red state" versus "blue state" geographic polarization at the
aggregate level popularized by the mass media in 2000 and 2004.

Thus, the raw material for campaign organization present at each of the
national conventions in 2004 had a distinctive character. The resources and enthusiasm of these party elites were critical to the success of both campaigns in
the close contest that followed. These differences also presented the presidential candidates with challenges. President Bush faced party elites drawn from
various conservative interests and with views that were often to the right of
most Republican voters and the country as a whole. Likewise, Senator Kerry
confronted party elites drawn from numerous liberal interests and with views
that were often to the left of most Democratic voters, not to mention the
general public. One of the most crucial functions of the conventions is to work
out this challenge in a productive fashion. Thus, the national conventions are
staging grounds for presidential campaigns, where the parties engage in compromising, coalescing, and introducing the themes and personalities critical
for the general election. In this regard, the conventions deserve more respect
than they typically receive.

NOTES

1. The literature on convention delegates is voluminous. The highlights include Paul T.
David, Ralph M. Goldman, and Richard C. Bain, *The Politics of National Party Conventions*
(Washington, DC: Brookings Institution Press, 1960); Herbert McClosky, Paul Hoffman,
and Rosemary O'Hara, "Issue Conflict and Consensus among Party Leaders and Followers,"
American Political Science Review 54 (1960): 406–27; Herbert McClosky, "Consensus and Ideology in American Politics," *American Political Science Review* 58 (1964): 361–82; Jeane J. Kirkpatrick, *The New Presidential Elite: Men and Women in National Politics* (New York: Russell Sage
Foundation, 1976); John S. Jackson, Barbara L. Brown, and David Bositis, "Herbert McClosky
and Friends Revisited," *American Politics Quarterly* 10 (1982): 158–80; Alan I. Abramowitz and
Walter J. Stone, *Nomination Politics: Party Activists and Presidential Choice* (New York: Praeger,
1984); Warren E. Miller and M. Kent Jennings, *Parties in Transition: A Longitudinal Study
of Party Elites and Party Supporters* (New York: Sage, 1986); Emmett H. Buell and John S.
Jackson, "The National Conventions: Diminished But Still Important in a Primary Dominated Process," in *Nominating the President*, ed. Emmett H. Buell and Lee Sigelman (Knox-

ville: University of Tennessee Press, 1991); John S. Jackson, "The Party-as-Organization: Party Elites and Party Reforms in Presidential Nominations and Conventions," in *Challenges to Party Government*, ed. John Kenneth White and Jerome M. Mileur (Carbondale: Southern Illinois University, 1992), 63–83; Richard Herrera, "Are 'Superdelegates' Super?" *Political Behavior* 16 (1994): 79–92; Richard Herrera, "The Crosswinds of Change: Sources of Change in the Democratic and Republican Parties," *Political Research Quarterly* 48 (1995): 291–312; John S. Jackson and Nancy Clayton, "Leaders and Followers: Major Party Elites, Identifiers, and Issues, 1980–1992," in *The State of the Parties*, 2d ed., ed. John C. Green and Daniel M. Shea (Lanham, MD: Rowman and Littlefield, 1996); John C. Green, John S. Jackson, and Nancy L. Clayton, "Issue Networks and Party Elites in 1996," in *The State of the Parties*, 3d ed., ed. John C. Green and Daniel M. Shea (Lanham, MD: Rowman and Littlefield, 1999), 105–19; and John S. Jackson, Nathan S. Bigelow, and John C. Green, "The State of Party Elites: National Convention Delegates, 1992–2000," in *The State of the Parties*, 4th ed., ed. John C. Green and Rick Farmer (Lanham, MD: Rowman and Littlefield, 2003).

2. Miller and Jennings, *Parties in Transition.*

3. Denise L. Baer and Davis A. Bositis, *Elite Cadres and Party Coalitions* (Westport, CT: Greenwood Press, 1988).

4. Denise L. Baer, "Who Has the Body? Party Institutionalization and Theories of Party Organization," *American Review of Politics* 14 (spring 1993): 1–38.

5. Buell and Jackson, "The National Conventions."

6. In the 2004 PES survey, we mailed a questionnaire to a systematic random sample of the delegates to both conventions using the official delegate roster provided by each national party. The questionnaires were mailed immediately after the national convention for each party. After one follow-up mailing, we received 458 usable returns for the Democrats, for a response rate of 45 percent, excluding undeliverable mail; for the Republicans, we received 502 usable returns, for a response rate of 46.5 percent, excluding undeliverable mail. The 2004 data was weighted for race, producing a weighted N of 500 cases in each party.

7. On previous PES surveys, see John S. Jackson and Robert A. Hitlin, "A Comparison of Party Elites: The Sanford Commission and the Delegates to the Democratic Mid-Term Conferences," *American Politics Quarterly* 4 (1976): 441–81; Jackson, Brown, and Bositis, "Herbert McClosky"; Buell and Jackson, "The National Conventions"; Jackson, "The Party-as-Organization"; Jackson and Clayton, "Leaders and Followers"; Green, Jackson, and Clayton, "Issue Networks"; and Jackson, Bigelow, and Green, "Leaders and Followers."

8. Jackson, Brown, and Bositis, "Herbert McClosky and Friends Revisited"; Kirkpatrick, *The New Presidential Elite;* Miller and Jennings, *Parties in Transition.*

9. Karen M. Kaufman and John R. Petrocik, "The Changing Politics of American Men: Understanding the Sources of the Gender Gap," *American Journal of Political Science* 43 (1999): 864–87.

10. In the PES surveys, Hispanic identification is included in the same measure as race.

11. John C. Green and Mark Silk, "The New Religion Gap," *Religion in the News* 6, no. 3, Special Supplement (2003): 1–3, 15.

12. Kirkpatrick, *The New Presidential Elite.*

13. Miller and Jennings, *Parties in Transition.*

14. Green, Jackson, and Clayton, "Issue Networks and Party Elites in 1996."

15. Herrera, "Are 'Superdelegates' Super?"

16. Herrera, "The Crosswinds of Change."

17. David, Goldman, and Bain, *The Politics of National Party Conventions;* Jackson and Hitlin, "A Comparison of Party Elites."

18. Joseph A. Schlesinger, *Political Parties and the Winning of Office* (Ann Arbor: University of Michigan Press, 1991).

19. "A Look at the Delegates to the Democratic Convention," *New York Times,* June 16– July 17, 2004; "A Look at the Delegates to the Republican Convention," *New York Times,* August 3–20, 2004.

20. Miller and Jennings, *Parties in Transition;* Jackson, "The Party-as-Organization."

21. Herrera, "The Crosswinds of Change."

22. There is an extensive literature on amateurs and professionals in party politics. Important work includes James Q. Wilson, *The Amateur Democrat* (Chicago: University of Chicago Press, 1962); Aaron Wildavsky, "The Goldwater Phenomenon: Purists, Politicians, and the Two-Party System," *Review of Politics* 27 (1965): 393–99; M. Margaret Conway and Frank B. Feigert, "Motivations, Incentive Systems, and the Political Party Organization," *American Political Science Review* 62 (1968): 1159–73; John W. Soule and James W. Clark, "Amateurs and Professionals: A Study of Delegates to the 1968 Democratic National Convention," *American Political Science Review* 64 (1970): 888–98; Kirkpatrick, *The New Presidential Elite;* Miller and Jennings, *Parties in Transition.* For a summary of the literature, see Thomas Carsey, John Green, Rick Herrera, and Geoffrey Layman, "The New Party Professionals? An Initial Look at National Convention Delegates in 2000 and Over Time," paper presented at the annual meeting of the American Political Science Association, Philadelphia, September 1, 2003.

23. Carsey, Green, Herrera, and Layman, "The New Party Professionals."

24. Denise L. Baer and Julie A. Dolan, "Intimate Connections: Political Interests and Group Activity in State and Local Parties," *American Review of Politics* 15 (summer 1994): 257–89.

25. Baer and Bositis, *Elite Cadres;* Green, Jackson, and Clayton, "Issue Networks."

26. Baer and Bositis, *Elite Cadres.*

27. Jackson, Brown, and Bositis, "Herbert McClosky"; Jackson, Bigelow, and Green, "The State of Party Elites," 54–78.

28. Jackson, "The Party-as-Organization"; Kirkpatrick, *The New Presidential Elite.*

29. McClosky, "Consensus."

30. McClosky, Hoffman, and O'Hara, "Issue Conflict."

31. For example, the CBS/New York Times Surveys found that 79% of Democratic delegates agreed that "the government should do more solve national problems," compared to 48% of Democratic voters. For the Republicans delegates, 85% believed the government was doing too much, compared to 60% of Republican voters.

32. Gerald Pomper, "Parliamentary Government in the United States?" in *The State of the Parties,* 4th ed., ed. John C. Green and Daniel M. Shea (Lanham, MD: Rowman and Littlefield, 2003); John C. Green and Paul S. Herrnson, eds., *Responsible Partisanship? The Evolution of American Political Parties Since 1950* (Lawrence: University Press of Kansas, 2002).

33. John S. Jackson and Nancy Clayton, "Leaders and Followers: Major Party Elites, Identifiers, and Issues, 1980–1992," in *The State of the Parties,* 2d ed., ed. John C. Green and Daniel M. Shea (Lanham, MD: Rowman and Littlefield, 1996); John S. Jackson, Nathan S. Bigelow, and John C. Green, "Leaders and Followers: National Convention Delegates, 1992–2000," in *The*

State of the Parties, 4th ed., ed. John C. Green and Rick Farmer (Lanham, MD: Rowman and Littlefield, 2003).

34. Jackson, Brown, and Bositis, "Herbert McClosky"; Jackson and Clayton, "Leaders and Followers"; Jackson, Bigelow and Green, "Leaders and Followers."

35. Jackson and Clayton "Leaders and Followers"; Jackson, Bigelow, and Green, "Leaders and Followers."

36. John M. Bruce, John A. Clark, and John H. Kessel, "Advocacy Politics in Presidential Parties," *American Political Science Review* 85 (1991): 1089–1106.

37. David, Goldman, and Bain, *The Politics of National Party Conventions;* Jackson "The Party-as-Organization"; Jackson and Hitlin, "A Comparison of Party Elites."

38. John H. Aldrich, *Why Parties?* (Chicago: University of Chicago Press, 1995).

5

THE UTILITY OF PARTY CONVENTIONS IN AN ERA
OF LOW VISIBILITY AND CAMPAIGN FINANCE REFORM
J. Mark Wrighton

OVER TIME, THE PROCESS by which Americans choose their chief executive
has changed dramatically. The process has progressed from individuals seeking
the presidency to party elites choosing their standard bearers to a democratization of the process through which the mass memberships of political parties
select nominees for the general election. Coupled with other changes in the
political system (i.e., the Progressive ballot and voter registration reforms of
the early twentieth century and more recent campaign finance reforms), these
modifications have had profound effects on the types of candidates who seek
the presidency, the attention paid to the process by the wider electorate and
the media, and the amount of resources required to win the office.

The principal vehicle by which the political parties choose their presidential nominees is the party convention. The nomination process has inherent
importance in that it sets the conditions of the general election, and who is
chosen to lead the ticket goes far in determining the party's electoral fortunes.
Indeed, party bosses understand well the impact that determining who will
carry their standards has on the general election.[1]

The nomination process itself has changed extensively over time. Each time
a change has occurred, the effect has been to open up, or "democratize," the
process further. In order to understand the current state of affairs in the American presidential election system, one must recall that significant changes have
come in the last thirty-five years as more registered partisans have gained access to the process through participation in party primaries to select delegates
to a national convention. The shift from party caucuses to a primary election
process for committing party delegates to candidates prior to the nominating
convention has further reduced the control party elites once had.

Recently, however, party chairs have found ways to affect the outcome of
the presidential nominating process by adjusting the process prior to the con-

vention. This has occurred principally through an ever-increasing frontloading of the schedule of state party presidential primaries. The resulting clustering of state primaries closer to the front of the process has made available many more delegates much earlier in the process. In 2004, the Democratic Party had—in Sen. John F. Kerry of Massachusetts—a candidate with enough delegates in hand to claim the nomination by March 2, an extremely early date. As we will see, such extreme frontloading places intense pressure on candidates to raise large amounts of money earlier and forces those without substantial resources to withdraw from the process sooner.

Furthermore, in the period leading up to the conventions, frontloading has virtually removed the suspense surrounding the identity of the nominees. At least one candidate in each party is assured of arriving at the convention with enough delegates for the nomination. Thus, for outside observers of the political process, conventions appear to have become nothing more than "unity" events or four-day commercials for the parties and their candidates. Yet the party conventions retain important purposes despite this lack of suspense.

Concomitant with the change from a party caucus process to a frontloaded primary for selecting presidential candidates is an escalating decline in the attention paid to the process. Although potential candidates consider runs for the presidency now almost four years in advance, the electorate seems not to pay attention to the process until the year—or sometimes not even until up to several months—before the election. Indeed, many voters now appear to be ignoring the conventions, thinking them to be no more than opportunities for speechifying with the usual partisan rhetoric.

Prior to the primary season, presidential candidates respond to demands placed upon them by this "invisible primary" by purchasing early paid media and seeking as much free media as possible. Doing so provides candidates opportunities to introduce themselves and their policy positions to those in the electorate who may be paying attention. With the assistance of an attentive media looking for stories, this ideally translates into a buzz, which assists candidates' fundraising and endorsements efforts later in the process of capturing the nomination.

As the summer of the presidential election year comes to a close, the parties try to attract viewers to their conventions by offering grand themes for their productions. In recent times, the parties have sought to attract viewers to their conventions and to entertain them with pop music acts scattered between the speeches, elaborate video biographies of the candidates, and "convention jockeys" on the floor and from remote locations.

For its part, the media—in its dual role as agenda setter and public mood reflector—may, at first, be reluctant to cover the process until candidates take sufficient steps to enter the race. Once this occurs, the "horse race" metaphor (Who is up? Who is down?) dominates the coverage.[2] Once the race is on, substantive issues of the moment may drop dramatically in their relative importance and coverage.[3]

Overlaid on the entire presidential election process is the ever-increasing requirement for large amounts of resources in order for a candidate to garner a nomination and for the parties to showcase their nominees. Getting through to primary voters who are not paying attention and generating a buzz about a candidacy require spending money early and often. A process of natural selection occurs to the extent that those candidates who are able to do this successfully and translate it into early success and momentum are the ones most likely—regardless of their objective ability to win the general election—to become the parties' nominees. Additionally, parties must raise and spend large amounts of money in order to capture the attention of and to influence voters during their conventions.

The demand for early and big money engendered by the process stands in marked contrast to the recent push for campaign finance reform, however. As the process has been opened up to more participation among partisans, the financing of American elections has been increasingly regulated. Reformers generally bemoan the amount of money in the political system and the perceived influence it may have, yet most reforms have the counterintuitive effect of increasing the amount of money in politics, reducing the accountability of that money—or worst yet for reformers—both. Additionally, the most recent round of reform has actually *increased* the influence that groups and individuals might have through donations to the party conventions.

This chapter explores the changes in the nominating process and their effects on the party conventions outlined above by going into more historical depth with some data to elucidate the trends. It also attempts to assess whether the party conventions continue to provide any serious benefit to the process or stand as the expensive partisan "commercials" they are charged with being.

A CHANGING NOMINATION PROCESS: COMING FULL CIRCLE?

During the period leading up to the conventions, potential party nominees campaign around the country and attempt to amass enough committed delegates to claim the nomination on the convention's first ballot. Each party—through a contested nomination process—has an implicit discussion about the issues of the day and how each potential candidate will address them. In order to become a party's presidential nominee, one needs to claim a majority of the party's available delegates.

The process of how delegates are committed to particular candidates reflects the general expansion of other electoral processes in the American political system. Over time, the process has devolved from relatively small numbers of partisan elites to mass partisan electorates participating in state-by-state elections to commit delegates to candidates. Additionally, the parties have dramatically frontloaded their primary schedules with the effect of making their conventions "coronations" of their nominees. This section explores the extent to which this process has changed and how those changes have affected the character of the parties' national nominating conventions.

For a relatively brief period of their history, U.S. political parties did not hold nominating conventions. In the early 1800s, there were meetings of the parties respective congressional caucuses. It was not until the 1830s, however, that parties began formally holding meetings of members from around the country for the purpose of nominating individuals to carry their standards in the general election for president.[4] Individual states did have processes by which they named delegates to these conventions, but the delegates usually were partisan officeholders in state legislatures. There was little suspense at these meetings, as the party bosses had conferred prior to the meeting—likely in the legendary "smoke-filled room"—and decided who the nominee would be. Each party luminary would then deliver a large bloc of delegates in support of the predetermined choice. This process held little external suspense, was not open to party rank and file, and provided a means by which those in control could maintain their influence and loyalty to the party through the rewards system.

Over time, the process opened up slightly as each state party organization began holding caucuses of party activists and elites in order to commit delegates to the national nominating convention. The caucus process forced presidential candidates to let go of the "front porch" style of previous campaigns, to begin addressing the concerns of different regions of the country, and to appeal to the local partisan elites in each state. However, "King Caucus"—while opening up the nominating process slightly—was still fairly unrepresentative of the parties' general memberships. The activists who participated in the caucus process possessed a smaller (albeit larger than the process with only state legislative partisans participating) variation in party loyalty and viewpoints than did the parties' broader memberships.

The turn of the twentieth century found a reform movement sweeping the nation. The Progressive movement—in addition to pushing for voter reforms such as the secret ballot and voter registration prior to elections—advocated a further expansion of the definition of those eligible to participate in the parties' nomination process. The movement supported a change from holding caucuses to a system of party primaries, the results of which the parties might use to commit delegates to particular candidates at the nominating conventions.

Over the course of the past century, the major parties have employed this method to an increasing degree, resulting in a much broader participation by rank-and-file members. In 1912, the Democratic Party held twelve primaries and chose 33 percent of its delegates by primary elections; in the same year, the Republican Party held thirteen primaries and chose 42 percent of its delegates through the more participatory process. By 2000, the parties held primaries in forty or more states and selected more than 85 percent of their delegates through a primary process.[5] As a result of the increased use of state party primaries as the means by which to commit delegates to candidates—and their subsequent frontloading, 1952 would become the last year in which the nomination process exceeded one ballot at the convention.

While the movement from caucuses to primaries represented an important change in the process, the last thirty years have seen more profound changes in how candidates collect delegates toward the number needed to capture the nomination. The major transformation in the process arose in the form of an ever-increasing frontloading of the primary schedule. Its most significant effects have been the demands placed upon candidates. Prospective presidential candidates must now raise money and support among early-state party elites sooner than ever before.

While the Iowa caucuses and the New Hampshire primary have maintained their relative positions at the outset of the process, the national parties have allowed more state party organizations to move their contests closer to the beginning. More and more, states have sought the advantages of greater influence and coverage by the candidates and the media associated with early primary contests. Indeed, an over-time glimpse at the relative percentages of delegates available early in the primary season reveals the extent of frontloading. In the 1960 Democratic primary season, 56 percent of the available delegates were not committed until the first week of May; in 1996, 51 percent of the party's delegates were available by the third week in March.[6] With a larger percentage of delegates available earlier in the process, the party nominations are now effectively settled in the six weeks following the Iowa caucuses.[7] Thus, while enhancing voter information as candidates make themselves known earlier in the process, frontloading produces significantly lower turnout rates later in the primary season as primary outcomes have less effect in determining the nominee.

With the parties' nominations effectively settled in March of the presidential election year, the conventions have become—to outside observers—events at which "coronations" rather than nominations occur. To some they may resemble the past process, if not in exact method then in effective outcome. While party bosses may not be choosing the nominees, an ever-decreasing number of state party organizations is effectively choosing them.

Furthermore, the five to six months between harvesting enough delegates to capture the nomination and the convention enhances the challenge of running for president by reducing the candidates' visibility among the electorate. While the extra time gives them the ability to raise and spend more primary dollars, candidates must work to overcome the temptation to "coast" into the convention. During the same lull in the action, the temptation for voters and the media may be to "tune out" once the parties have a nominee in hand.

DWINDLING INTEREST IN AND COVERAGE OF THE CONVENTIONS

Contrary to what one might surmise about the interest of the electorate in the presidential campaign, one does not observe an upward climb as the November election approaches. Rather, voter interest appears to peak when parties are in the final stages of determining a nominee. As explored above, frontloading has resulted in candidates amassing a majority of the necessary delegates very early. It should be no surprise then to see that voter interest in the 2000 presidential election campaign dropped precipitously after March.[8] With the conventions now occurring five to six months after the nomination process, one should expect a small number of viewers as well as sinking amounts of media coverage.

Figure 5.1 demonstrates the steady decline in television ratings for the party conventions.[9] There are at least three potential explanations as to why fewer viewers are tuning into the conventions. Fewer may watch the proceedings because the nominee is now "predetermined," they may not watch because the parties have stripped and scripted the conventions so that they now provide little substantive debate of the issues, or they may be getting more of their political information from other sources.

First, the frontloaded primary process now produces party nominees well in advance of the conventions. In the presidential election process, there is

FIG. 5.1. Television ratings and hours of coverage, 1960–2000

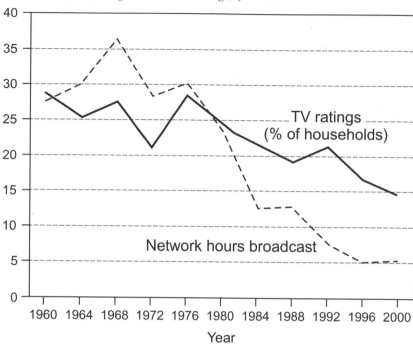

Source: Campaign Finance Institute.

nothing more dramatic than not knowing who the party's nominee will be as a party convention begins. Indeed, those who miss "the good old days" might well yearn for the now unlikely possibility of the "brokered" convention, in which no candidate arrives with a majority of delegates and speculation abounds about what deals may be necessary to cobble together a majority. The rule changes binding delegates to their preconvention commitments and expanding the use of the primary—derived from the McGovern-Fraser Commission study of the Democratic presidential nomination process—went far in removing much of the suspense from the conventions.

Second, because the conventions appear to have become "scripted commercials," voters may be tuning out. The 1968 Democratic Convention in Chicago stands as a potential watershed event in that the antiwar protests in the streets of the Windy City took attention away from and marred to some extent the proceedings in the hall. Since then, the parties have tightly controlled the events and messages of their conventions. In 2004, each party carefully structured its convention around a central theme and used the speakers on each night to communicate a finely tuned portion of the message the party wanted to convey to the electorate. Voters may simply be bored with the prepackaged political messages each convention now presents. Even partisans bemoan the lack of substantive discussions at the party quadrennial meeting.

Finally, voters are relying on a much wider array of sources for their political information. Within the television medium itself, there has been a dramatic shift away from the traditional networks toward cable outlets. There has also occurred a steep increase in reliance on Internet news outlets.[10] Instead of viewing an event that has little drama and appears to be scripted so as to remove much controversy, the electorate seems to be fragmenting as voters seek sources of information which better fit into their increasingly hectic lives and desire for reinforcement of their beliefs.[11] Thus, voters have found other ways to remain connected to the political campaigns.

The figure above also demonstrates that the number of convention coverage hours has dropped along with viewer interest. On its face, this should come as no surprise as the media is likely to deliver only what the electorate wants to see and in the amounts it desires. Indeed, television coverage has dropped to about one hour an evening during the four-day events. Television appears to have settled on covering what voters say they are most interested in seeing—the major speeches of each night.[12]

In addition to giving the viewers what they want—or maybe do not need given their reliance on the plethora of other sources of information available to them—the television networks may have also deemed the conventions as lacking in news. The lack of suspense and general (scripted?) agreement among partisans do not make for riveting television. Television has responded not only by reducing the amount of overall coverage but also by increasing the amount of analysis in an effort to "liven up" the event, but even that may have begun to ring hollow among the electorate.

Despite the drop in coverage and the number of convention viewers, the electorate appears to still be engaged with the presidential election process. Zachary Karabell—in his paper from 1998, "The Rise and Fall of the Televised Political Convention"—reminds us that conventions continue to have discernible impacts on the political process. Bounces and slumps out of the conventions still affect candidate fortunes in the general election. What is—or is not—said, how it is said, and how it plays in the electorate may contribute to the ultimate outcome in November. In the age of a transforming media, voters do not have to see them on television to hear about and to be affected by the conventions.

THE EFFECTS OF CAMPAIGN FINANCE REFORM
AND REGULATION ON CONVENTION FINANCING

The story of the American political regime continues to be one of gradual change. Over the course of 200 years, the boundaries of the nation expanded from east to west across the North American continent. The set of Americans eligible to vote has broadened dramatically over time from white, male property owners to any citizen aged eighteen or older. Additionally, the processes of American elections—including presidential ones—have changed over time. For example, by pressing for reforms such as the secret ballot and voter registration at the turn of the last century, the Progressive movement spurred dramatic change in the voting booth.

How candidates in the American political system finance their elections has—in relatively more recent times—been a major topic for reform-minded individuals. Just as reforms to the means by which presidential candidates collect delegates toward the party nomination have changed the way all involved behave, so, too, have changes to the system of financing elections changed the behavior of candidates, political interests, and parties.

In 1972, Richard Nixon set what was then a record for spending in a presidential election. The subsequent Watergate scandal raised concerns about the "cleanliness" of contributions to the Nixon campaign. Shortly thereafter, Congress—by amending a 1971 campaign finance law—enacted the first major campaign finance reform legislation, the Federal Elections and Campaigns Act (FECA), Public Law 94–283. There have been several subsequent changes to campaign finance rules, all of which have had implications for the political system at large as well as for the conventions in particular.[13]

In 1974, Congress limited the amount that individuals could contribute to campaigns to $1,000 per candidate per election. For presidential elections, Congress established a system of public financing for primary and general election candidates. This system includes a check-off provision on federal income tax forms to create and to maintain a public pool of funds for presidential candidates. FECA also limited the expenditures by candidates for public office.[14] The campaign law further established an oversight body, the Federal Election Commission, which regulates and enforces campaign finance rules, and provided a public grant program for major and minor parties to help fund their nominating conventions. Each major party receives an inflation-adjusted grant and cannot make expenditures exceeding the allocated amount.[15]

With the passage of the Bipartisan Campaign Finance Reform Act (BCFRA), Public Law 107–155, in 2002, Congress amended FECA and enacted a second major round of campaign finance reform. Among its major provisions was a doubling of the amount individuals can contribute to $2,000 per candidate per election, an indexing of this limit in future years to inflation rates, a ban on so-called soft money contributions to the political parties, restrictions on contributions by unions and corporations, and restrictions on electioneering activity by issue groups thirty days in advance of primary elections and sixty days in advance of general elections.[16]

In its infancy, the BCFRA proved to be quite controversial and has produced some unintended consequences. The legislation's electioneering and soft money ban provisions survived a court challenge—one based primarily on the assertion that they violated the tenets of the U.S. Constitution's First Amendment—put forward by political groups and party representatives in *McConnell v. FEC* (2004). Subsequent group activity in the form of 527 groups, which go unregulated by BCFRA in the amounts of money they can raise and spend, prompted a court challenge by the act's authors.[17] Finally, despite reformers' claims in 2002 that the legislation would help "take money out of politics," congressional and presidential candidates have raised and spent more money than ever before.[18]

These campaign finance regulations have had a significant impact on the American political landscape. As the rules have changed over time, individuals, candidates, and groups have adapted well in order to find legal, if not legitimate, means to maximize their ability to contribute to campaigns and to raise the funds necessary to meet the ever-increasing costs associated with crafting and disseminating a message. If one likens campaign cash to water—which always seems to find a way around barriers—it should be no surprise to learn, given the current state of campaign regulations, that groups are finding ways to influence the process through the party conventions.

In 1979, the Federal Election Commission issued regulations allowing host committees, organized in the cities awarded the party conventions, to contribute to party committees and also allow unions and corporations to give freely to those host committees.[19] Thus was born the "convention loophole." As the FEC's interpretation of its regulations has changed, the size of this loophole has changed as well. In 2004, the Campaign Finance Institute (CFI) produced

FIG. 5.2. Contributions to major party presidential nomination conventions, 1980–2004

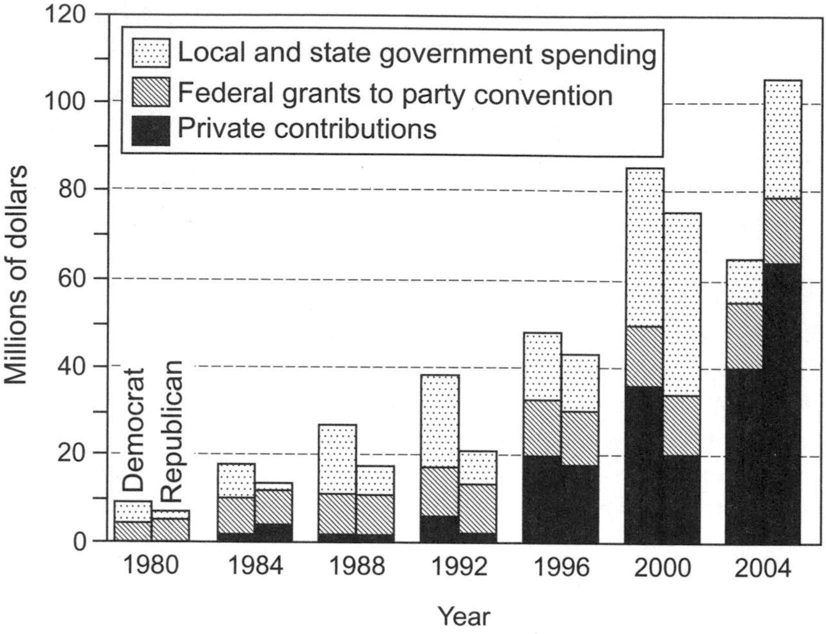

Source: Campaign Finance Institute.

a report detailing the growth of the loophole. In it, the CFI details how the commission has gradually relaxed its initial 1979 requirements that donors to convention host committees be local and that expenditures for convention expenses be in amounts proportional to what retailers might expect to recoup during the convention.[20] Because these exemptions provide resources above and beyond those supplied by the public grants-in-aid established in 1974, the amounts raised (and spent) on conventions grew exponentially in the next twenty years.

Figure 5.2 demonstrates this dramatic growth in contributions to the party conventions. First, one can see clearly the identical blocks of federal grants-in-aid given to the major parties every four years. (These are indexed to inflation, amounted to just under $15 million in the 2004 cycle, and derive from the Presidential Election Campaign Fund *before* any candidate receives matching funds.) Second, despite some variation in their contributions, it is clear that local and state governments view the conventions as worthwhile investments for their economies.[21] Third, and most importantly as to the concerns raised by reformers, there has occurred a marked rise in the amount of funds contributed by individuals and groups. Between the two major-party gatherings of 2004, the convention loophole generated $100 million in private donations, up from $9 million a scant three cycles earlier.

The CFI report characterizes this growth in private contributions as "inconsistent with the spirit, if not the letter, of BCRA's ban on national party soft money." Further, the CFI recommends that political parties pay for convention expenses with hard dollars—ones contributed to the parties under the regulated limits of campaign finance rules—and that host committees raise soft money for "civic promotion activities" only.[22] Doing so would tighten the convention loophole and reduce group influence in the nominating process. Recalling that changing the rules potentially alters outcomes, however, gives one pause to examine the implications of the full implementation of the CFI's recommendations on financing nominating conventions.

First, conventions—and by extension the entire political process—have become extremely expensive undertakings. Figures from the CFI's report provide a surprising glimpse at the enormous amounts of money necessary to conduct the conventions. The institute reports that the two parties were expected to spend, combined, a total of $76 million of the $100 million in private contributions on facilities, computer and technical support, and transportation.[23] These are costs associated with simply putting on the events and are certainly likely to rise in the future. In 2004, requiring the parties to use hard dollars, in conjunction with BCFRA's $25,000 maximum on donations to the party, would have compelled them to raise funds from at least 3,040 different individuals, if not more, as the number of donors willing to give at that level is constrained.[24]

Second, the massive fundraising effort simply to hold their quadrennial meetings would detract from the parties' other, equally important functions in the American political regime. Parties serve important functions beyond nominating candidates for election and seeking to win those contests. Besides contesting elections, the parties are vehicles by which new participants get their first experience in the political world. For better or worse, the political socialization process occurs in the context of the major political parties as parents pass on their political values, which—in turn—form the basis and energy of a generational renewal of the body politic. The adoption of the recommendations in the CFI report would likely compel the parties to choose between raising money for their conventions and doing this important outreach work.

Because these donations are made to host committees and other entities with the short-term interests of attracting conventions and then hosting them, the current system of financing conventions does not provide the electorate with any means to punish tainted donations. Simply put, private donations cannot be tied directly to the parties. It is, however, possible for the political parties to assist in reducing the perceived corruption of the current process without impairing their ability to perform important political socialization functions. Allowing parties to raise unregulated soft money for the dedicated purpose of financing their conventions would unite concerns about the sources of the money to entities with their long-term electoral interests in avoiding scandal. At the same time, the parties could remain important players in the process by which citizens participate in their government. Ideally, placing the responsibility in the hands of the parties—instead of host committees—would assuage reformers' concerns about soft money continuing as part of the process of convention financing.

THE CONTINUED IMPORTANCE OF CONVENTIONS
IN A PERIOD OF CHANGE

Given that the nomination process has lost much of its suspense, that the electorate and the media seem to have "tuned out" to the four-day party meetings, and that they have become expensive undertakings fraught with potential corruption and influence by donors, one might assume that conventions have lost their value in the American political system. Despite all of these concerns, however, they continue to serve important roles and deserve to continue to occupy a place in the presidential election process. The quadrennial party meetings serve as showcases for the basic political values of the American regime, providing a means by which candidates can fire up the troops and build support for future campaigns. They also function as vehicles through which the political socialization process occurs, which cements them firmly in the American political process.

First, political parties—like any other membership organizations desiring to perpetuate themselves—must act to pass on their lore. The national party meeting once every four years provides a singularly unique opportunity for members to renew connections and unify to get their nominee elected. Further, partisans can use their conventions to make new connections for future battles and races at state and local levels.

Second, the conventions provide an early opportunity for party candidates to begin the next "invisible primary." As noted earlier, the high demand for early support and resources has stretched the length of presidential elections beyond the four-year mark. The conventions provide a centralized opportunity for would-be candidates for president to meet important state party officials. Given their place at the beginning of the process, the Iowa and New Hampshire convention delegates receive extra attention from those considering a run for the White House. In addition to trying out their stump speeches and glad-handing prominent state officials, potential candidates can exhort the delegates to work hard for the current nominee.

Finally, conventions play an important role in the political socialization process. Delegates bring their children and other family members along to experience the circus atmosphere and to learn about the political process. Important values—such as solving political differences through the use of persuasion tactics and not violence—of our political society are passed on to the next generation. Thus, the republic is reenergized once every four years as parties convene. In recent cycles, both major parties have emphasized this important function by holding special youth-oriented events during the week and including youths in the convention programs.[25]

Of all of the rituals of American politics, only the presidential inauguration ceremony provides some of the same important—and intangible—benefits by emphasizing the republic's basic values of civil partisanship and conflict resolution. The conventions, however, represent unique opportunities for participatory politics. Concerns expressed over the modern conventions' lack of suspense, the dwindling voter interest and media coverage in them, and the large degree to which private contributions have become a major source of their funding fail to acknowledge the important contributions they make to the republic.

The one constant lesson derived from studying political processes is that changes to them inevitably result in changes to outcomes and candidate behavior. Further frontloading of the nomination process—potentially leading to a national primary, the possible replacement of traditional television network coverage by other media, and significant changes to the means by which they are funded may result in fundamental changes to the purposes served by the national conventions. Reformers would do well to remember their contributions to the American polity before calling for such changes.

NOTES

The author wishes to thank Lara M. Brown for her suggestions.

1. William Marcy "Boss" Tweed of Tammany Hall understood well the potential control over electoral outcomes afforded by controlling the nominating process when he remarked, "I don't care who does the electing as long as I get to do the nominating."

2. In 2000, the percentage of "horse race" coverage jumped to 71 percent (from 48 percent in 1996 and 58 percent in 1988 and 1992). See Table 6.2 in Stephen J. Wayne, *Is This Any Way to Run a Democratic Election?* (Boston: Houghton, Mifflin, 129).

3. In 2004, the media's obsession with the potential order of finish in the Democratic Party nomination race hit a zenith at a debate in New Hampshire when the moderator focused most of the discussion—much to the chagrin of some of the candidates—on the frontrunner status of former Vermont governor Howard Dean and his endorsement by former vice president Al Gore. Six weeks later, Dean's campaign fell apart after successive defeats in Iowa and New Hampshire.

4. For a description of the process leading up to the first nominating convention in Baltimore, Maryland, in May 1932, see Hugh Gregg and Bill Gardner, *Why New Hampshire?* (New Hampshire: Resources).

5. From Table 7.1 in Wayne, *Is This Any Way to Run a Democratic Election?*, 156.

6. Andrew E. Busch and William G. Mayer. "The Frontloading Problem" in *The Making of the Presidential Candidates, 2004*, ed. William G. Mayer (Lanham, MD: Rowman and Littlefield, 2004).

7. In 2004, Senator John F. Kerry accumulated a majority of available delegates after the March 9 primaries.

8. See Figure 4 from "Is There a Future for On-the-Air Televised Conventions" by Thomas Patterson, available at www.cfinst.org/eguide/partyconventions/background/papers.html (accessed October 17, 2005).

9. Preliminary figures for 2004 indicate relatively steady ratings.

10. For the specific figures, see Table 6.1 from Wayne, *Is This Any Way to Run a Democratic Election?*, 127.

11. There has even been an increase in the late-night comedy shows as a source of political news as voters can see them at a time when they are not otherwise occupied and in a format which may seem more entertaining than the real thing.

12. Voters are most interested in seeing the nominee's acceptance speech. For how voters rated other portions of the conventions, see Table 3 from "Is There a Future for On-the-Air Televised Conventions" by Thomas Patterson, available at www.cfinst.org/eguide/partyconventions/background/papers.html (accessed October 17, 2005).

13. Provisions of federal campaign finance laws are available at www.fec.gov/finance_law.html (accessed October 17, 2005).

14. The Supreme Court struck down FECA's spending limits on congressional candidates in *Buckley v. Valeo (1976)*. The decision did, however, uphold spending limits for presidential candidates choosing to take public funds available in the Presidential Election Campaign Fund. The decision also allowed uncoordinated "soft money" expenditures.

15. 26 USC 9008. In 2004, this grant totaled $15 million for each major party.

16. For a complete rendering of the BCFRA provisions, see http://www.cfinst.org/eguide/shays.html (accessed October 17, 2005).

17. Not only were these groups' activities unregulated but also they became campaign issues in and of themselves in the presidential election of 2004 as both major-party candidates faced well-financed attack campaigns from these groups.

18. The Center for Responsive Politics (www.opensecrets.org) reported that—as of August 2004—the two major-party presidential candidates had raised almost $600 million (accessed October 17, 2005).

19. *Federal Register* 44 (November 1, 1979): 63037, 63041–42.

20. "The $100 Million Exemption: Soft Money and the 2004 National Party Conventions," pp. 1–2, www.cfinst.org/eguide/partyconventions/financing/cfistudy.html (accessed October 17, 2005).

21. If not in the short term—as Boston discovered in 2004 with a negligible economic impact—then perhaps in the long term as an intense week-long promotion of the host city as a tourist destination.

22. "The $100 Million Exemption: Soft Money and the 2004 National Party Conventions," p. 42.

23. "The $100 Million Exemption: Soft Money and the 2004 National Party Conventions," p. 7.

24. To see just how constrained the donor population is, one may find relevant numbers at given contribution levels at www.opensecrets.org/bigpicture/donordemographics.asp?cycle =2002 (accessed October 17, 2005). In the last presidential cycle, 1999–2000, about 14,900 Americans gave more than $10,000.

25. In New York in 2004, the GOP introduced "convention jockeys," interviewers on the convention floor and at remote locations, in an ostensible effort to provide more variation in its convention program and to—perhaps—reach out to the MTV culture by emulating the music television channel's VJ (video jockey) concept.

6

NOMINATING CONVENTIONS, CAMPAIGN EVENTS, AND POLITICAL INFORMATION

Costas Panagopoulos

TO SOME EXTENT, THE aim of this volume is to assess if national presidential nominating conventions *still* matter, and, if so, how and why? This chapter examines the impact of conventions on the level of political information about presidential campaigns disseminated by mass media channels. Previous studies have presented evidence that conventions do in fact increase the amount of media coverage of political campaigns. The findings of the empirical analyses described below corroborate these results. Thus it seems that conventions continue to play an important role in the campaign process partly because they arm citizens with more political information that can be used to evaluate candidates and make wise vote choices.

POLITICAL INFORMATION

Scholars have suggested that the primary function of presidential campaigns is to generate information for the purpose of persuasion. Thomas Holbrook argues that campaign events influence the dynamics of presidential races because voters' opinions respond to information provided by these events. Hence, information is a crucial component of the online information processing model Holbrook describes. "As events unfold and the voter is presented with more information about the candidates, this information is incorporated into the voter's events tally." Voters use this tally to update their impressions. Events create information, which, in turn, affects voters' evaluations. "Voters stay online during the campaign and update their evaluations of the candidates as events unfold and new information is made available to them."[1]

Holbrook's analysis hinges on a crucial assumption: The information acquired during the campaign serves a valuable function for the voters.[2] Other scholars have reached similar conclusions about the role of political information in campaigns, arguing that information permits voters to refine their opinions and make more informed decisions. Andrew Gelman and Gary King argue that as voters absorb more information generated by campaign events, they become more "enlightened" about the choices available and become more sensitive to the types of variables that usually dominate voting behavior: partisanship, presidential performance, the economy.[3] This sensitization leads to informed choices and predictable election outcomes, provided that both parties run relatively effective campaigns.

Central to this line of reasoning about information-generating campaigns is the role of the mass media.[4] Political information generated by campaigns can only make a difference for voters if they are exposed to it. It is the mass media, claim Gelman and King, through its coverage of campaign events, that arms citizens with the much-needed information to make "enlightened" choices.[5]

Based on these claims, one could reasonably infer that greater levels of political information are useful for the electorate. Campaign events that augment the amount of political information available to voters (through the mass media) perform an important function during presidential campaigns. While some campaign events are spontaneous, conventions and debates are institutionalized elements of the presidential selection process. Do these campaign events—conventions in particular—affect the amount of political information made available to voters?

To evaluate this question, Holbrook examined patterns of newspaper coverage of the presidential campaigns in 1984, 1988, and 1992. Holbrook's measure of coverage was the number of paragraphs about the presidential campaign that appeared on the front page of the *New York Times*. Holbrook defends his choice of the *New York Times*, arguing that coverage in this nationally reputable source is likely to be similar to trends in the amount of coverage found in most other similar media sources, Holbrook's analysis of the three presidential campaigns he included in his study allowed him to demonstrate that conventions provide a "significant and large bump" in the amount of information generated.[6] Debates, on the other hand, do not appear to generate significantly more information.

Holbrook's finding is especially poignant when viewed in light of the claim that information generated early in the campaign is expected to exert a greater influence over voters because information's value declines as its cumulative amount increases (as Holbrook finds it does as the campaign nears the end).

Because conventions occur relatively early (many consider Labor Day as the unofficial start of the presidential campaign), information generated by conventions may be even more influential.

Do conventions continue to generate comparatively greater amounts of campaign coverage, thus augmenting the amount of political information available to voters? To investigate this question, I replicate Holbrook's analysis for the 2004 presidential election.[7] This approach updates Holbrook's original analyses using data from the 2004 cycle and facilitates comparisons to his original findings.

DATA AND METHODS

Following Holbrook, I use the amount of presidential campaign coverage (total number of paragraphs) that appears on the front page of the *New York Times* between June 1 and Election Day 2004. The count for each day is the number of campaign paragraphs, partial or full, that appear on the front page. Photographs and figures, such as poll results, are counted as paragraphs. To be included in the count, the story had to be about a candidate or personality involved in the campaign (including family members), issue positions, issues within the party, or public opinion toward any aspect of the campaign. Because incumbent presidents receive coverage for activities not related to the campaign, only those stories that are clearly about the campaign are included.[8]

Figure 6.1 presents the overall pattern of coverage during the campaign summarized as the average daily number of paragraphs for seven day periods. On a daily basis, the *New York Times* devoted on average 8.7 paragraphs of front-page coverage to the presidential campaign over the entire period of the study. The data presented display spikes in coverage during the Democratic convention, which took place is Boston, Massachusetts, from July 26 to July 29 and the Republican Convention hosted in New York City August 30 through September 2. The average number of front-page paragraphs during the conventions (as defined below) was 15.2, nearly double the overall mean. Attention to the campaign also climbed during the period surrounding debates in 2004, to 12.8 paragraphs on average. Yet the analyses below suggest this pattern does not hold for all debates in 2004. We do observe, however, a substantially higher than normal rate of coverage during the first presidential debate on September 30 and near the campaign's end.

To advance a more systematic analysis, I also replicate Holbrook's multivariate analysis to explain levels of campaign coverage using a set of explana-

FIG. 6.1. Media coverage of campaign 2004

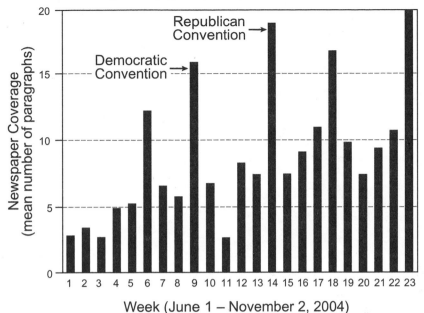

Source: Compiled by author.

tory variables. This analysis uses daily counts of campaign paragraphs as the dependent variable. The set of independent variables are identical to those employed by Holbrook and include dummy variables for each of the party conventions (coded 1 for the period between two days before and three days after the conventions and 0 for all other days), dummy variables for the presidential and vice-presidential debates (coded 1 for the day of the debate and the two days after the debate and 0 for all other days), and a counter variable for the increasing activity in the fall campaign (coded 0 for all days prior to September 1 and taking on an increasing value, in increments of 1, for each successive day).[9]

RESULTS

Table 6.1 presents the results of Holbrook's original analyses for 1984, 1988, and 1992. It also includes the results of the replication of the analysis using 2004 data. The 2004 results exhibit remarkable similarity to Holbrook's original findings and confirm many initial suspicions about patterns of campaign coverage. Campaign coverage, at least on the front page of the *New York Times*,

TABLE 6.1. Campaign events and political information

	1984	1988	1992	2004
Constant	7.36*	6.00*	7.06*	5.99*
	(.72)	(.82)	(1.03)	(0.64)
Democratic convention	16.44*	9.58*	15.31*	8.24*
	(2.51)	(2.59)	(2.82)	(2.13)
Republican convention	14.95*	8.65*	14.74*	10.05*
	(2.38)	(2.59)	(2.83)	(2.12)
First presidential debate	7.12*	0.78	−1.57	10.87*
	(3.47)	(3.56)	(4.81)	(3.59)
Second presidential debate	0.88	−0.21	−0.35	−0.36
	(3.55)	(3.63)	(5.49)	(3.63)
Third presidential debate	—	—	−1.19	3.41
			(4.21)	(3.66)
Vice presidential debate	0.75	0.98	-3.40	−3.36
	(3.49)	(3.59)	(5.20)	(3.61)
Fall campaign	−0.01	0.10*	0.24*	0.11*
	(.03)	(.03)	(.04)	(.03)
N	158	159	154	155
R-squared	0.36	0.16	0.34	0.05

Note: Dependent variable: *New York Times* coverage of campaign (front-page). GLS estimates derived using the Yule-Walker method for correction for serial correlation. Standard errors are given in parentheses. Estimates for 1984, 1988, and 1992 are reported in Holbrook (1996). Estimates for 2004 compiled by author.
*$p<.05$

was significantly greater during the period of both parties' conventions. Unlike Holbrook's original analyses, the first convention in 2004 (Democrats) did not increase coverage more than the second convention, but both conventions caused a spike in campaign coverage. The *New York Times* devoted more than eight paragraphs of additional coverage to the campaign during the Democratic convention in 2004 and more than ten additional paragraphs on average during the Republican convention.

Results presented in Table 6.1 also indicate that debates have the capacity to boost the overall level of campaign coverage, but only the first debate between President George W. Bush and Senator John F. Kerry did so in 2004. The other two debates—and the vice-presidential debates between Dick Cheney and John Edwards—did not significantly alter the amount of campaign coverage. Findings also suggest that campaign coverage increased during the fall and as Election Day approached.

DISCUSSION

The findings presented in this chapter reveal that presidential nominating campaigns significantly increase the amount of political information about the campaign provided by the media for public consumption. This information is useful in making informed decisions about vote choices and provides a valuable service to the electorate. Above and beyond other roles they may or may not play, conventions appear to continue to boost the amount of political information during presidential campaigns. The analyses above demonstrate that conventions are the only formal, institutionalized campaign events that *consistently* generate comparatively greater political information. Even as presidential debates can perform a similar function at times (as the first presidential debate did in 2004), debates' ability to generate greater political coverage and information in the media seems limited. By contrast, conventions appear to do so reliably. Of course, this result is facilitated by media organizations, but campaign events—like conventions—provide the impetus for relatively more campaign coverage and, ultimately, more information that voters can use.

NOTES

1. Thomas M. Holbrook, *Do Campaigns Matter?* (Thousand Oaks, CA: Sage, 1997), quote on p. 52.

2. Holbrook, *Do Campaigns Matter?*, 54.

3. Andrew Gelman and Gary King, "Why are American Presidential Election Polls So Variable When Votes Are So Predictable?" *British Journal of Political Science* 23 (1993): 409–51.

4. Holbrook, *Do Campaigns Matter?*; Gelman and King, "Why are American Presidential Election Polls So Variable"; Samuel Popkin, *The Reasoning Voter: Communication and Persuasion in Presidential Campaigns* (Chicago: University of Chicago Press, 1991).

5. Gelman and King, "Why are American Presidential Election Polls So Variable," 448–49.

6. Holbrook, *Do Campaigns Matter?*

7. Ibid.

8. Ibid., 68.

9. Ibid., 62.

7

CONVENTIONS FOR THE UNCONVENTIONAL
Minor Party Conventions, 1992–2004
John C. Berg

PARTY CONVENTIONS ARE USUALLY thought to serve a number of important functions. Officially, they choose candidates, determine platforms, set the party's rules, and elect the officers who will govern the party until its next convention. Unofficial functions are at least as important. Conventions can help bring contending factions together, inspire party activists to work hard on the campaign, and provide a way for the party to present itself to the public.[1]

For the major parties, only the unofficial functions retain their importance. For the last few decades, every major party nominee has won a majority of delegates before the convention and has then exercised nearly total control over the platform, the rules, and the choice of chair for the party's national committee.[2] Major party conventions have become pep rallies, designed to make the nominee look good on television and thereby earn a "convention bounce" in the polls. Paradoxically, this design had made the resulting conventions so devoid of real news content that the commercial television networks no longer provide gavel-to-gavel coverage.

Minor party conventions are another story. Despite the poor chances of the nominee's being elected, minor party nominations are frequently contested. In 2004, for example, the Green and Libertarian parties had nomination contests at their conventions. Minor party conventions also set the rules, determine the platforms, and choose the leaders for the party; in fact, the last function can be more important, as the nominee will probably lose but the leaders will continue to direct the party. Conventions also help give minor parties cohesion; they provide one of the few opportunities for party activists from different regions to get to know each other. Since minor party conventions generally receive little or no coverage on television or in other mass media, they can fulfill these functions (or fail to fulfill them) without the distortions induced by media pressure. The role of conventions in the development of the Green Party of the United States exemplifies the performance of these functions.

The Green Party conventions of 2000 and 2004 illustrate the Greens' development into an electoral party, a status that had not always been clear. When the U.S. Greens began, they were more movement than party, and their conventions, or rather "gatherings," made no nominations, determined no platforms (although they did agree on "ten key values," which have remained the center of the Green program), and decided only organizational questions—and those with considerable difficulty. These early conventions drew virtually no media attention. The Green conventions took on a more conventional form only after the party had begun to run candidates for president, a strategy adopted initially without a normal convention. The intervening years were marked by small conventions, often stalemated, in which feelings grew hot and eventually led to the splitting of the Greens into two competing national organizations.

BEGINNINGS OF THE U.S. GREENS

The U.S. Greens began in May 1984, when the success of Green parties in other countries, most visibly in Germany, inspired a group of ecological activists to meet as part of the North American Bioregional Congress and talk about "how to create a Green organization that could reflect the tremendous political and cultural diversity of this country, and also have a real impact upon the strange and often unseemly world of American politics." A follow-up meeting in St. Paul decided that it would be premature to launch a Green party until a grassroots base was developed; instead the meeting founded the "Committees of Correspondence, after the locally-based alliances of people from Maine to Georgia that helped to spark the American Revolution."[3] A Green clearinghouse was established, and the meeting adopted the "Ten Key Values" as the basis of unity for the U.S. Green movement.

The Ten Key Values (10KV) are most commonly given as "ecological wisdom, social justice, grassroots democracy, non-violence, decentralization, community-based economics, feminism, respect for diversity, personal and global responsibility, and future focus."[4] Some Greens have considered "feminism" to be ambiguous, or have doubted whether men can be feminists, and have replaced it with "post-patriarchal values"; the Green Party of the United States has expanded it to "feminism and gender equity."[5] The 10KV, which continue to be cited today, are meant to give the Greens a common philosophical basis, while leaving state and local organizations free to adopt their individual programs in accordance with the call for decentralization. The Greens believe that this philosophical basis makes them different from other parties. Accordingly, as John Rensenbrink observes, "self-study ... is often the favored initial activity of most [Green] groups. Once sufficiently familiar with the roots and scope of the Green movement and Green vision, and once feeling sufficiently comfortable with one another, groups will take on one or more ... other types of action."[6]

In the early years the Greens came together every year in a "Green Gathering." As the movement began to grow, there was considerable discussion about how a grassroots movement could maintain democracy at the national level, and two principles were adopted. In order to keep the organization committed and activist, membership would be defined as consisting of those who declared their adherence to Green values and who paid dues to the national organization. In order to prevent those who could afford to travel to national meetings from having disproportionate influence, members who did not attend those meetings could be represented by giving their proxies to designated representatives.

By the early 1990s, internal disagreements among the Greens had led to the growth of two loosely organized factions. These groupings took on various names over time, and there were many Greens who did not fit easily into either of them; so what follows is a simplification. The Left Greens were concerned to maintain a consistently progressive Green point of view which would combine a commitment to opposing racism, sexism, and homophobia and to supporting the working class with the characteristic Green environmental program. In order to maintain such consistency, they felt that it was important for new members to join the Greens only as a conscious choice, based on agreement with the Green program. The requirement that members pay dues—which were never very high—was meant to assure that such choices were meaningful. Left Greens also tended to think that nonelectoral organizing and protest were equally important as electoral campaigns, and that the latter without the former would quickly corrupt the Greens into a party just like the others. Their local orientation and commitment to including low-income members led to the adoption of proxy voting, seen as a way to keep national Green decision making from being dominated by lone activists who were able to travel to meetings but did not necessarily represent anyone but themselves.

The other major grouping, known at one time as the Green Politics Network (GPN), was defined by its commitment to running Greens for office. Members of this group were not necessarily less left than the Left Greens in their political views nor less convinced of the value of nonelectoral movement organizing, but they did tend to feel that there were already many organizations doing such organizing, and that the major contribution the Greens could make to the broader movement was to provide a voice for movement issues within the system of campaigns and elections. Consequently, this group paid more attention to the practicalities of electoral campaigns and to the need to comply with state and federal laws regulating such campaigns. Among other things, laws in many states required parties to have a statewide governing body and to open party membership to all voters who registered with the party. Left Greens objected to the latter, which posed the danger that the party could be taken over by those who did not share its aims, and state party organizations simply had no place in the existing Green national structure, which allowed only for locals and individuals as members.[7] Some GPN activists proposed changes in the bylaws to meet those concerns, but those changes were voted down—sometimes by a handful of people who each held many proxy votes. Rightly or wrongly, GPN activists began to suspect that these proxies might not represent actual members, and that the system was rigged against them.[8]

Frustrated by the national Green Party structure, leaders of a few state parties began to meet on their own, with no official link to the GPN, to discuss mutual problems and possible strategies. Since they were interested in electoral action, the idea of a Green presidential campaign came up. Various candidates were suggested and sounded out, and one of these, Ralph Nader, indicated that he would be willing to accept a Green nomination. At the same time, Nader insisted on some specific conditions. First, because he was deeply involved with many nonprofit organizations that he had founded over the years and did not want to subject those organizations' finances to scrutiny from the Federal Election Commission (FEC), he would raise and spend no more than $4,000 on his campaign, the level that would trigger FEC reporting requirements; individual state Green parties would have to raise and spend funds for his campaign independently. Second, he would not become a member, however that might be defined, of the Green Party.

Although these restrictions would hurt, those Greens who supported Nader thought that he would be a very strong candidate. Nader had been a consumer rights leader for more than thirty years, during which time he had fought and won battles with major automobile companies.[9] He had helped to create a new type of progressive entity, the public-interest law firm, and had founded several organizations, from Washington think tanks to the network of campus-based Public Interest Research Groups (PIRGs). He also had high visibility with a reputation for personal integrity. Many Greens thought that the visibility Nader would bring would compensate for his hands-off approach to the campaign; some even justified his approach, arguing that asking local activists to do the bulk of campaigning was in keeping with the Greens' spirit of local action.

Many aspects of a Nader campaign were controversial within the Green movement. Nader was not a Green and did not intend to become one; he did not share the Greens' commitment to combating racism, sexism, and homophobia; and many thought a presidential campaign would take too much money and energy away from organizing at the local level.[10] Moreover, there was no existing mechanism for nominating a Green presidential candidate. Anticipating bitter debate and another losing proxy battle if they took the issue to a national Greens Gathering, Nader's backers hit upon a novel approach. They would seek to nominate Nader as the presidential candidate of the Green Party of California. This would put him on the ballot of only one state, but it would also compel all other state Green parties to face the question of whether they, too, should nominate him. Nader entered and won the California Green primary in March, as well as primaries in a few other states with recognized Green parties. Then, with his candidacy an established fact, Mike Feinstein of the California Green Party (and an elected official in Santa Monica) invited Greens to an ad hoc gathering in Los Angeles in August. This conference, *not* an official meeting of the Greens/Green Party USA (G/GPUSA, combined four days of workshops and speeches with a presidential nominating convention on the fifth day. By August 19, the day the convention nominated him, Nader had already qualified for the ballot in twelve states.[11]

In 1996 Nader appeared on the ballot in twenty-one states, and qualified as a write-in in twenty-three more. He received 685,297 votes for president, 0.97% of the total, finishing a distant fourth; needless to say, he won no electoral votes.[12] Although these figures might suggest that the campaign was a miserable failure, it did not look way from the Green point of view. The purpose of the campaign had not been to win but to build the Green party; and the party had grown significantly in members and in geographic coverage. Shortly after the election, thirty-one state Green parties sent representatives to a meeting in Middleburg, Virginia, at which a new national organization, the Association of State Green Parties (ASGP) was founded. The ASGP, in some ways a successor to the GPN, was to become the vehicle for a second, more energetic Nader presidential campaign in the year 2000.

The ASGP held its first and only presidential nominating convention in Denver, Colorado, from June 23 to June 25, 2000. Forty state Green Parties were officially represented, with 375 delegate votes, allocated according to a formula that measured membership and Green Party state-level activity. At the opening session, 315 of these delegates were present, with more arriving during the course of the convention; proxy voting was not allowed.

Only a few state Green Parties, such as that of California, had the right to take part in their state's presidential primaries; most of the delegates had been chosen in party conventions. Procedures in Massachusetts were typical: all members who had registered as Greens were invited to the convention at the Friends Meeting House in Cambridge on March 25, and eighty-five attended. Two separate votes were taken, one to elect delegates and one to indicate preferences for the announced candidates for the Green nomination. In addition to Nader, two other candidates were running: Jello Biafra, an entertainer who had first become widely known as a member of the rock band the Dead Kennedys and had gone on to a solo career as a spoken-word performer; and Stephen Gaskin, the founder of a long-established agricultural commune and leader of the commune movement nationally. Joel Kovel, an author and professor at Bard College, had withdrawn his candidacy by the time of the Massachusetts convention. Delegates were chosen primarily for their willingness to travel to Denver at their own expense, but they were mandated to divide their ballots in the proportions of the preferences voted at the state convention—eleven votes for Nader and one for Biafra.[13]

In 2000, for the first time, Green leaders planned their party's convention with the broadcast media in mind. As a result, despite some oddities—to help keep business flowing on schedule, delegates were urged to "twinkle" their fingers in the air instead of applauding, and there was more emphasis on the legalization of industrial hemp than one would have found at the Democratic and Republican counterparts—the meeting was much more like a major party convention than like a typical gathering of the left. The speakers list emphasized representatives of international Green parties and leading figures from American political life, including John Anderson, a former member of Congress (R-IL) who had run a strong independent campaign in 1980; Ronnie Dugger, founder and leader of the Alliance for Democracy; Jim Hightower, former agricultural commissioner of Texas (an elected office), who was now supporting Nader; and Doris "Granny D" Haddock, a ninety-year old woman who had gained fame by walking across America in support of campaign finance reform. Tony Mazzochi of the Labor Party (which did not endorse candidates in principle) and Don Torgerson of the American Reform Party (the faction of the Reform Party that had supported Richard Lamm in 1996 and quit in protest over Ross Perot's tight control of the party) spoke in support of Nader. Many Green candidates for state and federal office spoke as well.

Aware of Greens' propensity to debate endlessly the fine points of issues, the convention organizers did away with the issue workshops traditional at movement meetings—the only workshops were campaign training sessions run by the Nader campaign organization in a separate hotel. Debate on the platform was limited to a yes-or-no vote.

The highlight of the convention, of course, was the balloting for president on the afternoon of June 25. It was clear that Nader would win, but each of the other declared candidates—including Kovel—spoke before the vote. Making it clear that they had run primarily in order to bring new constituencies into the Green Party and the presidential campaign, they all endorsed Nader. Nader did not speak for himself but had his name placed in nomination by Hightower. The result of the balloting, never in doubt, was 295 votes for Nader, 10 for Biafra, 10 for Gaskin, and 1 for "none of the above."

Ronnie Dugger then introduced Nader for his acceptance speech, which was broadcast on C-SPAN and covered in the *New York Times* and other newspapers.[14] The candidate was received with great enthusiasm—with the TV cameras rolling, most Greens realized that applause would come across better than "twinkling"—as he laid out the major theme of his campaign, the need to restore American democracy by taking power back from the corporations. He argued that conservatives as well as liberals should want this, that America needed to change direction—referring to "Granny D," he bemoaned the new reality that, in order to be heard, the average citizen needed to walk across America. Perhaps aware of some Greens' concern that he was too centrist, he also touched on a variety of issues dear to the left, including industrial hemp.

Despite the hemp, the twinkling, and the occasional tie-dyed shirt, the Green convention of 2000 was made for television, and resembled recent major party conventions in other ways. The nomination was settled beforehand, the platform was molded to suit the needs of the campaign, and—since the ASGP was a federation of state parties—there were not party leadership issues to be decided. It fell into the category of "nondeliberative events that ratify decisions already made."[15]

The Green Party gained visibility from the convention coverage, and, while Nader was well known already, the convention made more people aware that he was the Green candidate. However, this new visibility was not sufficient to affect the campaign strategy of the major parties. The Democrats and the Gore campaign, in particular, continued to ignore Nader and the Greens until much later in the campaign, as discussed below.

The professional tone set by the convention continued as the campaign began.[16] Although state and local Green parties joined in enthusiastically, the campaign was run by the Nader 2000 staff, which raised money, organized rallies, and printed literature. To the extent that funds allowed, state campaign coordinators were on the Nader 2000 payroll. William Hillsman, one of the architects of Jesse Ventura's Reform Party victory in Minnesota, was retained as a media consultant and made a quick impact when his ad parodying a credit card commercial, broadcast during the major party conventions, provoked a copyright infringement suit.

Although the campaign budget was far more than Greens were accustomed to, it was far from adequate for a modern national campaign. There was little television advertising and considerable emphasis on grassroots mobilization and free media. Nader used his unsuccessful demand for participation in the debates to garner press coverage—in Boston, for example, he obtained a ticket to watch the debates, got a television news crew to film him as he traveled to the site on the subway, and then got more press by suing the debate commission after he was excluded from the audience.

Large rallies in major cities were the most important campaign activities. By amassing paying crowds of ten thousand or more the campaign generated local press and demonstrated that Nader had significant popular support.

By mid-October polls showed support for Nader at 7 to 8 percent in California, Connecticut, New Jersey, and Rhode Island, 10 percent in Minnesota and Oregon, and 17 percent in Alaska. California and Alaska were not competitive, but in the other states—and in Washington and Wisconsin—the Gore campaign's strategists began to worry that Nader might win enough votes away from Gore to tip some states, and perhaps the election, to Bush.[17] The Gore campaign, which had been trying to ignore Nader, now struck back. Gore proclaimed his commitment to environmentalism while arguing that a vote for Nader would help elect Bush, and a group of major environmental organizations repeated the argument. Regular stories about Nader—albeit negative ones—began to appear in the election coverage of the *New York Times* for the first time since the Green convention at the end of June.[18]

While Gore was attacking Nader, Nader was targeting Gore, having made the strategic decision to campaign hardest in the swing states, including Florida, during the last few weeks before the election.[19] This decision may have been driven by a desire to maximize Nader's votes, rather than to hurt Gore, but understandably, this decision was not popular with Democrats.[20] Nevertheless the decision helped establish the Green party as an electoral force to be reckoned with. Ultimately, Nader got 2,882,782 votes, 2.74% of the total, finishing third—well ahead of Buchanan with 0.43%, but far behind the 50 million vote totals of Bush and Gore.[21] Nader also fell far short of the 5 percent cutoff needed to qualify the Greens for FEC general election matching funds in 2004. Most importantly, perhaps, Nader's active campaign in Florida won enough votes to change the outcome in that state, and nationally, from a Gore to a Bush victory.

Although the Nader campaign did not qualify for FEC general election matching funds, it did achieve several other important Green objectives. The Green Party reached a new level of success as a result of the 2000 campaign. Eight new state Green Parties grew out of the campaign, bringing the national total to thirty-four; party registration increased 63%, to 194,000; and the numbers of Green candidates for state and local office, and the numbers of such candidates who were elected, rose by the highest proportion since 1992.

The 2000 Nader campaign also brought an effective end to the bitter factional dispute that had plagued the Greens for at least five years. Both of the factions, the Association of State Green Parties (ASGP) and the Greens/Green Party USA (G/GPUSA) nominated Nader, but the ASGP was clearly the main campaign vehicle. After the election a group of leading members from both sides of the dispute drew up a compromise unity plan, which was adopted by the ASGP. When the G/GPUSA was unable to approve the plan (because of its proxy-voting system, which gave a handful of members a majority of the votes), that organization split, with most members going over to the pro-unity side. The ASGP then proceeded unilaterally to transform itself into the Green Party of the United States (GPUS), while its rival has been pushed to the margins of political life.[22]

The Green Party continued to grow through the next few years, running active campaigns and, most notably, almost electing the mayor of San Francisco. It entered the 2004 campaign season with the strongest organization it had ever had, but it faced two problems: Ralph Nader and George W. Bush.[23]

Tensions between the party and Nader went back to the 2000 campaign. Nader and his personal staff had been highly critical of Green Party organizational efforts during the 2000 campaign. In a postelection analysis of Nader's failure to get 5 percent of the vote, Micah Sifry cites several criticisms of the Greens by "a close Nader advisor." The Green nominating convention was too early to let the candidate maximize federal "primary season" matching funds, Greens cared more about state and local elections than the presidential campaign, Greens failed to organize for the mammoth rallies, and in October the ASGP issued a statement calling for the suspension of U.S. aid to Israel until it withdrew from the occupied territories, a position Nader did not share.[24]

From the other side, John Rensenbrink lists several Green grievances with Nader at the end of 2003. "His personal style is too aloof; he does not involve the party in his strategy planning; he is unilateral and mercurial in his actions; he is not a Green; he is in danger of becoming a 'perennial candidate'; his message is that of 'a one-noter' (the anti-corporate mantra); and . . . the net effect of these and other factors is a drag on the Green Party."[25] A further grievance was that Nader had refused to give the Green Party a list of those who had contributed to his campaign fund until two years after the election. Given these grievances and misunderstandings, the Greens were divided as to the desirability of nominating Nader again in 2004.

The Greens' second problem was George W. Bush and his remarkable ability to polarize American public opinion. When they were criticized by Democrats in 2000 for having cost Gore the election, Greens bore the criticism with equanimity, pointing to Gore's ineffective campaign, his inability to carry either his own state or President Clinton's, and the chicanery of the Supreme Court majority as the real reasons Gore lost. However, following Bush's declaration of the "War on Terror," and particularly after the U.S. invasion of Iraq, Greens began to feel the pressure of "Anyone But Bush."

Sometime in late 2003, Nader began to let it be known that he intended to run for president again, but this time not as a Green. As Ted Glick put it in his syndicated "Future Hope" column: "By all reports, he [Nader] is upset with the criticism that some former strong Nader supporters in the Greens have made of him, and he believes that the Greens aren't growing fast enough. He is reportedly saying that he does not want to announce as a possible Green Party candidate, raise lots of money and put in lots of energy and then, at the nominating convention in late June in Milwaukee, not be chosen as the candidate, or see the party decide upon a particular strategy for whomever is its Presidential candidate that he would have to abide by if chosen."[26]

Nader commented elsewhere that the Green convention was scheduled "too late" for him to run an effective campaign, but it is difficult to regard this as a serious point, since one of his complaints in 2000 had been that the Green convention was too early.[27] In any case, candidates customarily begin their campaigns well before the conventions at which they seek nomination.

Presumably Nader's real concern was that he might seek the Green nomination but have it denied to him.

Nader formally announced his independent candidacy on February 22, 2004. Although he did not participate in the Green Party's delegate selection process or enter any Green primaries, he made it clear that he would still like the Green Party to draft him, and ultimately worked with Lorna Salzman, a declared candidate who ran, in effect, as Nader's proxy. Meanwhile, Nader sought and won the nomination of the Reform Party and various single-state parties, while gathering signatures for independent ballot lines.

Nader's decision raises two questions about his motives: Why did he run? And why did he choose not to run as a Green? The first of these looms much larger within the United States than it does in other countries; the general attitude outside the United States seems to be that the voters are perfectly capable of making strategic decisions for themselves, so that if they chose to vote for a "lesser evil" in order to stop Bush, they would do so. However, in the United States the prevailing assumption among political activists is that voters are not capable of rational thought; it is therefore up to the parties and candidates to structure the strategic situation appropriately. Thus there was a "Ralph, Don't Run" movement among left liberals, including many who had supported Nader's candidacy in 2000. Nader's response to this group was that his campaign would energize new constituencies and ultimately help the Democrats defeat Bush.

As for Nader's decision not to seek the Green nomination, two explanations seem plausible. Either he thought it would be humiliating to undergo the Green Party's process of internal decision making, which would have required him to enter primaries, debate other candidates, and subject himself to the oversight of party decision makers; or he wanted to run without the ideological baggage of the Green label.[28] The latter seems more likely. Nader had always argued that small-town conservatives—the kind of people who organize to keep Wal-Mart out of their towns—should support his anti-monopoly agenda, and he seems to have believed that dropping the Green label, not to mention adding Reform, would help him with such voters. He must surely have realized that, had he entered Green primaries, in which many more people than the Green hard core could have voted, he would have won. So his shunning of the Green nomination is probably best understood as an attempt—largely unsuccessful—to shed his reputation as a leftist.

Whatever his motives may have been, Nader's decision to avoid the Green Party's delegate selection process made him ineligible for the party's nomination. However, the party could still endorse him, a decision which would leave state Green Parties free to offer him their ballot line or not, as they chose. By June 24, when the Green national convention met in Milwaukee, the Nader campaign was fighting for ballot access in many states, and the twenty-three states in which Green Parties existed would have given it an important boost. Nader did not attend the convention but announced on June 21 that Peter Camejo of California would be his running mate. Camejo was a leader of the California Greens and had been the party's candidate for governor during the Davis recall election, finishing third with about 3 percent of the vote. Camejo served as the leader of the Nader forces at the convention.

The leading candidate in the race for delegates was David Cobb, an attorney and long-time Green activist from Texas who had recently relocated to California and had run for attorney general in that state. Cobb was an effective campaigner in person but was little known to the general public. He promised to campaign hard and effectively but to concentrate on states where the two-party contest was not in doubt, in what became known as a "safe states" strategy. Coming into the convention Cobb had about 33 percent of the delegates; Camejo, Lorna Salzman, Carol Miller, and Paul Glover, each of whom had run as a Nader proxy in one or more states, had about 28 percent; 23 percent were uncommitted, 12 percent supported no nomination, and the remaining few percent were for Kent Mesplay. Following a Cobb-Camejo debate and the adoption of the platform, the balloting for the nomination began the morning of Saturday, June 26. In the first round, with most delegates pledged to a candidate, Cobb led with 308 votes, Camejo had 119, Nader 117, no nominee 109, Salzman 40, Mesplay 24, and others received a handful of votes. In the second round, delegates were free to vote as they wished, and candidates were required to sign a pledge to accept the nomination if they won—a step only Cobb, Mesplay, and Joann Beeman, a "favorite daughter" candidate from Michigan, did. The Nader forces asked delegates to vote for no nomination; if that position won a majority, the convention could then move to endorse Nader or, perhaps, in a compromise suggested by Camejo, both Nader and Cobb, leaving it up to each state Green Party to decide whose name should be placed on the ballot in that state. Cobb needed an additional seventy-seven votes and got them when the roll call reached Virginia, making him the Green nominee.[29]

Cobb won for a combination of reasons. On one hand, the "Anybody but Bush" sentiment was shared by many Greens, who did not want potential allies to see them as saboteurs. Cobb's "safe states" strategy appealed to this group; in reality, with the unknown Cobb as the party's standard bearer no such strategy was needed, as he was unlikely to get enough votes to affect the outcome no matter how vigorously he campaigned.

On the other hand, many who might have supported Nader felt insulted by his decision to avoid the primaries and his failure to appear at the convention. These decisions by Nader reinforced the bad feelings coming out of the 2000 campaign, leading many to feel that it was time for a Green candidate who was actually Green. Had Nader appeared at the convention, he would have gained many of these votes, perhaps enough to win the nomination. Had he run in the primaries, open to the broader public, he might well have come to the convention with the nomination sewed up in advance.

Because the Green nomination had still been in doubt when it began, the 2004 Green convention was *not* made for TV. Good coverage was still desirable, but that desirability was overridden by the need to make the contending groups within the party feel that the decision had been fair. As a result, the GPUS had restored the nominating convention to its historic functions: nominating a candidate for president and setting the party's political direction for the next four years.

Cobb's nomination was the main story of the convention for Green Party members; however, for the major parties and the national media it was that Nader had been denied that nomination. Once that happened, Cobb and the Greens disappeared from view. The Democrats continued to attack Nader but ignored the Greens. It might thus be said that the convention's only impact on the major parties came from what it did *not* do.

The healthy competition at the convention did not lead to a healthy campaign; in fact, the 2004 election was a fiasco for the Greens. The party's presidential candidate in 2000, Ralph Nader, was a well-known and widely respected national figure. He appeared on forty-four state ballots (including the District of Columbia), and received about 2,883,105 votes, finishing third. The Green candidate in 2004, David Cobb, was little known outside the Green party. He appeared on twenty-eight state ballots, and received 119,751 votes, finishing sixth. The party lost its ballot status in a number of states.

Do the U.S. Greens have a future? If so, it probably does not lie in presidential politics. The polarizing effect of George W. Bush seems certain to persist through the 2008 election, leaving little room for a Green alternative. However, the Greens continue to be active in state and local politics. Their first state legislator, John Eder of Maine, was reelected in 2004; a retiring Green on the San Francisco Board of Supervisors was replaced by another Green, Ross Mirkarimi; and the Greens kept their control of the village of New Paltz, New York, and the city of Sebastopol, California. The Greens' presidential candidate, David Cobb, has been playing a leading role in the postelection campaign to defend the right to vote and to have one's vote counted in Ohio and elsewhere. Perhaps the next evolutionary step for the Green national convention will be to move from being a place where nominees are selected to a gathering that sets the party's strategic direction.

NOTES

1. Terri Susan Fine, "Presidential Nominating Conventions in a Democracy," *Perspectives on Political Science* 32, no. 1 (winter 2003): 32–39.

2. Fine, "Presidential Nominating Conventions," 32.

3. Brian Tokar, *The Green Alternative: Creating an Ecological Future* (San Pedro, Calif.: R. and E. Miles, 1992), 52. Confusingly, another unrelated organization with the same name was started at about the same time by former members of the Communist Party USA who wanted to promote socialist politics while leaving its Stalinist heritage behind.

4. See, e.g., "The Ten Key Values of the Greens" at www.greens.org/values/ (accessed June 11, 2004).

5. Green Party of the United States, "Ten Key Values of the Green Party," www.gp.org/tenkey.html (accessed June 11, 2004).

6. John Rensenbrink, *Against All Odds: The Green Transformation of American Politics*, foreword by Ralph Nader (Raymond, ME: Leopold Press, 1999), 111–12.

7. This was not a paranoid fantasy. The lack of control parties have over their memberships enabled the controversial disk jockey Howard Stern to win the Libertarian nomination for governor of New York in 1994. Stern ran as a publicity stunt; he used his radio show to mobilize supporters to attend the Libertarian state convention and renounced the nomination a week after he had won it. See Kevin Sack, "Eyes Wide, Libertarians Pick Stern," *New York Times*, April 24, 1994, pp. 20, 40; "The Stern Gang," *New Yorker*, May 9, 1994, pp. 39–40. The more serious danger is shown in Patrick Buchanan's successful quest for the Reform Party presidential nomination in 2000; Buchanan's views on everything but free trade differed radically from those of most Reform activists, and many felt that his only goal was to win control of the $13 million in federal campaign funds that the party had qualified for by Ross Perot's performance in 1996.

8. See Rensenbrink, *Against All Odds,* for a full account of this conflict from the GPN perspective; for a view from the other side, see Howie Hawkins, "Individual Members: The Grassroots of Green Party Democracy," *Synthesis/Regeneration* 14 (fall 1997), available at www .greens.org/s-r/14/14–02.html (accessed June 11, 2004); Howie Hawkins, "Green Parties: Still Seeking Unity," *Z Magazine* 10, no. 3 (March 1997): 21–24.

9. Ralph Nader, *Unsafe at any Speed: The Designed-in Dangers of the American Automobile* (New York: Grossman, 1965); Thomas Whiteside, *The Investigation of Ralph Nader: General Motors Vs. One Determined Man* (New York: Arbor House, 1972); Charles McCarry, *Citizen*

Nader (New York: Saturday Review, 1972); Justin Martin, *Nader: Crusader, Spoiler, Icon* (Cambridge, MA: Perseus, 2002); Patricia Cronin Marcello, *Ralph Nader: A Biography* (Westport, CT: Greenwood, 2004).

10. He had told interviewer William Safire that he was "not interested in gonadal politics," (*New York Times,* March 21, 1996).

11. Walt Contreras Sheasby, "To Build a Party: Ralph Nader and the Green Candidacy," 1996, newsgroup posting, Grns.usa.forum (accessed June 6, 2004). Also see Rensenbrink, *Against All Odds,* 207–9.

12. Dave Leip, "Dave Leip's Atlas of U.S. Presidential Elections," www.uselectionatlas.org (accessed June 6, 2004).

13. In the event, one of the twelve Massachusetts delegates did not attend the national convention. The delegation caucused in Denver and agreed that the mandated vote for Biafra would be cast by Jon Leavitt, co-chair of the state party.

14. See, e.g., Michael Janofsky, "Nader, Nominated by the Greens, Attacks Politics as Usual," *New York Times,* June 26, 2000.

15. Fine, "Presidential Nominating Conventions," 32.

16. Material for the next five paragraphs is adapted from John C. Berg, "Spoiler or Builder? The Effect of Ralph Nader's 2000 Campaign on the U.S. Greens," in *The State of the Parties: The Changing Role of Contemporary American Parties,* ed. John C. Green and Rick D. Farmer (Lanham, MD: Rowman and Littlefield, 2003). See also Micah L. Sifry, *Spoiling for a Fight: Third Party Politics in America* (New York: Routledge, 2002), and Ralph Nader, *Crashing the Party: Taking on the Corporate Government in an Age of Surrender* (New York: Thomas Dunne, 2002).

17. Micah L. Sifry, "Nader's No Ventura, But . . . ," *NewsForChange.Com,* October 31, 2000.

18. John Nichols, "Nader: Fast in the Stretch," *Nation,* November 20, 2000.

19. Ibid.

20. See Barry C. Burden, "Ralph Nader's Campaign Strategy in the 2000 U.S. Presidential Election," paper presented at the annual meeting of the Midwest Political Science Association, Chicago, April 4–7, 2003.

21. Reported in *Ballot Access News* 16, no. 10 (January 1, 2001).

22. John Rensenbrink, "Challenge and Response: The Emergence of the Green Party in the United States," *Green Horizon Quarterly,* Feb. 2003.

23. Material for the remainder of this chapter is adapted from John C. Berg, "Surviving Nader? The Future of the U.S. Greens," paper presented at American Politics Group, Canterbury, UK, 2005.

24. Sifry, *Spoiling for a Fight.*

25. Rensenbrink, "Challenge and Response."

26. Ted Glick, "Jesse Then, Ralph Now?" Associated Press syndicated column, 2003.

27. *New York Times,* January 10, 2004.

28. Greg Gerritt, *Green Party Tempest: Weathering the Storm of 2004* (Providence: Moshassuck River, 2005).

29. Ted Glick, "Green and Growing," Associated Press syndicated column, 2004.

8

LIGHTS, CAMERA, CHAOS?
THE EVOLUTION OF CONVENTION "CRISES"
R. Sam Garrett

ON THE SURFACE, THE idea that presidential nominating conventions are prone to crises seems ludicrous. Because of the constant media coverage with which this book is concerned, presidential nominating conventions have become increasingly scripted to avoid any hint of dissent during the parties' media showcases. Given this backdrop, conventions should be the last place we observe any disruption that might be exploited by the media or an opponent—especially a crisis, which suggests fundamental disarray within the convention or lack of unity surrounding the nominee. However, a stroll through convention history reveals that disagreement, disharmony, and even crises are common.

This chapter enhances our understanding of presidential politics, presidential conventions, and the media by exploring how conventions have evolved. The changing nature of convention crises is an important but unexplored element of party politics. A half-century ago, when conventions were charged with real debate and decision making, uncertainty—and the potential for crisis—was common. After serious unrest at conventions in the 1960s, which played out before national television audiences, both major parties deemphasized actual decision making at conventions. Today, conventions largely ratify the choices primary voters have already made. Presidential conventions no longer face serious *political* crises that threaten their ability to function. However, modern attempts to control every facet of conventions are not perfect. *Message* crises, which represent departures from the planned party script, can still occur.

The shift from political crises to message crises at conventions provides a window into the changing nature of American political parties. During the last fifty years, American voters have increasingly strayed from parties, preferring the independent label or rejecting political participation altogether.[1] The evolution of presidential conventions from raucous events engaged in serious debate and decision making, to preplanned meetings which largely ratify previous choices, is another sign that while parties continue to play vital roles in American politics, campaigns are increasingly about individual candidates, not party labels.

This chapter employs an informal case-study method of various convention crises, especially since 1952. The 1968 Democratic convention receives special attention as an example of political crisis. The 1992 Republican and Democratic conventions represented different extremes of message crises. Using these cases as examples, the chapter focuses on "theory building," which explores new areas and searches for general patterns. Therefore, it begins a discussion about how convention crises have evolved over time and how the parties have responded by changing their nominating processes. The distinction between political and message crises provides a theoretical framework for a richer understanding of presidential conventions. Readers are invited to draw their own conclusions about where particular cases fit within that framework. Future research can and should revisit the discussion begun here.

The literature on crises in campaign politics, including presidential conventions, is quite limited. In fact, the term *crisis* is almost never discussed in any systematic way. The existing literature that actually seeks to define terms instead focuses on competing operationalizations of campaign scandals, usually limited to ethical transgressions.[2] The theoretical grounding for defining what precisely *crisis* means at presidential conventions is virtually nonexistent.

However, recent research on crisis management in congressional campaigns provides some clues to begin exploring convention crises. Campaign crises are complex, interactive events that disrupt campaigns' planned agendas and intended public messages.[3] Although the research cited above lays the groundwork for understanding crises and crisis management in congressional campaigns, systematic inquiry of crises at presidential conventions remains elusive. In tracing the evolution of presidential nominating conventions with an eye toward crises, I offer one interpretation of how those changes affect the kinds of crises and potential crises occurring at conventions. I suggest that two broad categories of convention crises are evident in the last half-century: political and message crises. Both reflect political professionals' emphasis on campaign crises as disruptive events that threaten the campaign's ability to control the media messages described elsewhere.[4]

A HISTORY OF CRISES AT PRESIDENTIAL NOMINATING CONVENTIONS

In the modern era of "scripted" presidential nominating conventions, even describing significant conflict—let alone crises—can be difficult. For decades, the leadership of both major parties has focused on producing media-friendly conventions that portray appealing, inspiring images of unity and energy. Anything that threatens such efforts is best handled off-camera, which is an essential logistical concern for convention organizers. According to veteran Democratic political consultant and experienced convention operative Joseph Napolitan, "The best convention efforts are quiet, unpublicized; you don't really want anyone to know what you are up to, or how successful you are at what you're doing. That's why candidates and their managers hold back the announcement of commitments [from delegates] until these announcements will achieve maximum impact."[5] It is worth noting that Napolitan made that statement in 1972, the first year the Democrats' "reformed" their convention, hoping to minimize conflict after the public disaster of the 1968 Democratic convention (discussed below). The trend toward convention order has intensified in the last thirty years, making conventions even more tightly managed today than Napolitan suggests.

However, presidential nominating conventions have not always been as predictable as they are today. They developed from a national need for an orderly process of selecting each party's nominees. Well into the 1800s, party caucuses within Congress selected each party's presidential candidate. After the tumultuous election of 1824, when the selection of Andrew Jackson as president was thrown to the House of Representatives after a discrepancy between the popular vote and the electoral college, the caucus system was discredited. In a search for greater predictability and less conflict, national parties began holding increasingly formal nominating conventions by the 1830s.[6]

The party-convention system brought order, which limited the potential for conflict and disruption on a national scale. However, this did not put an end to crises in party politics. Certainly, conventions during this era could not be accused of being the scripted, predictable gatherings most people find them today. In fact, conventions take root in a crisis of human terms. According to journalist Nicholas von Hoffman, the Anti-Masonic Party held the first national convention in 1831, after a rumor circulated that Mason William Morgan, who was allegedly "preparing to make public the secrets of the ancient order," had been kidnapped and murdered "to prevent him from carrying out his intention." Although the facts of the case remain unclear, Morgan's disappearance "spread the idea that the Masons were secretly anti-democratic aristocrats" and provided impetus throughout the country for a centralized political gathering to oppose the group. Ironically, after some searching, the party ended up nominating a former U.S. attorney general who happened to be a Mason himself.[7] Although the Anti-Masons and their cause didn't stick, political conventions as a method of presidential nomination did, as did early convention crises.

Less dramatic, but more politically significant, was the 1860 Democratic convention. In that year, the party was so divided over slavery that Democrats initially held two conventions. When they finally convened together in Baltimore, southerners boycotted the event after Senator Stephen Douglas of Illinois was nominated for president. The public split among Democrats helped carry Republican Abraham Lincoln to victory. In 1896, William Jennings Bryan did not even arrive at the Democratic convention as a presidential candidate. Instead, "the 36-year-old junior congressman from Nebraska stepped to the podium to voice support for a controversial resolution advocating the free coinage of silver. But his speech . . . so electrified delegates that they swept him to the nomination."[8] Events like these are hardly the stuff of the allegedly scripted, predictable conventions we know today.

Through most of the twentieth century, national conventions remained a hotbed of substantive debate about party platforms and sometimes-bitter controversies over presidential and vice-presidential nominees. In 1924, for example, Democrats exhausted an amazing 103 convention ballots before arriving at a nominee. More recently, the 1952 Democratic convention "drafted" Adlai Stevenson after three ballots, even though Stevenson had said publicly that he did not want to be nominated and did not have the drive to be president.[9] In selecting Stevenson, the delegates ignored primary results, where Tennessee senator Estes Kefauver had earned 3 million more votes than Stevenson.[10] The decision was one of the more prominent midcentury actions that made conventions of both parties seem undemocratic, later fueling the decline in deliberative conventions in favor of party primaries.

On a more public front, Republicans at the 1964 convention in San Francisco were greeted by 150,000 civil-rights protesters, the largest such gathering since the March on Washington the previous year. The protests were aimed largely at presumptive nominee and Arizona senator Barry Goldwater—a fact not missed by some of his opponents for the nomination, who attended the protests.[11] Nonetheless, Goldwater handily won his party's nomination on the first ballot.[12] Despite midcentury reforms of presidential nominating conventions, political crises—or at least potential crises—continued on the convention floor even until the 1980s. In 1976, for example, former California governor Ronald Reagan challenged incumbent President Gerald Ford for the party's nomination at the convention. Ford won the nomination by only 113 votes. In 1980, President Jimmy Carter faced a challenge from Senator Ted Kennedy.

All these battles can be classified as political crises because they signified deep divisions within the parties and at least temporarily delayed conventions from employing their full organizational resources in support of one candidate and one message. More importantly, during the last half-century, these political convention crises unfolded in public view. Especially in the "pre-reformed" era, such disruptions as the 1964 Republican convention or the multiple ballots of 1952 prompted millions of viewers around the nation to watch gavel-to-gavel coverage to see how the crises would be resolved.

The term *political crisis* need not imply that these events were detrimental to party success. Many were not. These events might not meet the conventional gloom and doom connotation of the word *crisis*. However, they all disrupted the conventions' and presumptive nominees' planned agendas and presentations. In turn, convention organizers and candidate staffers were distracted from their strategic plans in resolving each conflict—all of which are central elements to how political professionals define campaign crises.[13] This finding suggests two conclusions. First, in the absence of other theory about convention crises, there is no reason to suspect that political professionals' thinking about what constitutes crises in campaigns should not also apply to political conventions. There is little reason to doubt the validity of practitioners' experience and wisdom as the foundation of building theory about convention crises.[14] Second, political crises at conventions are more common than we might think, as becomes clear when crises become a variable used in analyzing conventions. A closer look at the 1968 Democratic convention reveals how dangerous such crises can be.

THE 1968 DEMOCRATIC CONVENTION: CLASSIC POLITICAL CRISIS

The 1968 Democratic convention represents a defining vision of deliberative, visual, and even physical political chaos. The Chicago convention occurred in the middle of a series of troubled party gatherings. In 1964 Democrats had suffered another political crisis over a convention seating controversy surrounding competing delegations from Mississippi, representing a split within the

Democratic Party on civil rights. In 1972, the Democrats competed over nominees even on the convention floor, and South Dakota senator and presidential nominee George McGovern did not give his acceptance speech until 3:00 a.m. Not only had Democrats suffered a political crisis in the turmoil surrounding their candidate, but they also faced a message crisis because no one had heard their candidate speak.

But the 1968 Democratic convention was the epitome of political crisis. The party "had to throw out the script," as National Public Radio host Robert Siegel said when introducing Walter Cronkite's 2004 commentary about his experiences covering the convention.[15] Convention delegates, and the party itself, were deeply divided over the war in Vietnam. Furthermore, thousands of protestors descended on Chicago to decry the war outside the convention hall. What ensured was a spectacular series of events (very unlike the scripted modern conventions discussed below) involving miscommunication, physical violence, public repudiation of convention host Chicago mayor Richard Daley, and a disastrous November outcome for nominee Hubert Humphrey, the sitting U.S. vice president.

Delegates gathered in late August 1968. Inside the hall, the convention split over Humphrey's more conservative policies toward Vietnam and the more liberal stance of George McGovern. However, a telephone strike in Chicago kept delegates unaware of the seriousness of the massive protests brewing a few miles away. Twelve thousand Chicago police dressed in riot gear, along with 7,500 troops each from the army and the Illinois National Guard and 1,000 Secret Service agents, attacked demonstrators with tear gas and billy clubs. Six hundred arrests were made, and "bloody confrontations were captured on TV."[16] As Cronkite recalled, convention delegates were unaware of the violence unfolding outside:

> Delegates had no idea what was happening. The amphitheater [where the convention was held] not only was surrounded by fences and barbed wire, it was isolated from any live coverage from Grant Park [where the demonstrations were being held]. Satellites and portable transmission gear lay in the future. We could have had live pictures, but a telephone workers strike had blocked installation of telephone lines to our remote camera units. So film and videotape shot in Grant Park had to be hand carried six miles to the amphitheater. A conveniently timed taxi strike further immobilized the city. It seemed that the only workers who were not on strike were the Chicago Police.[17]

The situation became chaotic at a time when it was particularly difficult for the convention to function and present a unified message: during prime-time roll-call voting. A vicious twenty-minute confrontation between demonstrators and various security forces, especially the Chicago Police, ensued around prominent downtown hotels, including one housing Hubert Humphrey. At the same time, lesser violence broke out at the convention. Police tried to remove a member of the Alabama delegation from the floor, allegedly at the direction of the U.S. Secret Service. Other delegations blocked the aisles to prevent police from removing the delegate, resulting in pushing and shoving.[18]

By 9:30 that night, videotape of the Grant Park demonstrations arrived at the convention hall. As the media aired the footage, "delegates watch, first in disbelief, and then in rage." Shortly thereafter, New York senator Abraham Ribicoff interrupted his speech nominating George McGovern, looked at Mayor Daley, and declared, "With George McGovern as president of the United States, we wouldn't have to have Gestapo tactics in the streets of Chicago."[19] Protestors were well aware of the media's coverage priorities and news cycles, and they staged demonstrations to play out on the evening news.[20] The convention was in shambles, having suffered a political crisis of epic proportions in the full glare of the media spotlight.

MODERN CONVENTIONS: LIMITING CRISES, DIFFERENT CONFLICTS

Until the 1960s, the key source of conflict—and the potential for crisis—surrounded *nominating* party candidates. Given the modern primary system, however, the presidential nominees from each party are well known long before the convention begins. Conventions are, therefore, more about affirming the party's choice and building unity than about the drama of deciding who will represent the party in the fall.

Byron Shafer argues that these "reformed" party conventions emphasize launching the general-election campaign but also make doing so more difficult as various factions compete for influence in shaping the party platform.[21] Because various interests within the parties have less power to directly exert their influence over nominee selection at the convention, the fight between factions shifts to influencing the party platform. This change has important implications for message crises at conventions.

Factional conflicts within the convention present at least two significant threats to the picture-perfect convention that is so essential to the intense media scrutiny of modern American politics. First, conflicts between party factions make it more difficult for convention organizers to present a unified message to the public, which is the essence of message crisis. "For what the nationalization of presidential politics, in concert with reform in the process of delegate selection, had really done to the convention was to replace a struggle over the construction of a nominating majority with a struggle over the presentation—and publicizing—of the central goals of *all* the major convention participants.[22] Even when outsider candidates are no longer realistic contenders for the nomination at the convention, loyalists can remain committed to the candidate in an effort to publicly force the party to embrace parts of the candidate's platform.

Reflecting on the shift in convention conflict from nomination differences to issue differences among delegates, Shafer writes, "The mix of (and distinctions among) independent issue activists, interest group representatives, and party officeholders, even when no alternative candidates survived [is] still a more common basis for convention disputes."[23] Progressive Democrat and Ohio congressman Dennis Kucinich exemplified this situation in 2004, when he refused to formally end his underdog presidential campaign, even long after Massachusetts senator John Kerry had secured enough primary votes to be guaranteed the nomination. Kucinich did not formally end his candidacy and endorse Kerry until July 22, just four days before the opening of the Democratic National Convention. Perhaps because of his tenacity, Kucinich received a prime-time speaking slot on the same night Senator John Edwards of North Carolina accepted the vice-presidential nomination. The speech offered Kucinich and his faction's interests widespread exposure at the convention. Increased pressure on factions to make their messages heard means that there is perhaps more potential for message crises at conventions today than in the past because diverse interests at the conventions have fewer and more restricted opportunities to advance their causes.

The second way in which conflicts among factions pose a threat to stable conventions is through undermining the body's legitimacy as a home for the party faithful, which also undermines the ability to present a unified message. Remember, in the "post-reform" era the convention in many ways is a nationally televised pep rally designed to educate the public about the presidential ticket and demonstrate party unity and enthusiasm surrounding that ticket. Displaying unity can be difficult if the convention delegates do not feel that their interests have been adequately addressed. Recent gatherings of both major parties have displayed this characteristic. In favor of order, Democrats barred antiabortion speakers from major speaking roles at their

1992 convention, frustrating then-Pennsylvania governor Robert Casey, who argued that debate within the party and its convention was central to the political process. Similarly, the 2000 Republican convention was criticized for being exceedingly scripted in reaction to public divisions at the 1992 and 1996 conventions.

It is precisely because of the unpredictability and disarray of the 1950s and 1960s—often the result of political factionalism as discussed above—that both parties moved away from conventions as deliberative bodies. I suggest that during the "reform" period beginning in the 1960s, potential crises at national conventions shifted away from *political* crises of deliberation and toward *message* crises of facilitating a unified, attractively packaged media event, not to mention maintaining public and media interest in conventions.

In response to the chaos of the 1968 convention, the Democratic Party charged its McGovern-Fraser Commission with reconsidering party rules and reforming the nominating process. One of the commission's major contributions was in formalizing the already powerful role that primary elections, rather than conventions, had obtained by the mid-twentieth century.

Republicans followed a similar path in emphasizing primaries over conventions, although the GOP has historically kept infighting within the party and at its conventions to a minimum. In more recent years, that unity and discipline has been the result of entrenched power among its right wing. This group began in the conservative movement stoked by Goldwater at the 1964 Republican convention and later threatened Ford's eventual nomination at the 1976 convention. The successors of the unified Republicans helped ensure intense discipline during the 2000 convention. The party has made significant overtures to some minority groups in recent years, especially Latinos, but remains largely homogenous. As a result, Republicans have enjoyed some immunity from convention crises, especially compared to the upheaval of traditional Democratic conventions. Republican discipline in presenting a unified public front epitomizes the importance of message at modern conventions and exemplifies message crises when party discipline fails, as the case study of the 1992 Republican convention demonstrates below.

In an interview, Lara M. Brown, who served as a John Edwards representative to the California platform-committee delegation at the 2004 Democratic National Convention, argued that the usual lack of crisis at Republican conventions is due to differences in how the Democrats and the GOP handle internal divisions. When asked about differences in maintaining conflicts at conventions, Brown responded:

The Republicans always do it better, and it largely has to do with the fact that Republicans are more focused on outcomes, and Democrats are more focused on process. So . . . Democrats really, truly believe that it is important to hear from [Rev. Al] Sharpton, and they will find a time for [him] to speak—maybe in the morning—[but] they still will allow it. The Republicans just would say, "No, sorry, we're not going to hear from the Log Cabin Republicans this time. This is just not going to happen. You guys can hold your own convention somewhere else, but we're not doing it."[24]

Around the same time conventions were reforming as a means of preventing uncertainty for both parties, important changes in American professional politics and campaign management were also underway. Both events solidified the transition from political to message crises at conventions. These changes not only decreased the strategic roles political parties play in campaigns generally but also put new emphasis on individual candidates, their messages, and precise "packaging" in campaigns and presidential conventions. This message discipline is hardly the stuff of political crises at conventions. But, it is clear from examining these changes why message crises (and preventing them) are so important at modern conventions.

Political consultants, the army of professionals specializing in general campaign strategy, media production, polling, research, and other campaign services, today exert far more influence on individual campaigns than do political parties. Even at modern party conventions, the presumptive nominee's campaign team has a leading role, often over the party itself, in shaping the convention program and imagery. As consultants and candidate-centered campaigns have become more prominent in the last forty years, parties have become increasingly irrelevant in campaigns of all kinds, including conventions. "As political parties lost control of campaigns, the essential nature of modern campaigns changed . . . When candidate-centered elections became the norm, campaigns had to focus on selling the candidate to a wide group of potential supporters," who are not necessarily partisan loyalists.[25] This evolution in American politics decreased the importance of conventions as decision-making bodies but also meant that individual candidates and their campaigns were allowed to exert precise control over convention events and messages. This change reduces the traditional potential for political crises at conventions and highlights the importance of presenting a flawless, unified convention message based on the leading candidate's priorities.

After the contextual changes described above, and convention reforms of the 1960s and 1970s, orderly conventions without political crises became the norm. Primaries grew increasingly important as power shifted away from convention delegates and toward primary voters. Convention delegates became increasingly tied, by custom and sometimes by party regulations, not to their own judgment but to the electoral votes they represented from the primary votes already cast in their home states. In reforming conventions away from the potential for *political* crises of major threats to convention unity and business, both major parties faced new challenges in their conventions. *Message* crises have become the modern symbols of serious conflict at party conventions, when crises occur at all. Although reformed conventions have brought order to the process, over time conventions have struggled with numerous internal and external challenges, some of which continue through the present day. Although they do not entail the turmoil and mayhem of past conventions, they still present potential message crises, albeit in less ominous forms than the political crises of the last fifty or one hundred years.

The 1976 Democratic convention in New York City contained a brief crisis that exemplifies the intersection of changing context that limited the potential for factional political crises and the dominance of preventing message crises at the convention. On July 4, 1976, the Israeli military raided the Entebbe, Uganda airport in a successful effort to retake a hijacked Air France jet and one hundred Israeli citizens taken hostage by Palestinian militants.[26] Before the Uganda crisis unfolded, the Democratic platform committee had met in June to set the programmatic agenda for the convention.[27] The convention's political director and longtime Democratic strategist Mark Siegel had the delicate task of balancing his professional duties for ensuring a disciplined convention, free from message crises, with the strong desires of some party officials and delegates to reopen the party's platform to praise the Israeli action. Siegel recounted the episode in an interview:

> God knows, ideologically, I was not offended by [the idea of reopening the platform]. But, as someone who was running the convention, I did not want the platform opened up again because then the left [wing of the party] might want to do something and the African-Americans might decide the civil rights plank isn't strong enough [etc.]. So, we came up with a compromise. . . . Wendell Anderson was the governor of Minnesota and the chairman of the Platform Committee. When he delivered the report of the Platform Committee, [his] opening remarks

had a sort of ringing section of three or four minutes on Entebbe. That's an example of crisis management, creative crisis management. "Yes, we're going to address it, but not in a way that opens up the flood gates."[28]

In essence, what would have probably been a political crisis in an earlier era became an example of successfully managing a message crisis. In 1992, the Republicans were not so lucky.

MESSAGE CRISES AT THE 1992 CONVENTIONS

The 1992 conventions for both parties represent message crises in modern conventions in different ways and for different reasons. The 1992 Democratic convention is widely regarded as one of the most scripted in modern political history. Convention organizers certainly enjoyed the lack of genuine *political* crisis. But, they did face new message challenges, even new potential crises.

In exchange for more political certainty, Democrats perhaps inadvertently invited *message* crises when journalists were so starved for newsworthy material that minor convention disputes became media centerpieces. *Washington Post* reporter Howard Kurtz profiled the media's attempts to find news amid a sea of harmony. Under the subheading, "Struggling to Find Angles Beyond the Script, Broadcasters Turn Up Minor Disputes," Kurtz wrote that, "Faced with the most carefully orchestrated Democratic convention in modern history, television tonight settled for whatever scraps of conflict it could find."[29] Kurtz explains that CNN, ABC, CBS, and NBC all hyped a dispute between presidential candidate and former California governor Jerry Brown and presumptive nominee Bill Clinton. Brown demanded that he be allowed speaking time at the convention, which did not mesh with the intense scripting the Clinton team had arranged. However, Kurtz suggests that the media exaggerated the seriousness of the dispute between Brown and Clinton, perhaps creating a crisis where there was none. "When CNN landed a live interview with Bill Clinton, anchor Bernard Shaw's first question was, 'What about Jerry Brown? Are you going to let him speak?' Shaw even asked Clinton about a minor seating dispute in the Virginia delegation."[30]

Although Brown delegates did manage to create "a din that delayed the convention for several minutes" at the height of prime-time television coverage, the conflict did not change the outcome of the convention, nor did it threaten the convention's ability to do business, as would a classic political crisis.[31] But, because the media fixated on minor events, convention officials, and even Clinton himself, were forced to address them. As we saw at the beginning of the chapter, it is on these distractions from the convention's (and in this case, the candidate's) planned business and intended message that political professionals focus when they talk and think about campaign crises. This finding helps explain not only why staged, scripted conventions are so important for political professionals working around conventions but also why those professionals are so concerned about any hint of discord that could eventually develop into full-blown convention crisis if not properly managed in advance.

The 1992 Republican convention represents the opposite extreme from the scripted Democratic gathering that year. Republicans faced a message crisis due to *lack* of control. The George H. W. Bush campaign was criticized for failing to formulate a coherent message, which some argued fostered the president's defeat the following November. Halfway through convention, prominent *Washington Post* reporter David S. Broder wrote that "the featured prime-time speakers the Republicans have presented [including a former president and three previous or future presidential hopefuls] did more to showcase their own ideas and personalities than to answer the questions voters have about Bush."[32] Even at presidential conventions devoted to modern candidate-centered campaigning, the question of which candidate's campaign the convention centers around is not always clear, particularly during message crises displaying a lack of party unity, or at least a lack of coordination, which is so essential in staging modern conventions.

The 1992 Republican convention speech by conservative activist and presidential challenger Patrick J. Buchanan is a prime example of message crisis. The Bush campaign and convention organizers were aiming for a moderate message emphasizing his international accomplishments and attacking the Democratic Congress on domestic issues.[33] However, Buchanan delivered a scathing attack on Clinton and focused much of his remarks on divisive social issues. As news photographers captured a troubled-looking first lady Barbara Bush, Buchanan attacked Hillary Clinton's "radical feminism" and warned that Bill Clinton would usher in an era of "unrestricted abortion on demand." In one of the speech's most notable passages, Buchanan declared, "There is a religious war going on in our country for the soul of America. It is a cultural war, as critical to the kind of nation we will one day be as was the Cold War itself."[34] Even some delegates in the normally unified Republican faithful were uncomfortable with the speech's tone.[35] Although the speech appealed to Buchanan supporters and the party's most conservative elements, it had caused a prime-time crisis for the Bush campaign and the moderate message it attempted to portray.

A lack of coordination had led to disagreements over when Buchanan should speak, if at all, and a lack of "vetting" and similar message discipline. Former Republican National Committee chairman Richard Bond later revealed that Buchanan had landed the prominent opening-night speaking slot largely by default, as convention organizers were concerned about providing him a platform too close to the speeches later in the week by Bush, Dan Quayle, and their families. According to Bond, "So, we ended up putting Pat on the first night, and with the effect of the media seizing upon what they saw as narrow-mindedness or intolerance in the Republican party, which I regret. I don't know to this day, because of this split operation [in organizing the convention], whether anybody screened Pat's speech. I know that I did not. We probably should have been more forceful in saying, now listen, here's our plan, this is what we want to stick to, this is the theme, but that never happened from my end."[36]

MEDIA COVERAGE, CRISES, AND CONVENTIONS

In an effort to have more scripted conventions for the sake of political order, convention organizers have, in some ways, created more potential for crises by limiting the old-fashioned debating opportunities that made previous conventions contentious and interesting. Indeed, although the disharmony displayed at the 1968 Democratic convention or the 1992 Republican convention represent crises in one sense or another, they at least kept the public's—and the media's—attention. In both cases, the attention was mostly *not* the kind party officials wanted. But, the potential for conflict, and sometimes genuine crisis, ensured that the party message would be carried in the media. This is the dilemma modern conventions face: whether it is better to avoid any hint of crisis or even conflict through tightly scripted conventions and get little media coverage, or to allow for a more open debate—and the conflict that goes with it—which yields more media attention. Clearly, the leadership of both parties has chosen the former strategy. The media has followed suit.

Modern conventions thus have traded one kind of crisis for another. Both parties have virtually eliminated the *political* crises, which stalled the conventions' ability to do business and sometimes conveyed fractured, bitterly divided gatherings. But, in bringing increased political order, modern conventions also open themselves to *message crises* in lack of coverage and lack of interest. Modern conventions can be just plain boring. This causes political journalists and producers to focus on whatever conflict they find, sometimes implying crises based on minor disagreements.

The raucous pre-reform conventions occurring through the 1960s were appealing to the media in large part because they often embodied uncertainty. In the traditional days of national conventions, when these bodies engaged in genuine debate and substantive political decision making, the media was attracted to covering conventions because their inherent uncertainty made them newsworthy. Certainly, when political crises occurred, the media was there, and they knew that viewers would eagerly follow. Conventions also had the good fortune of being in the right place at the right time, during the dawn of widespread television penetration in the 1950s and 1960s. Indeed, the first major national effort to televise the 1952 conventions was regarded as such an important technical achievement for the broadcast industry that "completion of the nationwide coaxial cable for television transmissions was expedited specifically to provide coverage of the conventions." In an era when live events dictated television coverage, political conventions full of potential crises were a perfect fit for television networks. "In turn the audience for this coverage was immediately and then reliably huge. Such coverage was thus institutionalized, convention after convention."[37]

It is easy to understand why the media, and readers and viewers, preferred the days when conventions were actually deliberative bodies with potential crises. Uncertainty makes news. It also fits media coverage priorities emphasizing conflict and competition in elections.[38] Similarly, people process information based on simple, easy-to-use mental frames and symbols, and tend to remember negative information.[39] Conflict and crises certainly fit the bill. This also helps explain why the media emphasizes message crises even when they are minor events. In short, the media liked political crises at traditional conventions because they knew the audience did, too.

Without such uncertainty and with heavy scripting barring serious political crises in modern conventions, the media and the public have largely stopped paying attention. "The combined ABC, CBS, and NBC coverage for each convention dropped from about 20 hours in 1992 to just 11 hours in 2000, while ratings dipped by a third over the same period."[40] In 2004, these networks devoted just three hours to covering each convention, although many more hours were shifted to cable affiliates such as MSNBC.[41]

Media organizations argue that in reducing convention coverage they are simply following public will. Even in 2004, when public interest in the election was dramatically higher than normal by some measures, interest in following the conventions was notably low. For example, one week before the Democratic National Convention in late July, 46 percent of adults in a national survey reported that they recalled seeing a campaign news story on television in the last day, compared to only 28 percent in a similar poll from 2000. More dramatically, in the same poll, 63 percent of respondents said they had thought about the election in the last twenty-four hours, compared to only 30 percent in the 2000 poll. Despite this increased attention to the campaign and media coverage surrounding the campaign in 2004, only 31 percent of respondents reported that they "planned to watch some or most of the Democratic convention, a very modest increase from the 28 percent who said so [in 2000]."[42]

LOOKING AHEAD

Whether scarce media coverage of modern conventions is good for democratic society remains an open question.[43] However, the eventual consequences of the combination of declining media coverage and low public interest suggest potential institutional crises for future conventions. The question of popular legitimacy is perhaps the greatest threat to a viable future for presidential conventions. It is highly unlikely that conventions will cease to function as we now know them anytime soon. But, if the trend of declining public interest in conventions, declining news coverage, and the perception that conventions do little formal business except ratify political decisions made months ago continues, it is possible that the public faith surrounding conventions will become so eroded that their political legitimacy will fall into question. This is essentially what happened after the 1960s and 1970s reform efforts in both parties, which gave most real political decision-making power surrounding party nominees to primary voters rather than convention delegates. As von Hoffman observes, "Direct voting seems much 'more democratic' to us moderns than sending delegates off to choose a nominee for us. We live in a time when the referendum is coming to compete with legislatures, when direct polling of our opinions in all sorts of forms, from television's 900-number call-in elections to public opinion surveying, seems to us to be the democratic thing."[44] Nonetheless, von Hoffman also argues that the media uses conventions as professional networking opportunities, and as Kurtz observes, depend on conventions for material, even if the conflicts within those stories are sometimes overemphasized.[45]

Security at conventions is also an issue. The chaos at the 1968 Democratic National Convention was so profound that party organizers from both sides have worked feverishly ever since to ensure it would not be repeated. This translates into meticulous concerns for even the physical setting for conventions, especially in the ability of that setting to impose literal order for the proceedings and in so doing prevent a damaging media spectacle. For example, "the desire to maintain the autonomy of the convention against demonstrators in 1972, keeping in mind the Democratic debacle in Chicago in 1968, led to a choice of Miami Beach, where a causeway facilitated crowd control."[46] Given post-September 11, 2001, concerns about terrorism, the chaos of the 1968 Democratic National Convention pales in comparison to the human and political devastation a terrorist attack or other major emergency could have on future conventions. This distinction between human and political crises is important to consider as we look ahead to future conventions and look back on the lessons from this chapter.

Any massive physical emergency at future conventions could have profound impacts. Whether terrorist attack, earthquake, or flood, the most serious threat from such an event is to the physical safety of delegates, candidates, the media, and all the other workers and hangers-on in attendance. The political implications resulting from such a massive disruption also would threaten a convention's ability to function and deserve serious consideration, although the party national committees could presumably resolve these problems privately if necessary. The political fallout of a physical crisis would certainly not have the same emotional or human toll as would the physical consequences of widespread injury, death, and physical ruin. However, the administrative and physiological disruption to the American political process of candidate nomination could be substantial.

Although scenarios like these would have seemed fanciful just a few years ago, the massive security planning in place for the 2004 Republican and Democratic national conventions suggests otherwise. A few months before the 2004 conventions, Democratic consultant Mark Siegel reflected on this most serious and new form of potential crisis. It is worth noting that Siegel volunteered these comments while elaborating on an answer to a question that had nothing to do with security, suggesting that convention organizers are clearly concerned about physical crises at future gatherings. "There's internal crises and external crises. What we're all afraid of, of course, is that there would be a terrorist attack during one or both of our conventions and that's the ultimate crisis. Convention planners have no control over it. It would be totally disruptive. The media would be taken by it. You wouldn't have coverage of the convention. You would have coverage of 1,200 people dying in a subway attack on New York or whatever monstrosity we could think of. You can control what's inside [the convention], but you really can't control what's outside in the new world."[47]

This chapter demonstrates that through a unique theoretical perspective, new insights can be learned about even the oldest of political institutions. By no means should future scholars overemphasize the roles crises play in presidential conventions. But considering the evolution of crises and crisis-management at presidential conventions can help us better understand the evolution of conventions—and parties—themselves.

NOTES

The views expressed in this chapter are those of the author, and do not necessarily reflect the views of the Congressional Research Service or the Library of Congress. This chapter was completed while the author was a Ph.D. candidate at American University's School of Public Affairs and Assistant Director for Research at the Center for Congressional and Presidential Studies. American University's School of Public Affairs, the Center for Congressional and Presidential Studies, and the Dirksen Congressional Center provided financial support for a related research project. I thank Costas Panagopoulos for the opportunity to contribute this chapter. I also thank the political professionals who participated in interviews. Karen E. T. Garrett provided invaluable support, as always.

1. The increasing number of Americans claiming to be independents is well documented in Norman H. Nie, Sidney Verba, and John R. Petrocik's *The Changing American Voter,* enlarged ed. (Cambridge: 1979). However, Bruce E. Keith, David B. Magleby, Candice J. Nelson, Elizabeth Orr, Mark C. Westlye, and Raymond Wolfinger argue in *The Myth of the Independent Voter* (Berkeley: University of California, 1992) that most independents retain partisan views.

2. See Lara Michelle Brown, "The Character of Congress: Scandals in the United States House of Representatives, 1966–1996" (Ph.D. diss., University of California, Los Angeles, 2001); John G. Peters and Susan Welch, "Political Corruption in America: A Search for Definitions and a Theory," *American Political Science Review* 72:974–84; Stephen C. Roberds, "Sex, Money and Deceit: Incumbent Scandals in U.S. House and Senate Elections, 1974–1990" (Ph.D. diss., University of Missouri-St. Louis, 1997); and James T. Smith, "The Institutionalization of Politics by Scandal and the Effect on the American View of Government" (Ph.D. diss., University of Nebraska, 2002).

3. This is a simplified version of political professionals' definitions of campaign crises in the congressional context. For a detailed account, see R. Sam Garrett. "'Adrenalized Fear': Crisis-Management in U.S. House and Senate Campaigns" (Ph.D. diss., American University, 2005); and R. Sam Garrett "Concepts, Crises and Campaigns: How Political Professionals Define Electoral Crisis," *The Journal of Political Marketing* (2006).

4. Garrett, "Concepts, Campaigns and Crises," and "'Adrenalized Fear.'"

5. Joseph Napolitan, *The Election Game and How to Win It* (Garden City: Doubleday, 1972).

6. James P. Pfiffner, *The Modern Presidency* (New York: St. Martin's, 2004), 19.

7. Nicholas von Hoffman, "Conventional History: The Rise and Fall of a Political Institution," *New Republic* (1995).

8. Rolando Garcia, "Modern Political Conventions Belie Raucous Past," Reuters, July 25, 2004, available at www.reuters.com/newsArticle.jhtml?type=topNews&storyID=5764873 (accessed July 26, 2004).

9. See Paul F. Boller Jr., *Presidential Campaigns,* rev. ed. (New York: Oxford University Press, 1996).

10. Von Hoffman, "Conventional History," 26.

11. This summary is adapted from UPI newsreel footage aired on July 27, 2004 by C-SPAN2 in conjunction with the fortieth anniversary of Barry Goldwater's 1964 acceptance speech.

12. Boller, *Presidential Campaigns,* 309.

13. See Garrett, "Concepts, Campaigns and Crises," and "'Adrenalized Fear.'"

14. In relying on practitioner expertise to guide theory building on an unexplored topic, the chapter takes a grounded-theory approach; see Barney G. Glaser and Anselm Strauss, *The Discovery of Grounded Theory: Strategies for Qualitative Research* (Chicago: Aldine, 1967).

15. "Remembering the Democratic National Convention of 1968," broadcast on *All Things Considered,* 8:00 p.m. ET, July 23, 2004, National Public Radio transcript.

16. "Conventions Past: 1968: Antiwar Riots Engulf Democrats," www.npr.org/news/national/election2000/demconvention/past.1968.html (accessed July 27, 2004).

17. Quoted in "Remembering the Democratic National Convention of 1968."

18. Walter Cronkite quoted in "Remembering the Democratic National Convention of 1968."

19. Ibid.

20. Zachary Karabell, "The Rise and Fall of the Televised Political Convention," discussion paper D-33 (Harvard University: The Joan Shorenstein Center, 1998).

21. Byron E. Shafer, *Bifurcated Politics: Evolution and Reform in the National Party Convention* (Cambridge: Harvard University Press, 1988).

22. Shafer, *Bifurcated Politics,* 148–49, emphasis in original.

23. Ibid., 185.

24. Telephone interview with author, April 30, 2004. In fact, the Democrats did allow Sharpton to speak in prime time that year. Representing the impossibility of total scripting despite party officials' best efforts—and perhaps a brief message crisis—Sharpton reportedly gave a different speech than the one Kerry campaign officials had vetted. He also spoke for twenty-four minutes instead of his allotted six. Many of Sharpton's remarks included harsher attacks on President George W. Bush than convention organizers had wanted and were featured prominently in media coverage.

25. Ronald J. Hrenbenar, Matthew J. Burbank, and Robert C. Benedict, *Political Parties, Interest Groups and Political Campaigns* (Boulder: Westview, 1999).

26. "1976: Israelis Rescue Entebbe Hostages," news.bbc.co.uk/onthisday/hi/dates/stories/july/4/newsid_2786000/2786967.stm (accessed July 29, 2004).

27. Congressional Quarterly, *National Party Conventions, 1831–1992* (Washington, DC: CQ Press, 1995).

28. Personal interview with author, May 10, 2004, Washington, D.C.

29. Howard Kurtz, "Brush Fires in the Forest of Newsmakers; Struggling to Find Angles Beyond the Script, Broadcasters Turn Up Minor Disputes," *Washington Post,* July 14, 1992, p. A18.

30. Ibid.

31. Ibid.

32. David S. Broder, "Coherent Message Elusive: At Halftime, GOP Hunts for Theme," *Washington Post*, Aug. 19, 1992, p. A1.

33. Congressional Quarterly, *National Party Conventions.*

34. Patrick J. Buchanan, "1992 Republican National Convention Speech," Houston, Texas, Aug. 17, www.buchanan.org/pa-92–0817-rnc.html (accessed July 28, 2004).

35. Broder, "Coherent Message Elusive."

36. Quoted in Charles T. Royer, ed. *Campaign for President: The Managers Look at '92* (Hollis, NH: Hollis Publishing, 1994), 206.

37. Shafer, *Bifurcated Politics,* 229, 227.

38. Thomas Patterson, *Out of Order* (New York: Knopf, 1993).

39. See David O. Sears, "The Role of Affect in Symbolic Politics," in *Citizens and Politics: Perspectives from Political Psychology,* ed. James H. Kuklinski (New York: Cambridge University Press, 2001); and Murray Edelman, *Constructing the Political Spectacle.* Chicago: University of Chicago Press," and John Mark Hansen, "The Political Economy of Group Membership," *American Political Science Review* 79, no. 1(1985): 79–96.

40. Rick Klein, "An Unconventional Production: Lagging TV Rating Spur Fresh Approach," *Boston Globe,* (April 27, 2004).

41. Thomas Patterson's "Vanishing Voter" project provides additional data and analysis on convention audiences and broadcast coverage over time at www.vanishingvoter.org.

42. Mark Jurkowitz, "In Poll, Most Say They Won't Watch," *Boston Globe,* July 23, 2004.

43. See Karabell, "Rise and Fall."

44. Von Hoffman, "Conventional History."

45. Ibid.

46. Nelson W. Polsby and Aaron Wildavsky, *Presidential Elections: Strategies of American Electoral Politics,* 4th ed. (New York: Charles Scribner's Sons, 1976).

47. Mark Siegel, interview with author, May 10, 2004, Washington, D.C.

9

REWIRING THE CONVENTIONS (AGAIN)
The Internet and Innovation in Politics and Media
Michael Cornfield

THE AGE OF ONLINE politicking has arrived. After ten years of public use, the Internet has achieved the status of a major medium for public affairs. In the run-up to the 2004 elections, approximately 75 million adult Americans turned to the Internet to get political news and information, discuss candidates and debate issues in e-mails, and participate directly in the political process by volunteering or giving contributions to candidates.[1] The blogosphere emerged as an important forum for politics, while videos made expressly for the web became a significant vehicle for persuasion and discussion. The online politics trend continues to project upward. Although the rates of people coming online and converting from dial-up to broadband connections have declined, growth persists. Survey research suggests three reasons why: people's experiences with the Internet are positive, the generation of soon-to-be adult Americans uses the medium more than its elders, and high-speed connections encourage longer usage times and more sophisticated behavior.[2]

This trend seems likely to have an effect on the institution of the political convention. During the second half of the twentieth century, the Democratic and Republican parties thoroughly altered their conventions to accommodate live television. What will they do in the first half of the twenty-first century as American use of the Internet continues to expand and evolve? A corollary question concerns the adaptations to come from journalists covering conventions. Television, radio, newspapers, and magazines must increasingly compete with blogs, search engines, and other web sites (including their own, e.g., CNN television vs. cnn.com) in relaying news and commentary about conventions to the public. The competition further spills over into e-mail and instant messaging.

What follows are reflections on change and continuity in political conventions as they connected to the citizenry via satellite, cable, broadband, and wireless Internet, and how the events were linked to the digital communication revolution. These reflections are based on analogical lessons from the advent of television, a sense of the basic structural properties of the Internet relevant to political communication, and early signs from the 2000 and 2004 conventions.

REWIRING FOR TELEVISION: "FROM DECISIONS TO IMPRESSIONS"

During the 116 years of national political conventions before television (1828–1944), party leaders and activists gathered in a city for a week's time in order to make a cluster of decisions crucial to an upcoming presidential election. Foremost among these decisions, of course, was the selection of the nominees for president and vice-president. Delegates were important decision makers; they were not obliged by a primary vote or other mechanism to stay with a particular candidate. Those convened also settled upon a theme and platform for the fall campaign. A successful convention enabled the party to emerge unified, its internal divisions over issues and candidates submerged to the desire to win the White House and other offices on Election Day.

Convention weeks were a writer's feast of speeches, deals, roll calls, confrontations, compromises, walk-outs, lock-outs, end-runs, procedural gymnastics, and assorted surprises. Journalists flocked around convention decision makers, rabble-rousers, and hangers-on, gleaning what they could and stringing it into narratives for publication. Convention stories reconstructed the movements of candidates and bosses between hotel suites and auditorium halls. They allowed readers to gain appreciation for the characters of these party leaders and to see some of the strategic maneuvering behind the headlines and oratory. Some of the longer narratives by such figures as H. L. Mencken, Theodore H. White, Norman Mailer, and Hunter S. Thompson are still worth reading for their literary panache and historical insight.

Enter television. Beginning in 1948, substantial numbers of Americans were able to watch parts of a convention's proceedings from remote locations, without a lot of editing.[3] Delegates and scribes now had to step over broadcast cables laid through the municipal auditoria (which gave way to sports arenas in the 1960s). The defensive footwork was an omen of their waning importance. Soon skyboxes were built in the arenas to house and display the broadcast anchors. Their extemporaneous narration to the television audiences swelled from captioning the proceedings, to interrupting them, to banishing them to the background and C-SPAN. By the 1980s, the political actors of conventions past were reduced to being extras in crowd scenes.

Why the demotions? As the live television audience climbed to tens of millions of prospective voters, party leaders realized that what this mass saw and heard of a convention would prove so indelible that they could ill afford to have decisions worked out even in partial view. A speaker paying tribute to the nominee could steal the spotlight. A long night of bargaining might result in the participants working out an acceptable arrangement but looking undisciplined and boring to the distant observers. Worst of all, violence might break out, or even the threat of violence in the form of displayed fury. Angry images would be hard to soften or expunge in the minds of viewers.

To convention managers, the risk that live television could turn off viewers (and their symbolic surrogates, the broadcast anchors and correspondents) outweighed any potential benefits from onsite politicking. Thus, the main party goal for a convention in the television era became a scripted show. It was less satisfying as a political experience but sounder as an electoral strategy. Campaign principals began to plan convention broadcasts as though they were long advertisements for which they had to pay production but not placement costs. Political decisions about the ticket, theme, and platform were pushed farther and farther back before convention week. After Estes Kefauver defeated John F. Kennedy for the 1956 Democratic vice-presidential nomination on the third ballot, no ticket roll call ever went past the first ballot. As the proliferation of primaries and then the front-loaded primary calendar all but assured that the nominee would be decided in early spring, party leaders began using late spring and summer to vet vice-presidential candidates, plan the convention show, and get into position for the fall campaign.

In a parallel development, print storytellers realized that their reconstructions of convention events now had to offer more than just an account of what happened, since television viewers would have seen (or would think they had seen) everything important by the time they picked up a periodical. Ironically, the more conventions became scripted, the more viewers were correct in thinking that they were. To avoid superfluity, print journalists had to play off the broadcasts and provide analysis, anecdote, and attitude. They had to put what had already registered inside the mass audience's head into fresh perspective. This adjustment was not limited to conventions and other events; after television came on the scene the Pulitzer Prizes, awarded yearly to print journalists, added categories in criticism, feature, and explanatory writing.[4]

So, over half a century, conventions were transformed. What happened then and there mutated from a political assembly into a television special. Production superseded interaction: the number of narrators, live and delayed, direct and indirect, exceeded the number of delegates. R. W. "Johnny" Apple, writing a valedictory column after covering twenty national political conventions for the *New York Times* between 1968 and 2004, put it succinctly: "Over the last four decades, almost everything about conventions has changed. I started when they were all about decisions; now they are mostly about impressions."[5]

Convention narrators—that is, journalists and their spin-conscious sources—came as a matter of course to voice their impressions of the stage-craft and televisual effects; oftentimes, these were worked up into evalua-tions of the managers' competence and the tickets' flair. The narrators folded into their accounts impressions of the mass audience, as those were manifest through television ratings and poll results. Nor were impressions limited to the parties and candidates; broadcast correspondents were judged along with the politicians. The interest in political and media star making—a default topic for consideration given the paucity of decision making going on—resulted in a Möbius strip of summitry at the 1980 Republican convention. Former president Gerald Ford ascended to the anchor aerie and told Walter Cronkite of CBS in a live interview that he would accept a place on the Republican ticket with presidential nominee Ronald Reagan so long as he could become a "co-president." This public statement so offended the Reagan team that they squashed the initiative while Cronkite attempted to confirm it.

In the closing years of the twentieth century, the manufacture of impres-sions started backtracking along with the decisions. Both preconvention activ-ity and its narration became increasingly concerned with the management, publication, and assessment of audience expectations of how well the show would go. Recursive loops of logic swathed these expectations in ribbons of ritualized prose. A consultant would tell a reporter that his candidate did not have to deliver "the speech of his life," and then analysts would discuss the consultant's tactical prowess in "downsizing expectations." All this ancillary talk made it harder to have a clear-cut reaction to actual performances. The conventions degenerated from climactic into anticlimactic occasions, where-upon disappointment became a prefabricated expectation.

And then, just as Johnny Apple exited, new cables were laid for another kind of Apple (as in computer). What does this second rewiring—partly wire-less, in fact—portend for conventioneers and their chroniclers?

STRUCTURAL EFFECTS OF THE INTERNET

Three features of the Internet and the digital communications system of which it is a part bear on the politics and journalism of presidential nominating conventions: direct access, profuse choice, and legible response.

Thanks to the Internet, it is now much easier for individuals to communicate directly with distant, potentially large, groups of people. Say I have an observation to share, a story to tell, an idea to propose. To make my message available to the public, all I have to do is put it online. This can occur without big expenses, physical time, space constraints, or bureaucratic considerations—each a significant filter, or gate, intrinsic to mass media publication. Of course, direct access to the Internet is no guarantee of a satisfactory public reception. But I can also use the new medium to improve the odds of my message being considered by the people I want to hear it in the manner I want them to hear it. I can assemble and enlist a network of supporters; the more e-mail addresses and web links I have, the better the chance that they, and their contacts, will listen to what I have to say.

Direct access applies to consumption as well as production. Indeed, that may be where the larger impact of the Internet resides. Just as television shifted the power of message distribution from convention organizers and accredited participants to broadcast producers—from the arena floor to the control room—so the Internet seems likely to effect an out-migration of this power to its many users.[6] Individual consumers increasingly possess remote controls regarding which messages they see. Everyone who has direct access to a terminal possesses enhanced discretionary authority over the sources and circumstances of their convention information intake.

Direct access is a blessing for democratic politics. More people can be heard in public and choose whom to listen to than in the television era. But a curse comes along with the blessing.

It is well beyond the scope of this essay to estimate the number of messages processed in a convention day by the average delegate, candidate, journalist, and citizen in 1920, 1960, and 2000. But it seems a reasonable guess that the tens of millions of adult Americans with direct access to the Internet not only face more messages from more senders at convention time than their predecessors, but there are more things to do with them. View. File. Edit. Reply. Forward. Delete. Save. The Internet makes social communication extensible as a series of discrete options. So does the cell phone and related mobile devices. That results in a profusion of choices.

At the individual level, profuse choice induces anxiety.[7] With the sovereignty of the broadcast shattered, distraction replaces attention as the default condition of a person immersed in a convention. Like a social climber at a cocktail party, as an online conventioneer my hand may symbolically rest in the hand of one other person, but my eyes and eyes are conditioned to scan the room in a continuous search for other possibilities.[8] The links, buttons, and insets challenge me to focus on one message at a time. At the societal level, the multiplication of options accentuates the fragmentation of the audience and all that that implies for the capacity of a candidate or broadcaster to "cut through the clutter" and make a big impression. Today's targeters aim numerous messages at demographic and geographic subsets of the mass audience and deliver those messages through specialized channels from cable to magazines to blogs. Coherence becomes a paradoxical challenge for convention executives and performers, as the party attempts to send out a message of unity through hundreds of cross-cutting channels.

The phenomenon of convention managers and participants on site and beyond cycling through scads of messages would seem to guarantee chaos. Yet the Internet can be harnessed to computer programs so as to monitor and fine-tune communications more than was possible in the prewired and broadcast-wired eras. Consider that staple of a political convention, releasing red, white, and blue balloons from the rafters to stir up the crowd at the conclusion of the nominee's acceptance speech. This started as a gimmick, a minor item for feature stories. Then it became a rehearsed contrivance ("RELEASE BALLOONS, TEN MINUTES OF CHEERING"). Now imagine virtual balloons dropping across a computer screen, each inviting end users to click on it and go to the campaign web site. This type of balloon drop is a countable phenomenon in the aggregate, in groups, and even individually. Like the corporate telephone recording promises, it can be monitored for quality purposes. This illustrates the strategic value of legible responses: if I keep track of what the responses are to the messages I send out through the Internet, and I know what I want well enough to establish success criteria (click-through rates, donation rates, e-mail subscription rates), I can optimize the quality of my communications over time. I can see which sites are eliciting the greatest numbers of positive responses and divert my resources from the poor-performing sites to them.

The legibility of responses to convention messages underscores the capacity of the Internet to generate instantaneous political action. Real-time sign-ups to volunteer for a campaign, or to subscribe to campaign email, can be interpreted as promissory votes. Additionally, feedback data can be incorporated into subsequent iterations of a message and so become part of the show, as when fundraising totals are reported in telethon-style running tallies. ("Look how many balloons have been 'popped' by people joining our party in the last hour!") Sometimes, for better and worse from a party's perspective, a message or even a piece of a message takes on a life of its own. Sound bites, photographs, tables, and texts have become sudden topics of discussion in the blogosphere, generating buzz that spreads offline into society.[9] The virtual balloon may be cut from the convention campaign web sites and pasted onto other sites. The feedback can help political executives deal with this kind of development as well.

What then, happened with the Internet during the conventions of 2000 and 2004? The second wiring entails a complex shift of consciousness and behavior; direct access, profuse choice, and legible response are complicated phenomena to assimilate. Consequently, the transformation has been spotty.

2000: SPARKS OF INSPIRATION AND FAILURE

Internet entrepreneurs in media and politics looked to the 2000 conventions in Philadelphia (GOP) and Los Angeles (Democrats) as opportunities to experience the same rocketing success as they had seen in high-profile commercial ventures during the tech boom of the late 1990s.[10] The old media covered these ventures as news and appropriated some Internet jargon; one *New York Times* correspondent filed stories under the header "Political Surfing." But any sympathy accompanying the curiosity soon turned to disappointment and deadpan ridicule. The consensual story line about the internet and the 2000 political conventions was that the new media fizzled.

Convention watchers were offered imaginative ways of using the Internet to play at being delegates, reporters, directors, and focus group members. The C-SPAN web site allowed its visitors to choose among several camera angles fixed on the official proceedings, including one aimed on the public affairs network's own control booth. The web site of pseudo.com, a start-up Internet programming network, went one technical step further and enabled Internet users to rotate a camera positioned in the hall. Another start-up, speakout .com, constructed an instant response meter for convention followers to rate what they were hearing and seeing on a scale of zero to one hundred. Results were posted the next morning.

The Republican Party invited its supporters to become "dot-com delegates," who could download a credential suitable for framing, but do little else. The only access the credential provided was to a web site with "talking points" given to party spokespersons, a chat room to be filled with other dot-com delegates, and a form to pose questions to a Republican official. The Democrats placed a video chat room on the podium so that convention speakers could interact (and be seen interacting) with web site visitors before or after their appearances in the arena.

Turnout for these initiatives was light, as election officials might say. Investors expecting mass audiences in the millions wound up with counts in, at best, the tens of thousands. Sites operated by well-known media organizations such as cnn.com and msnbc.com attracted the big traffic numbers. Chat rooms were largely vacant regardless of who ran them, with rants taking the place of anticipated dialogue. There were glitches in some of the fancier technological plays, giving convention narrators a handy symbol for the "Internet goes bust" story line.

But other things were happening in which the small scale of response constituted experimental progress. Protesters established mobilization sites (which still exist at r2kphilly.org and d2kla.org) filled with tactical and legal advice as well as links to indymedia.org, a locus for what has lately been termed *distributed, citizen,* or *grassroots* journalism.[11] Anyone could contribute an article, photo, or video clip. Site visitors could also participate in the "editorial collective," by which they could rate contributions and thereby affect the order of placement.

The web master of georgewbush.com proudly informed a high-tech news service that the site had accepted seven hundred donations during the convention. In the context of old media expectations, and of the Bush campaign's coffers, this number looked pathetically small. But it was a harbinger of Howard Dean's 2003 campaign breakthrough with small donations. Along "Internet Alley" outside the convention arenas in tents on the parking lots, conventioneers gave interviews to an estimated one hundred sites, mirroring targeted communications flourishing via talk radio and cable television. This, too, presaged the inclusion of web-based news and discussion outlets in outreach strategies to come.

2004: FINANCIAL BOUNCES AND BLOGGER BALLYHOO

The 2002–2004 election cycle marks the point in history when presidential campaigns figured out how to make some of the Internet's distinctive qualities pay off on a continual and systematic basis. In the four years following the 2000 conventions, the number of eligible voters looking online for news and information about the campaigns doubled, from 34 to 63 million, representing 31 percent of the U.S. adult population. The Howard Dean for president campaign came and went, leaving in its wake a treasure chest of innovations and a year of sustained attention to online politics from the national political community.

At the Democratic convention in Boston, "Internet Alley" morphed into "Blogger Boulevard," a collection of 123 individuals and small groups who ran web sites relying on the increasingly popular software template to post diary-style entries in reverse chronological order. There were fewer bloggers at the Republican convention in New York City. But at both conventions, they linked to each other's sites, cross-referenced each other's comments, and put a burr under the saddle of conventional journalists, who criticized them for a lack of professionalism. While this was to some extent true, such complaints looked petty and even hypocritical in the wake of several scandals at leading news organizations. The average convention blogger might not fact-check or strive for impartiality as well as the average news media outlet. But some of those that did worse succeeded by nonjournalistic standards. And some of the blogs did better at journalism. Indeed, a blog scored what may have been the only scoop associated with the 2004 conventions when someone posted word that the Kerry campaign was painting the word *Edwards* on its plane, a sure sign that John Edwards would be the vice-presidential nominee.

At any rate, old or mainstream media (MSM) carping was ineffective. Blogging continued to grow while MSM audiences continued to decline (at a much slower rate). Who could blame the audiences for defecting? The broadcast networks continued to pare down the number of hours they allocated to live coverage, and the parties continued to stress programmatic blandness and repetition. The Democrats dubbed their four nights "Plan for America's Future," "A Lifetime of Strength and Service," "A Stronger More Secure America," and "Stronger At Home, Respected in the World," while the Republican titles were "A Nation of Courage," "People of Compassion," "Land of Opportunity," and "Safer World, Hopeful America."

For their part, the parties had begun to see success in terms other than media ratings and even polls. On each side of the partisan divide, leaders were counting the money coming in and using the Internet to spread the message. The parties were joined by advocacy groups taking advantage of a new campaign finance law that enabled large donations to be funneled into financing political communications and organizing on behalf of a presidential ticket in all but name. For example, Americans Coming Together (ACT) launched a web video featuring comedian Will Ferrell impersonating the president; it was downloaded more than a million times, with more than thirty thousand viewers clicking through to the site to enroll as volunteers in ACT's grassroots campaign. And for sheer impact during the summer of 2004, nothing matched the cross-media campaign—blogs, e-mail, and web sites included—mounted by Swift Boat Veterans for Truth and its conservative supporters. Neither ACT nor Swift Boat Veterans played a significant part in the 2004 political conventions, but both keyed off the conventions in distributing these well-traveled messages.

REINVIGORATING CONVENTIONS WITH THE HELP
OF THE INTERNET . . . AND "AMERICAN IDOL"

What can we expect in 2008, 2012, and beyond, as online communication continues to permeate political conventions? The greatest and quickest changes seem likely to develop in connection with convention coverage. The Internet has rocked the business model and vocational ethics of twentieth-century journalism. The predictable prominence of conventions makes them a likely event for continued experiments in citizen journalism, remote-controlled cameras, and blogging, as we have already seen, as well as the encyclopedia entries that materialize with breaking news at Wikipedia. Meanwhile, the cost-conscious broadcast networks may be open to cutting exclusivity deals with the parties, now that objectivity standards have been demythologized.[12]

As for the parties and the presidential contest, a common topic of speculation revolves around the possibility that political victory could result from a creative and compelling use of the Internet with respect to a convention. It's a fun approach to considering the future, and the possibility has a surface logic. After all, in large sectors of the marketplace, including the media, success depends greatly on technological innovation; that is why so many corporations allocate resources to ongoing research and development. Governments lavish similar support on projects for reasons of national security (as illustrated by the seminal role played by the Defense Advanced Research Projects Agency in creating the Internet). As a result of corporate and government efforts in this regard, each campaign cycle features an array of new digital communication technologies for parties and candidates to try out in the electoral arena. Surely, one of these years, the argument runs, someone will pull off a technological coup de theatre during a political convention (or campaign generally) which will amount to an electoral coup de grace as well.

The problem with this expectation is that, on the whole, technological innovation has been a marginal and sporadic factor in electoral politics. Start with political long shots. They have a strong incentive to experiment with an emerging technology because the novelty often gets them an extra dollop of badly needed public attention. But while Internet dabbling and even proficiency won such presidential nomination outsiders as John McCain (2000), Steve Forbes (2000), Howard Dean (2004), and Wesley Clark (2004) a few headlines and, in the cases of McCain and Dean, some badly needed cash, these net-savvy campaigners were unable to offset the insider advantages of incumbency, wealth, law, and tradition. The reason is pretty clear: If Internet technology favors anyone in politics, it is activists over the disengaged.[13] Yet activists are as likely to be insiders as outsiders. The John Kerry campaign (2004) raised a huge amount of money online. A revolutionary alliance between a disengaged and underrepresented segment of the population and a technological and political genius-outsider remains the stuff of fantasy and flawed history.[14]

To be sure, technological innovation can contribute to political victories short of revolution, or even an election upset. The George W. Bush campaigns used the Internet well to mobilize resources in the 2000 Florida postelection controversy and again in 2004 to organize and monitor its ground troops. So a credible argument can be made that the Internet gave the Bush campaigns a decisive edge in the close races against Gore and Kerry. But in a close race, as in all electoral contests, there are many ingredients to victory; awarding the "decisive edge" in a close race to just one of those ingredients (if not the Internet, then the religious right, or the Bush family nexus to oil money) stretches a case beyond the evidence.

In order for the Internet to confer a systematic edge in electoral politics, the swing vote population in the proverbial center would have to coincide with the early adapter population, and a decisive number in this congruent population would have to have a continuing reason to favor campaigns that share its penchant for technological innovation. Neither condition has been met. The early adapters included Republicans, Democrats, Libertarians, and people who shunned electoral politics altogether, while the swing voters included many middle and late adapters.[15] And while early and heavy Internet use may incline people to care more about such issues as privacy, pornography, universal service, tax moratoria, and so on, no single ideology or agenda of Internet users has emerged, as evidenced by the existence of multiple and various advocates and advocacy groups oriented to the issue set.

There will be Internet-oriented innovations in political conventions, and the best prediction to make about them is that the who, when, and so what will be a random assortment of occurrences. Instead of getting more specific, I close with a suggested innovation, one that upholds the ideals of a liberal democratic republic: the parties should borrow a page from reality television, and stage "American Idol"–style contests in public speaking as a way of boosting popular interest and involvement in the conventions.

Reality television puts everyday Americans into contrived situations so that the rest of us can watch them succeed and fail. These situations range from game-show innocuous to frat-house sadistic. Sometimes there is an interactive component where the viewing audience gets to vote on which contestants get to move on to the next episode. The bottom line is that reality television shows are inexpensive to stage and hugely popular when well constructed. During the 2005 season, over half a billion votes were cast for contestants who performed on the Fox network.[16]

In 2004 the parties sponsored with MTV an essay-writing contest for Americans ages eighteen to twenty-four; the winners got to speak at the conventions. Essay-writing, however, lacks the excitement of performance, and fewer people feel qualified to judge essays than public speaking. Fewer may feel qualified to write essays, too; more than 100,000 people auditioned for the chance to become this year's national pop music "idol."

The parties would benefit from even 1 percent of that audition total. To save costs, auditions could be conducted in the form of two-minute videos submitted online or through the mail. Staffers could then cull twenty-five or so worthy entries. A panel of celebrity judges could cut that to ten, as Paul Begala did in 2004 for a DNC make-us-a-television-ad contest. Party "members" (e-mail subscribers) could then vote for the best of the ten. The top two, three, or four entrants would compete in a live runoff on one of the first convention nights, with beauty-contest-style interviews by the celebrity judges and speech performances followed by a twenty-four-hour voting period.

There is a potential ballot-stuffing problem. Viewers of "American Idol" got a lesson in this in 2004 when the Hawaii-based fans of Jasmine Trias took advantage of the state's exclusive time zone to call on behalf of their favorite daughter. But if people signed up with a party to stuff a ballot, so long as it got stuffed on behalf of one of the party-approved contestants, it would still be worth it to the parties and the public. The parties would reap e-mail addresses as the price of admission, and if they were duplicates or lurkers from the opposition in the harvest, so what? The extra cost of communicating with these people would be nil. Meanwhile, the politically disaffected would have an incentive to pay closer attention to the presidential campaign. Many would get involved with the parties in the course of voting for a favorite.

This idea is a transitional one, the equivalent of putting vaudeville on television. In time, as more people become accustomed to the Internet as a political recruiting and organizing tool, medium-specific forms and formats will develop. Meanwhile, as wireless access to the Internet proliferates, politics as a social activity will go back on the move. Conventions will fan out from the arenas and into other city locations, indeed, in multiple cities. The MeetUps and House Parties staged during the 2004 campaign are a preview of this third stage of the evolution: from decisions, to impressions, to mobilizations. My idea draws on the appeal of popular entertainment to invest the mobilized with decision-making power.

The radical potential of Internet technology may lead some to ask, why bother to continue with political conventions? Why not just disintermediate the entire process, and have partisans and journalists leave the building (listening to Elvis on their IPods)? The spectacle is trite beyond redemption. The security risks are great for as long as the war on terror continues. The decision work can be distributed and then aggregated, perhaps to better effect.[17]

The best reason to keep holding conventions anchored to a single building in a single city flows from its ritualistic function. Even when they lack political, news, and entertainment value, conventions remain important because Americans need a special recurring time, a holiday if you will, for their political parties to mark themselves to the general public and renew themselves in the stream of history. The heightened transparency of the event's proceedings through the Internet will only enhance the fundamental mystery of how it all comes together or falls apart.

NOTES

The author gratefully acknowledges the assistance of Ilyse Veron in researching and drafting portions of this essay.

1. Lee Rainie, Michael Cornfield, and John Horrigan, "The Internet and Campaign 2004," Pew Internet & American Life Project report, March 6, 2005, www.pewinternet.org (accessed June 10, 2005).

2. See the reports, data, and commentaries at www.pewinternet.org for continuing documentation of the growth of Internet use and political importance.

3. There was a limited television broadcast of the 1940 Republican convention.

4. Robert J. Donovan and Ray Scherer, *Unsilent Revolution: Television News and American Public Life* (New York: Cambridge University Press, 1992), 273.

5. R. W. Apple, "From Decisions to Impressions in 4 Decades," *New York Times,* September 3, 2004.

6. Two good books published the same year have titles emblematic of this change: Martin Plissner, *The Control Room: How Television Calls the Shots in Presidential Elections* (New York: Touchstone, 1999), and Andrew L. Shapiro, *The Control Revolution: How The Internet is Putting Individuals in Charge and Changing the World We Know* (New York: Public Affairs, 1999).

7. Barry Schwartz, *The Paradox of Choice: Why More is Less* (New York: HarperCollins, 2004).

8. Linda Stone calls this "continuous partial attention," not to be confused with multitasking. The former is less purposeful than the latter. For more on the concept, do an Internet search on the term, as there is no good summary statement as yet.

9. Michael Cornfield, Jonathan Carson, Alison Kalis, and Emily Simon, *"Buzz, Blogs, & Beyond: The Internet and the National Discourse in the Fall of 200,"* www.pewinternet.org/ppt/ BUZZ_BLOGS_BEYOND_Final05–16–05.pdf (accessed June 10, 2005).

10. Parts of this section are drawn from Michael Cornfield, "The Internet and the 2000 Republican Convention: An Appraisal," Joan Shorenstein Center on the Press, Politics, and Public Policy, Harvard University, www.ksg.harvard.edu/presspol/Research_Publications/ Reports/conventioninternet.PDF.

11. Dan Gillmor, *We the Media: Grassroots Journalism by the People, for the People* (Sebastopol, CA: O'Reilly, 2004).

12. For this idea and much more worth pondering on the topic of media old and new and political conventions, see Jay Rosen's *PressThink* posts for July through September 2004 at journalism.nyu.edu/pubzone/weblogs/pressthink.

13. Bruce Bimber, *Information and American Democracy: Technology in the Evolution of Political Power* (New York: Cambridge University Press, 2003); Bruce Bimber and Richard Davis, *Campaigning Online: The Internet in U.S. Elections* (New York: Oxford University Press, 2003).

14. Some Internet enthusiasts foresee a Martin Luther of the Internet, that is, a leader of a rebellion who relies on a new medium (in Luther's case, the printing press) to accomplish the revolution. These enthusiasts overlook the heavy and effective use of the printing press by advocates of the Counter-Reformation. The printing press was a necessary but not a sufficient condition of the Reformation.

15. See Bimber, and Bimber and Davis, note 12; also Kevin A. Hill and John E. Hughes, *Cyberpolitics: Citizen Activism in the Age of the Internet* (Lanham, MD: Rowman and Littlefield, 1998).

16. "Underwood the New 'American Idol,'" www.cnn.com (accessed May 27, 2005).

17. On the capacity of a dispersed population to exceed the intelligence of experts, see James Surowiecki, *The Wisdom of Crowds* (New York: Doubleday, 2004).

10

LOSING CONTROL?
The Rise of Cable News and Its Effect
on Party Convention Coverage

Jonathan S. Morris

Peter L. Francia

BEFORE THE LATE 1960S, party leaders dominated the nomination process. They controlled party delegates and brokered the deals that determined the party's presidential nominee. In 1968, however, Democratic Party leaders were unable to control their convention in Chicago. Anti–Vietnam War protestors clashed with Chicago police outside the convention, while conservative and progressive Democrats battled inside. The fractured convention damaged the party's image and contributed to the defeat of its presidential nominee Hubert Humphrey.

To prevent a repeat of the 1968 debacle, the Democratic Party created the McGovern-Fraser Commission, which led to several significant reforms in the nomination process. Under the new rules, rank-and-file party members, rather than party leaders, became instrumental in determining the party's presidential nominee. Candidates who won the primaries and caucuses earned "pledged delegates" and could secure the nomination before the actual convention took place. By 1976, both parties had completely transformed their nomination process by determining the presidential nominee before the convention.[1]

This new process eliminated the unpredictability of multiballot voting during the convention and reduced the infighting on the floor which characterized earlier conventions. With virtually no suspense or conflict to report, many in the mass media argued that the party conventions had transformed into "infomercials" that were no longer deserving of extended media coverage.[2] By the 1990s, the big three broadcast networks (ABC, CBS, and NBC) steadily reduced their television coverage of the conventions.[3]

While the major networks reduced coverage in the 1990s, cable news networks began to fill the void. CNN, MSNBC, and Fox News covered each night of the conventions during prime-time hours and, in the process, experienced a significant increase in their television ratings. Fox News, in particular, was the big winner. Its audience increased more than four-fold from 2000 to 2004.[4]

This rise in cable coverage is a potentially important development. Cable networks have a growing audience, but more importantly they cover the conventions quite differently from the traditional news networks. Cable news networks devote very little attention to the scripted speeches delivered on the convention floor and instead focus on commentary from opinionated talk-show hosts, such as Bill O'Reilly of Fox News or Chris Matthews of MSNBC. Cable news networks also invite Hollywood celebrities and controversial political figures as program guests to generate debate and conflict. This style of coverage reduces the convention and its speakers to little more than a backdrop for cable's talk-show style format.

The consequence of this development is that the political parties have lost control of how the media cover their conventions. Ironically, the parties' desire for stricter control of information has actually given them less control over how their conventions are portrayed to the American public. By pushing away the major networks with tightly scripted conventions, parties have left cable news networks to fill the vacuum with their brand of sensational, conflict-oriented coverage.

TELEVISION COVERAGE OF THE PARTY CONVENTIONS

Early television coverage of the party conventions was quite extensive. In 1952, the networks televised over 128 hours of both conventions. There was also a large viewing audience. One-third to one-half of the American public watched at least some portion of party conventions on television,[5] and the average household viewed more than ten hours of the coverage.[6]

With such a large and attentive audience, parties began to alter their convention proceedings to account for the rise of television and entered an era of "cordial concurrence."[7] During this time, the parties and the networks cooperated to create a television product that was newsworthy and entertaining but still allowed the parties to convey the image they desired.[8] However, in the serious competition for television ratings, networks began to cut or even eliminate coverage of the more mundane procedures.[9] Instead, the networks began providing journalists and commentators more time for analysis and discussion, and focusing more coverage on the conflict between different factions within the party.

To regain control of the conventions, both parties implemented new procedural reforms during the 1970s. While the convention delegates officially voted for the party's nominee at the convention, rank-and-file voters effectively determined the winner of the nomination through primary and caucus elections, which occurred months before the party convention. These procedural reforms transformed the party conventions from a deliberative event that determined the party's presidential nominee to one that more closely resembled a pep rally and coronation for the nominee. Moreover, the parties also discouraged "party mavericks" from speaking at the convention and increased security to thwart protestors inside and outside the convention halls.

Under this new choreographed environment, television journalists complained that the conventions were little more than infomercials and therefore not worthy of major news coverage. Ted Koppel and the crew of ABC's *Nightline* actually left the Republican National convention in 1996 after the second day of coverage, claiming that they were "bored and had better things to do."[10] During the Democratic convention of 2004, CBS anchor Dan Rather summed up his views on the modern-day conventions: "I wish I could take a stronger argument to my bosses (for more coverage). But it's basically an infomercial. The people who run the conventions have given the networks every reason to pass up the full coverage of the past by squeezing out any real news. I understand it's a public service, but most would need a speed-yawning course to get through it."[11] NBC's Tom Brokaw echoed a similar sentiment. While covering the last night of the Republican convention, the last of his career, he complained that, "These events are managed down to the last semicolon. That's why I find it hard to climb those stairs and get into the anchor chair anymore."[12]

Not surprisingly, the amount of airtime devoted to convention coverage has decreased precipitously, as have the ratings. In the 1960s, networks provided more than thirty hours of gavel-to-gavel coverage. By 2004, the networks covered just three hours over four nights.[13] Network television ratings are also down from 30 million viewers in 1960 to just 15 million in 2004.[14] Given the drop in ratings, there is speculation that at least one of the three major networks may not cover the 2008 conventions at all. The cable news networks, however, have been more than happy to fill in the coverage gap.

CABLE COVERAGE OF PARTY CONVENTIONS

While network coverage and television ratings have declined, the party conventions have actually had the opposite effect for cable news networks. During the 2004 Democratic convention, CNN averaged 2.3 million viewers during the prime-time hours of 8 p.m. to 11 p.m., Fox News averaged 2.1 million view-

TABLE 10.1. Television ratings for Republican convention

	AVERAGE VIEWERS PER NIGHT (IN MILLIONS FROM 10 TO 11 P.M.)			
Channel	Night 1 8/30	Night 2 8/31	Night 3 9/1	Night 4 9/2
Fox News	3.9	5.2	5.9	7.3
CNN	1.3	1.5	1.2	2.7
MSNBC	0.8	1.6	1.2	1.7
ABC	N/A	4.3	3.3	5.1
CBS	N/A	4.4	2.6	5.0
NBC	N/A	5.1	4.5	5.9

Source: Nielsen Media Research.

ers, and MSNBC averaged 1.3 million viewers.[15] During the 2004 Republican convention in September, Fox News made history by drawing in a larger audience than ABC, CBS, and NBC during each of the three nights the networks covered it (see Table 10.1). Furthermore, according to data collected by the Pew Research Center, those individuals who relied on cable news as their primary source of political information followed the Republican convention more closely than others (see Table 10.2).

Indeed, cable networks are not only drawing an increasing share of the television audience, they are also aggressively promoting their coverage of the conventions, unlike the network stations. In the weeks preceding the conventions, Fox News, CNN, and MSNBC ran extensive advertising campaigns about their upcoming convention coverage and anchored their prime-time coverage around their most compelling and colorful journalists. Fox News' Bill O'Reilly aired his program *The O'Reilly Factor* live from the convention halls, as did CNN's Larry King and MSNBC's Chris Matthews.

However, this development was more significant than simply moving the convention coverage from network to cable channels. The style of coverage from cable news networks is very different from the type of coverage that the major networks have long provided. Cable hosts, such as O'Reilly, King, and Matthews, have turned party convention coverage into a talk-show environment that features pundits, journalists, elected officials, and entertainment celebrities as guests. While there was some coverage of the happenings at the podium, cable news coverage often cuts off speakers for commercial breaks or for the journalists to interject discussion and analysis of ongoing or upcoming

TABLE 10.2. Attention given to the convention

PRIMARY SOURCE OF NEWS	AVERAGE ATTENTION GIVEN TO REPUBLICAN NATIONAL CONVENTION[a]
Cable	2.70
Network	2.13
Newspapers	2.36
Radio	2.41
Internet	2.37

Source: Pew Research Center (September 2004).
[a]1 = followed not at all closely; 2 = followed not too closely; 3 = followed fairly closely; 4 = followed very closely.

events. For example, on the Tuesday night of the 2004 Democratic convention (when there was no broadcast network coverage), Bill O'Reilly continued his discussion with actor Ben Affleck rather than show Senator Edward Kennedy's speech at the podium. "The good speech is coming up," O'Reilly said referring to upcoming keynote address by Barack Obama. "You're not missing anything."[16] The night before, O'Reilly also chose to ignore all but a few minutes of Al Gore's speech.

Beyond the tendency to ignore the podium speakers and business on the floor, cable hosts and their guests often engaged in heated arguments on subjects that had little or nothing to do with the party or the convention procedures. Perhaps the most infamous altercation in 2004 occurred between *Hardball* host Chris Matthews and Democratic senator Zell Miller, who was the keynote speaker at the Republican convention. Matthews's aggressive interviewing style irritated Miller, who responded with insults and threats. At one point, Senator Miller stated, "I wish I was over there, where I could get a little closer up in your face" (they were speaking by remote television connection), and "I wish we lived in the day where you could challenge a person to a duel."[17]

When the coverage was not oriented around talk-show banter, it seemed to focus heavily on frivolous topics and events, such as Teresa Heinz Kerry's altercation with a Pittsburgh newspaper reporter where she was caught on camera telling him to "shove it." Indeed, this incident was profiled as one of Bill O'Reilly's "talking points" in his opening monologue. During the Republican convention, analysts ridiculed President George W. Bush's twin daughters' less-than-stellar speech.[18]

FIG. 10.1. Vote decision made during conventions, 1960–2004

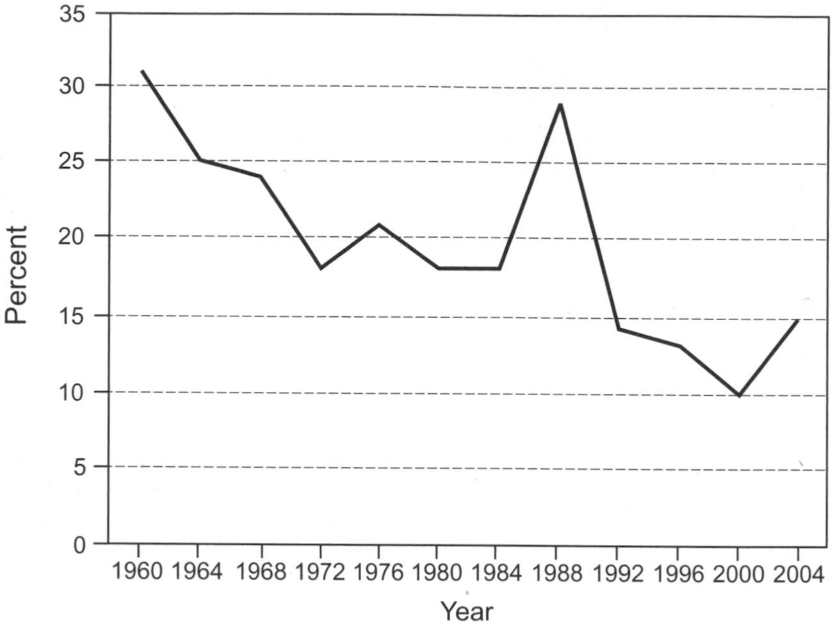

Source: National Election Studies.

The rise of cable news and its very different approach to covering the party conventions is a significant development with important implications. National conventions, which date back to 1831, provide an opportunity for the major parties to present themselves and their vision of the future to the mass public.[19] Fewer Americans watch the conventions on television than in decades past, but as Figure 10.1 demonstrates, 15 percent of the electorate still makes its decision on whom to vote for during one of the conventions. This 15 percent is more than enough to influence the outcome of a competitive presidential election, which certainly explains why the parties wish to keep the conventions so tightly scripted.

However, the parties' tight control over the conventions has pushed away the major networks. The parties' desire for tighter control of information may have actually given them less control over the flow of information as cable news networks have filled the vacuum with their brand of sensational, conflict-oriented coverage. While the preceding discussion has presented several examples of today's cable coverage of party conventions, empirical corroboration is necessary to demonstrate if broader differences exist between cable and network news. Our study examines transcripts of cable and network coverage of the conventions in 2004. Based upon the reasoning outlined above, we expect that cable news networks devote significantly more time to commentary and analysis from their hosts than do the major networks. We also expect cable coverage to spend less time on policy issues but more time covering conflict, sensationalism, and negativity than traditional broadcast coverage.

RESEARCH DESIGN

To test our expectations, we conducted a content analysis of transcripts of the Democratic and Republican conventions obtained from Lexis-Nexis. We searched all Fox News and CNN transcripts during the eight nights of coverage devoted to the conventions in the summer of 2004 during prime-time viewing hours (8 p.m. to 11 p.m., forty-eight hours of coverage total for both channels). To make our search criteria as broad as possible, we obtained all transcripts that mentioned the nominee of that convention (Bush or John Kerry) at least once. This search yielded over 1,400 pages of prime-time transcripts. We also analyzed the very limited coverage offered by CBS news in 2004 (only fifty-two transcript pages) as an example of network news coverage.

Our analysis focused on the content and tone within the transcripts. We also analyzed who was speaking at any given time. To analyze content, we searched for the frequency of several keywords and phrases in the transcripts. For example, to test how often CNN, Fox, and CBS covered the Swift-boat Veterans for Truth controversy regarding Senator Kerry's service during the Vietnam War, we counted the number of times that any variation of the term *swift-boat* was mentioned on each channel. Statements from the podium (or the floor during roll call) were not examined for tone or content.

CABLE VERSUS NETWORK CONVENTION COVERAGE: A COMPARISON

The cable news environment has indeed affected media coverage of the party conventions. First, very little of the happenings at the podium are actually covered during prime-time cable news coverage. Less than 7 percent of the coverage on our cable news sample actually contained material directly from the convention podium. Additionally, a great deal of this programming was not live podium coverage but video clips that showed only a few dozen seconds of sound bites. In stark contrast, network coverage devoted 80 percent of its airtime to live coverage of what was going on at the podium (see Table 10.3). While some of this difference is an artifact of the networks' decision to air

TABLE 10.3. Focus of convention coverage

	CABLE NEWS (%)	NETWORK NEWS (%)
Podium coverage	7	80
Host commentary	53	19
Guest interviews	40	1

Note: Percentages denote percent of lines spoken in transcripts.

only three hours of coverage per convention (thus focusing primarily on times when key speakers are addressing the delegations), this stark difference is indicative of a larger trend in television news in which cable news coverage resembles a talk show and the networks provide skeletal coverage of key addresses. While several scholars have argued that broadcast network coverage of presidential politics is increasingly journalist-centered and less apt to cover candidate sound bites, it appears that this tendency does not apply to convention coverage.[20] Thus, there is little time for discussion and banter among the journalists covering the event for the networks. The talk-show environment was what dominated on cable. Each night of coverage on Fox News began with Bill O'Reilly and was then followed by *Hannity & Combs* and *On the Record with Greta Van Susteren*. CNN's coverage was primarily *Andersen Cooper 360* and *Larry King Live*. It was through this lens that cable television conveyed the parties to the voters.

What is the image that comes through on cable? As we have already demonstrated, very little of its convention coverage follows what is happening at the podium. The individuals dominating the screen were the hosts and their guests. The hosts themselves, however, received the majority of airtime. Our analysis of the 2004 transcripts found that the hosts spoke 53 percent of the lines in our entire cable news sample, while guests or interview subjects spoke 40 percent of the total lines. On the networks, only 19 percent of the lines came from the host and other corresponding journalists, and much of that total came from short introductions and bios for speakers at the podium. Take, for example, how Rather introduced John Edwards's daughter Cate before she spoke at the podium:

> DAN RATHER, host: Now here's what's going to happen. Cate Edwards, the oldest of three Edwards children living; they lost a son in 1996. Cate Edwards will introduce her mother Elizabeth, who in turn, will

then introduce Senator John Edwards. That's going to be the play here. The hall is absolutely packed. It has not been for every hour of every day of this convention. But as is the usual case in conventions, when the vice presidential nominee delivers his acceptance speech, the hall fills up. Cate Edwards with her entrance. Recent graduate of Princeton University, 22 years old.

MS. CATE EDWARDS: Hi. Hi. I'm Cate Edwards . . .

Rather's only additional comment during the Edwards speeches was to provide similar information on Elizabeth and John Edwards as they were introduced:

RATHER: Elizabeth Edwards married John Edwards in 1977. This month they celebrated their 27th wedding anniversary. She is a graduate of the University of North Carolina Law School where she met her husband. She's appreciated for her down-to-earth, real neighborly qualities. She is 55 years old.

RATHER: John Edwards was born in South Carolina, grew up in the Piedmont area of North Carolina, town of Robbins. High school football running back, son of a mill worker, proud graduate of public schools, graduate of North Carolina State and the University of North Carolina Chapel Hill Law School. He is a Protestant Christian, worships at Methodist churches. The roll-up to John Edwards' address is the song "Higher and Higher." Edwards' mom and dad are here tonight, Wallace and Bobbie.

This benign commentary constituted a much smaller portion of the cable news coverage. Instead, the hosts were more long-winded and much more speculative. For example, consider the following commentary by the CNN host Wolf Blitzer and a few of his correspondents:

JEFF GREENFIELD: The best way I can show you this—and we don't often show conventional wisdom—is what's called the Iowa electronic markets. This is a betting pool, a nationwide betting pool where people are invited to come in and risk a buck. The higher the price of a candidate, the more likely people think he is to win. And you can see just about 10 days ago, Kerry and Bush were dead even and the last 10 days, it's going to cost you a lot more to buy a Bush contract than a Kerry contract. This isn't a poll asking who do you want to win, but who do you think. So there is a sense out there—it may be driven by swift votes or it may be driven by commentators—that things have moved slightly in the president's favor.

WOLF BLITZER, CNN ANCHOR: It's not necessarily a scientific poll or anything like that. And it's not just for people in Iowa, either.

GREENFIELD: It's a nationwide thing. And historically, this has been more accurate than most of the fancy scientific opinion polls.

BLITZER: Going into this contest, Judy, the president, the incumbent, where he is right now, is this where the Republicans would like him to be?

JUDY WOODRUFF, CNN CORRESPONDENT: No, they'd love for him to be well ahead. And, in fact, Wolf, when you think of the powers of the incumbency, the fact that he's had the White House with him, he's been able to travel around on Air Force One, he's been able to raise more money than any Republican in history. But, in fact, they know the war in Iraq which has divided this country, economic difficulties and a lot of Americans out of work, when you put that in, this has been a nail-biting election for Republicans all year long.

GREENFIELD: And the proof of that, Wolf and Judy, is that historically, if a president or anybody who comes with a 50 percent job approval rating or more, an incumbent wins. If under 50 percent, they lose. And where is Bush in the numbers? Just about even. That's why one of the subtexts of this convention—we're going to hear about strength and terrorism—is as the Republican chairman said, to put him in a position where people can see him not as a president, but as a good guy. They still believe that the likeability, the kind of folksiness of George W. Bush, despite his aristocratic heritage, is one of his strongest points. And they're going to be hitting that very hard all week.

Although the talk show environment dominated cable news coverage of the convention, this extended coverage did not focus much on policy issues. Discussion of policy positions of the parties and their candidates was virtually nonexistent, while discussion of public opinion polls and political strategy was much more prevalent. In total, cable news devoted just 4 percent of its content to discussing where the party or the candidates stood on specific issues of public policy.

TABLE 10.4. Issue content of convention coverage

ISSUE/TOPIC	NUMBER OF TIMES ISSUE/TOPIC WAS MENTIONED IN TRANSCRIPTS (EXCLUDING PODIUM SPEECHES)	
	Cable news	*Network news*
Medicare	6	0
Social Security	9	0
Swift-Boat	101	0
Shove it	23	. 0
Polls	126	1

In hundreds of pages of transcripts, neither the journalists nor the guests on Fox News nor CNN mentioned the issues of Medicare or Social Security more than a handful of times. Other issues or events, such as the standings in the polls, the Swift-Boat Veterans controversy surrounding John Kerry's past antiwar activities, and Teresa Heinz Kerry's confrontation with a reporter, garnered much more attention (see Table 10.4). Obviously, none of these topics were covered by the CBS journalists, as they had little opportunity to discuss issues and events during their small allotment of coverage time.

Beyond the tendency to ignore policy, the cable news environment took on an aggressive tone. Not only did the talk-show environment provide for pontification and speculation (as detailed above), but it also allowed discussions that sometimes became adversarial. Our examination of the network news transcripts uncovered no adversarial conflict between the journalists and/or invited guests, but more than 30 percent of the segments we sampled from cable news contained at least some adversarial verbal conflict, and 15 percent of the lines contained clearly negative statements about the parties and/or candidates. In many instances, the conflicts were quite rancorous. Consider the exchange during the Republican convention between Fox News' Sean Hannity and Tad Devine, a senior advisor for the Kerry Campaign:

HANNITY: Joining us now, senior adviser to the Kerry campaign, Tad Devine. Tad, I've got to tell you, I find it laughable, for all you Democrats to be so outraged over the truthful outlining of the record of John Kerry, when for a year, your leadership, Ted Kennedy and Howard Dean and the friends of John Kerry have accused this president of lying, misleading, of hyping, advancing theories he knew about 9/11 ahead of time, concocting war for political gain. You know, let's be real with the American people. You're not outraged over the remarks. You're trying to score political points, correct?

TAD DEVINE: No, that's wrong, Sean. Listen, last night's performance by Zell Miller was outrageous. And for Dick Cheney to do what he did, to question John Kerry's fitness to be commander in chief is an outrage. I mean, this is a guy, Dick Cheney, who got five deferments during the Vietnam War, questioning John Kerry who served heroically.

HANNITY: I thought you weren't going to—I thought we weren't allowed to bring that up, Tad?

DEVINE: I just brought it up, Sean. Did you hear it? You know, let me tell you, Dick Cheney is the last guy in America who should be questioning John Kerry, OK? The last guy.

HANNITY: Well, excuse me. He has a history of leading America through two wars, while your guy was against the Cold War. Your guy didn't want the death penalty for terrorists. Your guy voted against every major weapons system we now use. And after the first Trade Center attack, he didn't show up for intelligence meetings, and he wanted $6 billion in cuts. That means he's made the wrong decisions throughout his career, which makes him unfit, doesn't it?

DEVINE: No, it doesn't, Sean. Let me tell you about Dick Cheney's history. His history is that the company he led, Halliburton, is now under federal—three separate federal investigations. That's Dick Cheney's history. His history is . . .

HANNITY: Halliburton. Here we go . . .

Often, these types of arguments became so heated and uncivil that the individuals were simply talking over one another. When such incidents occurred, the voice recognition in the transcription computer could not accurately record what was said and would simply denote the presence of "crosstalk" on the transcript.[21] An analysis of the cable news transcripts found that crosstalk was noted 146 times over the eight days of coverage. Our analysis of network transcripts uncovered not a single incident of crosstalk.

While adversarial exchanges did not dominate cable news coverage, they were frequent enough to leave a possibly lasting negative impression with passive television viewers who may have been watching just a few minutes of coverage. This type of adversarial talk show coverage on television is often more entertaining than typical coverage.[22] However, research has also shown that such hostile negativity can also influence how viewers perceive politicians, parties, and the electoral system as a whole.[23]

Cable news was more likely than network news to focus on sensationalism. For instance, the controversial Bush twins' speaking role at the Republican convention was covered frequently by cable news providers, and they were lambasted by a number of commentators. Consider the following comments:

> JEFF GREENFIELD (CNN): I think charity would suggest that we pass— quickly pass the Bush twins' attempt to be humorous. I think both in the hall and outside the hall, that was the one note that they would have an erasure. They would probably let them do—have a do-over on that one, Aaron.

> KONDRACKE (Fox News): Now, I would add that if there's a first children's contest, I would think that Vanessa and Alexandra Kerry whopped the two Bush girls by miles. I mean they came off frankly as ditzes and you wonder how, you know, whether they should have been on the program at all.

> MARA LIASSON (Fox News): Yes, I think the Bush twins were trying to poke some fun at themselves and at their image. They seemed to confirm it tonight, their image of giggling teenagers who were more interested in clothes and rock concerts than they are in anything serious.

These are certainly critical comments, but they were relatively infrequent. Our analysis found that the Bush twins were mentioned in 13 percent of the cable transcripts we sampled. Another controversial figure frequently covered was filmmaker Michael Moore, whose anti-Bush documentary film *Fahrenheit 9/11* appeared in theaters that summer. Moore attended both conventions but had no major role in the proceedings. He was mentioned eighty-five times on CNN and Fox News but not at all on CBS. Take, for instance, the following news clip from Aaron Brown's coverage on CNN during the Democratic convention:

> BROWN: John Kerry would be the first to admit it: He's not Mick Jagger or even Michael Moore. The first doesn't seem to be a problem. Ah, but the second.
>
> Here's CNN's Tom Foreman. (BEGIN VIDEO CLIP)

UNIDENTIFIED MALE: Michael! Michael!

UNIDENTIFIED MALE: Michael! Michael!

TOM FOREMAN, CNN CORRESPONDENT (voice-over): All over Boston, ever since the convention started, it has been Moore, Moore, Moore.

MICHAEL MOORE, POLITICAL ACTIVIST: You're supposed to be able to believe the president. You're supposed to.

FOREMAN: Michael Moore's relentless attacks on President Bush with his film *Fahrenheit 9/11* and now in person have earned a hero's welcome. He was even seated with former President Jimmy Carter who is not talking publicly about it, while Moore is saying plenty.

MOORE: He said to me, "I can't think of anyone I would rather have to sit with me tonight than you," and . . .

FOREMAN (on camera): How do you feel about that?

MOORE: I was so blown away.

FOREMAN (voice-over): Moore says he's an Independent, not a Democrat, and some top Democrats don't like all the attention he's getting, but he has struck a chord, railing against the war, Republicans and the media.

MOORE: We need you to ask the questions! Demand the evidence. Demand the evidence. Don't ever send us to war without asking the questions.

FOREMAN: That said, he has no plans to endorse John Kerry.

MOORE: When John Kerry becomes president on January 20th next year, on January 21st, that camera lens of mine is going to be pointed at him, because that's my job.

FOREMAN: Are you going to go to the Republican convention?

MOORE: I already have my credentials for the Republican convention and so do my 25 bodyguards.

FOREMAN: But Moore dropped plans to attend the latest premiere of his film, a short distance from President Bush's ranch in Texas. Despite his courting of the media here, Moore says he does not want the story to be all about him. Tom Foreman, CNN, Boston.

Similarly, there is a growing tendency for the cable stations to invite entertainment celebrities to appear on their programs during the convention (as Michael Moore did). This practice would qualify as another aspect of sensationalism. Our analysis found that cable featured entertainment celebrities as guests on 8 percent of the news segments. This figure is certainly an increase from the number of celebrities featured on the networks, which was zero, but celebrities constituted a relatively small fraction of the talk-show guests, who were mostly pundits, journalists, and party officials. When entertainment celebrities did appear on the cable talk shows, it provided for some interesting moments. Consider Affleck's comments to Matthews during a broadcast of *Hardball* during the Democratic convention:

> BEN AFFLECK, ACTOR: Well, I mean, I think it's a very difficult question, which is why you see the Kerry campaign sort of straddling the line right now. There's a sort of a—conservative tendency toward, you know, don't do too much that may alienate the middle, but you also have to *enervate* the base. And I think that—that is going to be the issue of this campaign.

While Affleck's comments seemed benign, several observers noted the following day that the term *enervate* refers to the process of destroying something by depriving it of strength. This misuse of vocabulary, of course, was widely cited on hundreds of web logs as evidence that perhaps Ben Affleck was out of his league.

CONCLUSION

On Wednesday night of the Democratic convention on CNN, media critic Howard Kurtz observed that, "with the lack of hard news here, any little controversy, we the 15,000 journalists assembled here at the Fleet Center are going to jump on it." His colleague Jonah Goldberg agreed, saying that "when you have everything so minutely controlled and micromanaged that the slightest thing that goes off script just consumes the media to a big degree. But basically, what I don't like about this convention is that it's so fake. It's an infomercial. They should be selling steak knives." Our study suggests that Kurtz and Goldberg certainly have a valid point. The age of television ushered in the era of the controlled party convention, where all intraparty conflict and debate is hidden from the cameras. It is this environment that has prompted the broadcast networks to cut its coverage of the party conventions. Cable news stations, however, have been more than willing to step in and provide exhaustive coverage throughout the entirety of prime-time viewing hours. Unfortunately for the convention planners, cable news coverage does not necessarily put a friendly face on the party.

A talk-show environment has come to dominate cable news coverage of the conventions. The public hears very little directly from the parties and their selected speakers, and journalist commentary occupies the majority of airtime. This commentary is not oriented around policy or the qualifications and background of the nominees. On the contrary, policy discussion is almost nonexistent in comparison to banter on topics such as public opinion polls and political strategy. Heated arguments are as frequent as policy discussion, and overall negativity persists.

The parties have made strategic errors by turning their conventions into empty infomercials. This approach was successful in keeping broadcast networks from covering intraparty disputes over nominees and platforms, but cable news has proven they can fill the news cycle without such fuel, and the parties have little to no influence over the topics of discussion. In this respect, the parties have created a situation that has put their image, and perhaps their electoral fate, in the hands of political talk-show hosts on cable. Outside the realm of conventions, the effects of ideologically charged, conflict-ridden talk shows are mitigated by the fact that most viewers are watching the programs as supplements to news obtained by more traditional means (primarily newspapers and anchor-based television news coverage). During the conventions, however, the cable news stations have decided to showcase these talk shows as the primary sources of news during prime-time hours. The talk-show circus is not tempered by traditional coverage, and thus the parties' images among the mass public (many of whom are not accustomed to political talk-show theatrics) are at the mercy of endless spinning and arguing between pundits and politicos.

It would appear that the lesser-known presidential candidates are put at a particular disadvantage by cable news convention coverage. In 2004, for example, the Democratic Party went to great pains to highlight the record and accomplishments of nominee John Kerry, who was not nearly as familiar to the voting public as President Bush. While the Democrats were persistent in selling Kerry as a distinguished senator and war hero, the message was largely lost as pundits and journalists endlessly critiqued every conceivable aspect of the convention and Kerry himself. In 2008, both parties may likely run up against a similar dilemma, as there will be no incumbent president or vice president seeking the White House for the first time since 1952. With the American voting public evenly divided by party identification, the outcome of the general election may very well hinge on which party does a better job presenting their candidate to the television audience during the conventions. The most successful party will be the one that devises a message strategy that accounts for the fact that millions of swing voters will be watching the convention through the prism of the cable talk-show melee on Fox News and CNN. It would behoove both parties to devote greater resources toward sharpening their message on the talk shows as opposed to the stage and the podium.

NOTES

We wish to thank Amanda Hodges and Rebecca Buzzard for their assistance on this project.

1. Nelson W. Polsby, *Consequences of Party Reform* (New York: Oxford University Press, 1983); Robert E. DiClerico and Eric M. Uslaner, *Few Are Chosen: Problems in Presidential Selection* (New York: McGraw Hill, 1984); William Crotty and John S. Jackson III, *Presidential Primaries and Nominations* (Washington, DC: CQ Press, 1985); Howard L. Reiter, *Selecting the President: The Nominating Process in Transition* (Philadelphia: University of Pennsylvania Press, 1985).

2. Neil A. Lewis and Bill Carter, "TV Networks see Decline in Viewers; Cable Gains," *New York Times,* July 27, 2004, P8.

3. Zachary Karabell, "The Rise and Fall of the Televised Political Convention," discussion paper D-33, The Joan Shorenstein Center at the John F. Kennedy School of Government, Harvard University, 1998.

4. Howard Kurtz, "Convention Oratory, Increasingly Shoved Aside," *Washington Post,* August 2, 2004, C1.

5. Gladys E. Lang and Kurt Lang, *Politics and Television: Re-Viewed* (London: Sage, 1984).

6. Karabell, "Rise and Fall."

7. Larry David Smith and Dan Nimmo, *Cordial Concurrence: Orchestrating National Party Conventions in the Telepolitical Age* (New York: Praeger, 1991).

8. Tom Rosenstiel, *Strange Bedfellows: How Television and the Presidential Candidates Changed American Politics* (New York: Hyperion, 1993).

9. Smith and Nimmo, *Cordial Concurrence;* Karabell, "Rise and Fall."

10. David Broder, "Restoring the Conventions' Vital Function," *Washington Post* September 11, 1996, A23.

11. Lewis and Carter, "TV Networks see Decline."

12. Bill Carter, "Left to Reflect on Week's Poor Ratings," *New York Times,* September 3, 2004, P11.

13. The networks did not cover the second night of the Democratic National Convention, nor did they cover the first night of the Republican Convention. During each of the other three nights, one hour of coverage was slotted on each network from 10 to 11 p.m.

14. Thomas E. Patterson, "Election Interest is up Sharply, But Convention Interest is Not," a release from the Vanishing Voter Project, July 21, 2004, www.vanishingvoter.org (accessed November 5, 2005).

15. Kurtz, "Convention Oratory."

16. Marlon Manuel, "Election 2004: Democratic Convention: Network Coverage Leaves no Time for Juicy Details," *Atlanta Journal-Constitution,* July 30, 2004, 3B.

17. Lisa deMoraes, "Matthews and Miller: Spitballs at 10 Paces," *Washington Post,* September 3, 2004, C7.

18. Allessandra Stanley, "Fast, Frisky, and Caffeinated, Fox News Looked Right at Home All Week," *New York Times,* September 3, 2004, P11.

19. Byron E. Shafer, *Bifurcated Politics: Evolution and Reform in the National Party Convention* (Cambridge, MA: Harvard University Press, 1988).

20. James Fallows, *Breaking the News: How the Media Undermine American Democracy* (New York: Vintage, 1996); Daniel C. Hallin, "Sound-Bite News: Television Coverage of Elections, 1968–1988," *Journal of Communication* 42 (1992): 5–24; Thomas E. Patterson, *Out of Order* (New York: Vintage, 1994).

21. The Lexis-Nexis transcripts denoted such incidents with "(CROSSTALK)." This notation was easy to identify as it was in capital letters and placed within parentheses on its own line of text.

22. Richard Forgette and Jonathan S. Morris, "The State of the (Dis)Union: The Effects of New Media Coverage on Perceptions of Congress," paper presented at the annual meeting of the Midwest Political Science Association, Chicago, April 10, 2003.

23. Forgette and Morris, "The State of the (Dis)Union"; Diana C. Mutz and Byron Reeves, "The New Videomalaise: Effects of Televised Incivility on Political Trust," *American Political Science Review* 99 (2005): 1–15.

11

MASS MEDIA AND THE DEMOCRATIZATION
OF PRESIDENTIAL NOMINATING CONVENTIONS
Terri Susan Fine

PRESIDENTIAL NOMINATING CONVENTIONS DEMONSTRATE critical intersections among political parties, the mass media, and the public. Political parties and the mass media are crucial instruments of democracy. Although both have contributed to the decline of the deliberative nature of such gatherings, the solution to the problem can be found at its source: there is strong potential for parties and the media to recast presidential nominating conventions as deliberative and meaningful.

NOMINATING CONVENTIONS: THE INTERSECTION
OF POLITICAL PARTIES AND THE MASS MEDIA IN A DEMOCRACY

Parties became central to the government when they first formed in the late eighteenth century. The elections process naturally organized itself around a two-party system reflecting the Federalist/Anti-Federalist divide that dominated politics at that time. Parties in the United States also took on a decentralized character. Original party goals continue to be reflected in twenty-first-century party activity as office-holders shape, implement, and adjudicate public policy according to party principles. Achieving these goals requires that parties successfully manage elections, guide public policy, build grassroots membership, and encourage voter support.

Key scholars argue that democracy would be impossible without parties even though the U.S. Constitution makes no mention of them and the United States is the world's longest running representative democracy.[1] Because parties are considered core instruments of democracy, should parties fail, so too might democracy. Similarly, the mass media play a critical role in a democracy because they can provide the public with information about the government to which it would otherwise have no immediate access. The mass media support a key democratic role by serving as public watchdogs.

E. E. Schattschneider argues that parties articulate mass-based policy preferences that can then be implemented by party members holding public office.[2] A competitive party system where more than one plan and more than one set of leaders seeks favor with the electorate brings forward the best possible options.[3] The only way for the public to learn of party plans and options is through the mass media. The media enhance public knowledge by cultivating an informed electorate capable of making choices based on more, rather than less, information. The notion that parties bring together an otherwise amorphous electorate that has difficulty developing cleavages and articulating policy preferences, while the mass media educates the public of those preferences, suggests that parties and the media encourage informed democratic participation. Without parties to articulate the issues and the mass media to present them, the public would be unable or would have inordinate difficulty crafting and putting forward policies and programs.

Parties engage in interest aggregation and interest articulation. They facilitate interest aggregation by bringing public voices together in a manner clarifying policy preferences and political views. There is a minimal and implicit expectation that party members holding public office will support their party's principles and issue positions. By communicating public views to the government through their members, parties perform interest aggregation. Party conventions have the structures in place encouraging interest articulation (through coalition building and caucuses) as well as interest aggregation (through the platform writing and adoption processes). The mass media promotes party accountability of these processes because they report on party principles and issue positions while they also research and reveal to the public whether party members are adhering to formal party stances. Such accountability encourages party leaders to take those positions that they are willing to support and follow.

Nominating conventions provide party elites with the opportunity to develop consensus among mass-level adherents through the mass media. Conventions also give parties the opportunity to define and formally launch their presidential campaign. "The speeches on the candidates' behalf at the convention and their acceptance speeches are the opening shots of the fall campaign."[4] The national parties, while they enjoy a closer relationship with the president and Congress when compared with state and local parties, meet infrequently. Their nominating conventions function as their quadrennial meeting.

These principles can be considered within the context of three dimensions of democratic theory: accessibility of leadership, voter goals, and the character of participation.[5] Gerald Pomper agrees with those theorists, such as William Kornhauser, who argue that accessibility of leadership is the most important.[6] Without it, the nature of what voters want, and the means by which they express it (participation), would go unheeded. Inaccessible party leaders magnify the negative aspects of liberal democracy such as the public's freedom to not participate.[7] It is incumbent upon the parties, as conduits serving the interests of the public and government, to motivate public participation. Party efforts to mobilize public engagement enhance the positive aspects of liberal democracy, integrating political expression into policy decisions.

Nominating conventions follow these considerations because they give otherwise decentralized and disjointed parties the opportunity to act as one for several days every fourth summer. In many respects, conventions give tangible meaning to the many roles that parties play in their efforts to organize public preferences.

The mass media play an important role in advancing these three principles of democratic theory. Political leaders become accessible when the media makes the public aware of their roles and activities because those leaders may be more likely respond to public concerns once they understand that the public knows of their activities. Voter goals relating to enhanced, rather than minimized, knowledge of party activities are also promoted by the mass media, as is the character of participation. If the parties seek to inform the public of their programs and plans, and the media are successful in communicating those plans to the public, then the quality of political participation is enhanced. As the parties are taking part in interest aggregation, it is in a party's best interest to insure that voters are aware of its efforts to articulate those preferences. Such efforts will make for a more informed voter who is more likely to support a party's candidates once it is clear that the party is responding to those preferences.

Conventions also allow interests to communicate and formulate policy recommendations through conflict and compromise. Such opportunities allow interests to be articulated in a manner facilitating conflict resolution.[8] These opportunities demonstrate the importance of party conventions despite others' concerns that, since conventions now legitimate rather than make key party decisions, they are no longer necessary or warranted.[9] The mass media play an important role when they inform the public of the party's efforts to resolve its internal conflicts peacefully, as it may better appreciate how the party functions in its interest aggregation and articulation roles.

Mid-twentieth-century conventions succeeded in building consensus among various party factions and acting deliberatively. Convention delegates enjoyed a meaningful role in deciding who would be nominated while nominated candidates were expected to follow party principles. Convention attendees were integral to writing and adopting the party platform. The media played an important part in informing the public of these delegate activities as the networks broadcast convention deliberations for several hours each day.

Many aspects of party conventions remain unchanged over time. Conventions still occur over several days—rather than during a single day, several weeks, or months—and the platform is adopted before the president and vice president are formally nominated. The procedures governing nominations and platform adoption require that an absolute majority of delegates formally approve of the nominees and the platform while separate ballots are cast for president and vice president. Procedures for making and discussing business, such as *Robert's Rules of Order,* have been utilized for some time.[10]

Nominating conventions emerged in 1832 when Andrew Jackson was nominated for president by an entity other than Congress. Twelfth amendment requirements that the president and vice president be elected as a team render it necessary that candidates run as a team. A natural extension requires that candidates be nominated as a team. One viable candidate for each office remains by the time balloting takes place even though the actual balloting for president and vice president is conducted separately.

Standard convention practice meant that party leaders would name the persons they believed provided the best combination of presidential capability and electability. Variations on this process changed convention politics until the 1950s.[11] It was important that party leaders selected presidential candidates (and to a lesser extent vice-presidential candidates) who were electable on their own merits and would make the party itself attractive.[12] Victorious nominees were and continue to be under pressure to insure that the party will retain its hold on the presidency. A party may suffer a death knell of sorts should its nominee fail to secure the presidency or fail as president. Because low presidential approval is linked to congressional party turnover, voters use midterm congressional elections to express their increasing disapproval following the high approval points that regularly occur during the honeymoon period (the first one hundred days of the presidential administration).[13] The president's party generally loses congressional seats during midterm elections (although there are key exceptions, most recently 2002). While such losses are to be expected, failed presidencies make for graver losses than average in congressional elections.

Parties are pressured to make the best selection for the short and long term. Those responsible for choosing the nominee would be those most familiar with party goals and the complexities of the political process, campaign politics, and presidential responsibilities. Logically, the persons undertaking this task would be active and engaged party leaders.

While these approaches have dominated presidential nomination politics, much has changed over the last half century. In the 1950s, conventions governed by party elites would target insiders rather than outsiders (literally those not attending the convention). Those inside the hall constituted the key audience. Their views, concerns, and deliberations determined convention outcomes.

Significant rule changes also ensued after the 1968 Democratic National convention. These changes, coupled with trends already taking place (no multi-ballot conventions, increased media attention and direction, the enhanced role of the presidential nominee in selecting the vice-presidential nominee and overseeing the platform) warrant attention.[14] They were formulated and implemented because of the parties' concerns that they remain conduits to the government for the public and necessary components of a democratic polity.

The 1968 Democratic convention culminated a long period of public disengagement from government as well as the Democratic Party's detachment from the public. Anti-Johnson protests heated up on university campuses, which, coupled with declining public support for Johnson's Vietnam policies, led to enough early caucus and primary losses in the spring that Johnson withdrew on March 31, 1968.[15] Martin Luther King was assassinated in Memphis just two weeks later, promulgating louder public outcry against race discrimination. Robert F. Kennedy, the frontrunner once Johnson withdrew, had easily clinched the nomination by the California primary. Greater disengagement ensued when Kennedy, the popular and logical Democratic choice, was assassinated in Los Angeles on June 4, the night of the California primary.

These concerns festered through the summer and ultimately led to rioting and violence at the Democrats' convention in Chicago. The riots and the subject of these protests damaged the Democrats' image so much that they lost the next two presidential races to an arguably easily beatable candidate. (Richard Nixon had angrily withdrawn from politics after losing the California governor's race in 1962.) In response, the Democratic Party adopted rule changes altering the political landscape in which presidential candidates were nominated. The Republican Party did not incorporate rule changes per se. Rather, they altered their approaches in a manner reflecting the democratization of the nominations process.[16]

The changes sought to create a nominations process that was "open, timely, and representative."[17] In essence, the rule changes democratized the nomination process by opening it up to more rank-and-file party members and making it easier for a broader array of candidates to receive delegate support at nominating conventions. The opportunity to secure delegate slots was also democratized when the Democrats, through formal rule changes, and the Republicans, through affirmative recruitment efforts, sought to bring more women and minorities into the nomination process. For example, the Democrats required that one half of each state party delegation be comprised of women. Initial Democratic reforms also required a certain percentage of younger (under thirty) and minority delegates. The Democrats have since discontinued quotas linked to race and age.[18] Diversity among and across state delegations is now broader as a wider array of voices, representing various minority groups and candidates, is now a regular component of party nominating conventions. Consensus among competing party factions who would share in their desire to enjoy victory for their party is now encouraged.

One effort at democratization required that state parties demonstrate that their delegate selection procedures were not discriminatory. One easy way to achieve this goal was holding primaries (perceived as open) rather than caucuses (perceived as closed). As a result, while fifteen states held primaries in 1968, thirty-five did so in 2004. Proportional representative systems have also been adopted to better reflect primary voters' preferences. The proportion of votes necessary to receive delegate representation at the convention was lowered to insure that candidates who did not win a state's primary with a majority vote would still retain a voice at the convention.

THE PROBLEM: WEAKENED PARTY CONTROL

OVER PRESIDENTIAL NOMINATING CONVENTIONS

Presidential Nominations

The advent of primaries has affected who gets nominated as well as the influence that the nominee has when selecting the vice-presidential nominee.[19] Since 1972, current and former governors, persons with no national-level political experience, are far more likely to seek and secure their party's nomination because it is much easier to do. Since the first reforms went into effect, of the fourteen persons nominated between 1972 and 2004, four were current or former governors (Ronald Reagan, Jimmy Carter, Michael Dukakis, Bill Clinton,

George W. Bush), three had U.S. Senate experience (George McGovern, Robert Dole, John Kerry), three were current or former vice presidents (Walter Mondale, George H. W. Bush, Al Gore) and two were incumbent presidents (Nixon, George W. Bush).[20]

The advent of primaries means that parties exert less control over choosing their own nominees. It is much easier for someone who is neither well liked nor well known to pursue the nomination through a primary system when compared with a caucus system.

> The primary has also changed the distribution of power within the party. It clearly enhances the power of the party's candidates and the party in government at the expense of the party organization. Because candidates (especially incumbents) can defy the party organization and still win its nomination, the idea of party "discipline" loses its credibility. This sets the United States apart from many other democracies, in which the party organization has a lot of power over the party in government. Just as the direct primary undercuts the ability of the party organization to recruit candidates who share its goals and accept its discipline, it prevents the organization from disciplining partisans who already are in office.[21]

Paul Beck and Marjorie Hershey further add that one of the unintended effects of the direct primary is that the mass media's power is now much broader than it has been in the past. "Television image-building has come to substitute for the kind of labor-intensive door-to-door campaigning that strong party organizations traditionally supplied."[22]

The nomination itself, which had previously been used as a means to broker votes, now affords the nominee the opportunity to unify his party behind his candidacy. This is a meaningful shift. Previously, nominations gave parties the opportunity to foster unity behind the nominee. This relationship is now reversed. The presumed nominee now uses his nomination to foster party unity.

Since the presumed nominee is already known, he also becomes the convention focus. Attention is siphoned off other party building activities. For example, while nineteenth-century nominees did not even attend conventions, the nominee's acceptance speech is now an integral and much anticipated part of the convention. Recently, presumed nominees broke tradition by visiting the convention the same evening that the state delegations voted. Clinton, George H. Bush, George W. Bush, and Gore each made cameo appearances at their conventions the night before delivering their acceptance speeches. The acceptance speech is the formal conclusion of the convention and serves as the official kickoff to the presidential campaign.

The convention will continue showcasing the current administration, extolling the president's party less while giving more attention to the presidential candidate. The challenging party will emphasize its nominee at the party's expense. The shift from party nomination convention to presidential nomination convention, while considered synonymous terms in the past, will be much less so in the future. The consequences for candidates will be continued efforts aimed at independent moderates because the nature of presidential voting has taken on such appeals in the recent past.[23] The party will be expected to follow. This also means that the presumed nominee's efforts to target those voters utilizing nonparty cues may lead the nominee to distance himself from his party's platform. These concerns are elaborated on later.

Vice-Presidential Nominations

Vice-presidential nominations have changed significantly over the past fifty years. It was once quite common to select nominees from a diverse pool of possible candidates, all having the potential to balance the presidential ticket.[24] They were also identified and selected by party leaders. Political leaders' perceptions of balancing the ticket outweighed other considerations such as the presumed nominee's desire to overcome his own shortcomings. Clear differences result when a running mate's sole purpose is to overcome the nominee's own deficiencies rather than considering broader party deficiencies and/or constituent cohorts, although the two were not mutually exclusive. The candidate best able to serve the party's interest may also play a role in overcoming the presidential nominee's personal deficiencies.

Richard Nixon and Dwight Eisenhower provide a powerful example, as their personality differences would likely have prevented Nixon from being selected in 1952.[25] Yet Nixon's experience and his strong Republican commitment complemented Eisenhower's deficiencies. Eisenhower's detachment from selecting Nixon as his running mate set the tone for eight years of personality misfires and communication difficulties.[26] Nixon's congressional experience and California roots may not have been perceived by Eisenhower as ticket balancing even though such forces played a key role in Nixon's selection by party leaders.

In 1988, a nearly opposite occasion provoked surprise. George H. W. Bush selected Indiana U.S. senator Dan Quayle as his running mate. He was not on the political radar screen of party leaders' short lists, yet he balanced many of Bush's perceived deficiencies. Quayle was younger, more conservative, and a member of a two-career household, he had young children and a consistent antiabortion record, and he brought regional balance to the ticket.[27] It was Bush's perceived deficiencies, rather than a sole emphasis on Republican priorities, that secured Quayle's nomination. An emphasis on party priorities may have seen as a more suitable running mate a candidate with more congressional experience who was better known. Quayle enjoyed neither national name recognition nor popularity before becoming Bush's running mate in 1988.

Another vice-presidential selection strategy is to identify a worthy competitor whose delegate and public support brings overall strength to the ticket. This brought both Lyndon Johnson and George H. W. Bush their party's nods in 1960 and 1980, respectively. Choosing a vice-presidential candidate from among the pool of presidential nomination seekers invites support from a constituency that might otherwise consider the opposition.

The Reverend Jesse Jackson expected that Michael Dukakis would select him as his running mate for that very reason in 1988. Jackson had secured substantial numbers of African American delegates. He believed that his impact on the nomination, by motivating African Americans to register, vote and be campaign activists, warranted the nod. In Dukakis's case, placing Jackson on the ticket would not help him get elected.[28] For one thing, the Democrats had already nominated a "message" candidate in 1984 with Geraldine Ferraro as the first woman vice-presidential candidate from a major party, but a favorable monolithic voting block among women did not materialize.[29] Women did not vote for Mondale-Ferraro because of her candidacy; women who voted for Mondale-Ferraro were already predisposed to supporting the Democratic ticket.[30] African Americans, unlike women, demonstrate much stronger monolithic Democratic voting tendencies.[31] Dukakis would have gotten the black vote with or without Jackson on the ticket.[32]

Such strategies emphasize ticket balancing geared toward reducing the presidential nominee's liabilities, unlike the past, when more attention was given to respecting party elites' preferences. Bill Clinton may have epitomized this approach when he selected a fellow baby boomer, southerner, and moderate in 1992. Of course, Gore's congressional experience provided a certain balance and advantage. In many respects, selecting Senator Gore marked a new emphasis on the presidential nominee preference versus party leadership preference.

Clinton's decision to nominate a fellow southerner also reflects a trend that has impacted nomination politics. Similar nominations will likely follow. Personal mobility has significantly increased while personal roots are less easily determined. Regional distinctions become blurred as regional in-migration and out-migration lead to far more heterogeneous communities as people move around the country for employment opportunities, education, or a better quality of life. Roots are more fragile and more difficult to cement.[33] Regional ties as meaningful vote-choice motivators will hold a less crucial place among voter priorities. This means that strategies focusing on choosing a vice-presidential candidate from a geographic region that differs from the presidential nominee's as a means to garner votes from that region will be a diminishing factor in vice-presidential nominee selection.

Taken together, future vice-presidential nominees may be selected from a pool of applicants whose credentials minimize the presumed nominee's personal and political deficiencies. These patterns also suggest that "message" candidates will not find their way onto the ticket as few groups demonstrate strong monolithic voting patterns. And, regional balance will play a much more muted role in vice-presidential selection. Such possibilities were realized in 2000 and 2004 when both vice-presidential nominees heralded from small electoral vote states (although Richard Cheney, from Wyoming, was already vice president when he ran for reelection in 2004).

The Party Platform

In addition to presidential and vice-presidential nominations, party conventions also became the vehicle for parties to develop platforms—the parties' written statements of intent, record, and rhetoric. The platform itself, while it provides the opportunity for the public and the opposing party to hold that party accountable for its actions, has largely become an instrument over which competing intraparty factions argue.[34]

Platforms communicate party goals. Theoretically, party responsibility is achieved when candidates incorporate platform pledges in their campaign strategy and office-holders use them for policy guidance. Platforms encourage those seeking a wide range of offices to advance party policy. These documents are ratified by a representative delegation of the mass membership, thereby encouraging candidates to further party unity on the campaign trail.[35] Platforms also provide office-holders with written guidelines that can promote cohesion within institutions among individuals serving different constituencies. Single-member district systems create entire legislatures of persons representing districts that do not overlap. U.S. representatives are elected by constituencies completely distinct from any other. Platforms represent opportunities to organize and bring party members together on policy questions. Even presidential nominees will distance themselves from their party's platform unless they exert significant control over its framing. Nominees are more inclined to take such action because of the increasing proportions of political independents and weakly affiliated opposing party members. Personal appeals and single issues may draw such voters to those candidates.[36]

Yet nominating conventions continue to attract deeply committed party members. Convention delegates tend to take more extreme positions on particular issues, such as abortion rights, than does the partisan electorate.[37] Recent evidence suggests that convention delegates have grown more polarized on issues such as social welfare, racial, and cultural issues than in the past.[38] Such polarized views do not reflect the increasing proportions of moderates and political independents in the electorate whose votes the parties hope to capture. The platform then reflects the policy views of ideological extremists and smaller proportions of the electorate. It does not guide the campaign, as many argue that it should or used to, nor does it serve as a vehicle for either direction or accountability in government, as its writing and adoption processes would suggest. Further, platforms rarely unify parties. Following platforms does not occur nearly as often as platforms reflect party principles.[39]

Platforms do serve key party functions such as providing opportunities for mandates.[40] However, these opportunities have largely disappeared. One aspect of platform writing which has not changed, and which is likely to remain in the future, is that it provides the sole source of competition and uncertainty at conventions. Minority planks reveal intraparty factions and how such cohorts negotiate consensus and broker differences.[41]

The meaning behind the platform has also changed. Fifty years ago, those writing it were more inclined to consider it a document emphasizing party goals. The 1940 Republican platform provides an example: "The acceptance of nominations made by this Convention carries with it, as a matter of private honor and public faith, an undertaking by each candidate to be true to the principles and program herein set forth."[42]

More recently, the presumed nominee expects that he will exert control over the platform. He readily distances himself from it should he believe that platform pledges will cost him votes because such pledges will not reflect well on him to various potential constituencies. President George H. W. Bush lost control over the 1992 platform when key Republicans swayed it against his views.[43] Robert Dole distanced himself from his party's platform in 1996 when it contained clear, unequivocal language against abortion. Dole understood that the Democrats would shackle the platform to him, and his chances of winning among pro-choice moderates and weak Republicans would shrink even further.[44]

The party platform will remain conflictual despite public ignorance and presidential candidates' propensity to distance themselves from it. This is particularly true as the presidential and vice-presidential nominations are now in the hands of primary voters. Platform conflicts and their resolution may be in vain because minority plank advocates will not see their positions implemented even if they do end up in the platform. The party in government does not feel compelled to follow the platform unless it is consistent with either presidential or congressional goals already in place.

This discussion illustrates the important evolution of platforms in the last fifty years. Whereas in the past they were framed according to party goals and expectations, they now tend to represent presidential candidate goals. Should these differ from party goals, the party may decide to take action that will help gain the presidency even if that means contradicting its own pledges from past years.[45] Candidates, rather than be bound by the platform, will actually distance themselves from it should they believe that it will hurt their chances of winning.

These three convention activities demonstrate the critical changes that have occurred over the last fifty years in how party conventions function. These changes also reflect party efforts to democratize and broaden their support bases. The political environment in which party structures exist has changed significantly as the percentage of partisans has declined and the number of primaries and candidate-centered campaigns has increased. The individual and collective impact on conventions is found in the three convention activities.

These changes have naturally resulted in convention coverage adjustments. Now that the presumed nominee is determined months in advance of the convention and the vice-presidential selection is announced and the platform is written soon before the convention begins, media convention focus has shifted. One change in media focus is that now attention is paid to pundits guessing who might be the presumed nominee's vice-presidential selection. Before the convention starts, and before the vice-presidential nominee is announced to the public, the strengths and weaknesses of the presumed presidential nominee are emphasized in the context of who might be his strongest vice-presidential choice. Areas of contention on the platform also receive media coverage, particularly those that are most likely to divide the party.

Several aspects of the convention itself have changed because of the broadcast media. "The presence of media coverage encourages party leaders to aim for a carefully crafted picture of the party's strength and vision; this tends to deprive conventions of much of the drama, the sense of carnival, that was so much a part of their tradition."[46] The broadcast media, coupled with key political changes, has created a meaningful shift in convention audiences. Living room observers have replaced convention participants as the key audience to whom the party directs its message. Delegates become less significant in the electoral process, while the opinions of voters at home may impact how the parties and candidates shape the general election campaign season that follows the convention.

Network coverage, which in the past broadcast several hours of convention coverage per day, is now generally limited to no more than two to three hours (and sometimes less) leading up to the 11 p.m. newscasts on the East Coast. This insures that no critical convention events take place after 11 p.m., thereby allowing televised news to follow immediately after the most important speeches. Coverage outside of these few evening hours is usually limited to twenty-four-hour cable news channels, although most cable channels do not provide gavel-to-gavel coverage where only official convention activities are broadcast. Extensive commentary and interviews, on and off the convention floor, is liberally interspersed with speeches. Key convention speeches are now scheduled to occur during that primetime slot; the more important the party perceives the speech and speaker to be, the later the speech will be broadcast. Jesse Jackson experienced this approach first hand. Declining Democratic Party reliance on Reverend Jackson as an important player in its efforts to recruit African American voters was seen in its decision to schedule his post-1988 convention addresses earlier in the evening. Jackson was given a primetime, one-hour, end-of-evening speaking time that year but was not accorded the same opportunity in later years. More recently, his speaking time has been limited to less than twenty minutes and has been scheduled to end before prime time. Because convention coverage is driven by East Coast time, key convention activities begin even earlier when the convention city is in an earlier time zone so that key convention events still end by 11 p.m. on the East Coast. In 1996, Republican convention deliberations in San Diego ended by 8 p.m. nightly.

The scheduling of key speeches is just one way that the media presence has impacted how the parties handle their own conventions. Media presence also affects how television audiences respond to visual and audio information.

Visual cues become a key basis for how convention watchers form opinions about the parties. Decisions about the color scheme and design of the dais and the colors and manner of organizing the balloons that are dropped at the end of the presidential nominee's acceptance speech are linked to the recognition that the mass media plays a critical role in presenting the parties to the public. In 1992, for example, the Republicans hung nets filled with balloons of one color each (red, white or blue) while the Democrats filled each balloon net with different colors. Some Democrats and analysts criticized the Republicans for their opposition to integrating many colors in one balloon net, which was, to some, suggestive of the party's views on race relations! That same year, former California governor Jerry Brown ran against then-Arkansas governor Bill Clinton for the Democratic nomination. Brown secured several California delegates, many of whom opposed the death penalty. These delegates planned to sit together on the convention floor, wearing the same florescent anti–death penalty t-shirt in order to attract media attention. Heads of the California delegation, anxious to show party unity, assigned seats to their state delegates, which resulted in Brown's supporters being interspersed among the Clinton delegates who outnumbered them.

The role of the mass media in the three formal convention activities (presidential nomination, vice-presidential nomination, adopting a platform) is thus understood in two ways. First, the growth of the mass media as a primary news source has meant that party decisions about the scheduling and execution of conventions are now largely tied to how the mass media choose to present them to the public. The parties lose significant control over their own conventions in their efforts to reach out to the public during this crucial campaign period. Second, the mass media's efforts to secure their own audience means that the timing and content of their programs will likely impact whether and how the public responds to the party's efforts to secure voter support through its convention.

In his well-known *Parties and Elections in America: The Electoral Process,* L. Sandy Maisel is both encouraged and resigned when considering future conventions in light of those in the recent past. While he notes that party conventions lack the decision-making authority and purpose that they once did, he also recognizes that current circumstances do not preclude them from again becoming highly charged political and emotional events that enjoy a distinct place in the presidential campaign season.[47]

Maisel notes that parties cannot perform their interest articulation and interest aggregation roles unless they are democratic and deliberative. Recent changes in party nominating convention rules, as well as key changes in the political and media environments in which parties and conventions function, has meant that parties are far less deliberative in their nomination functions than they were a half-century ago. Party conventions play a key role in serving democratic goals, and those goals have gone unmet because of structural changes in the nominating process. Adding to this concern is that the mass media has contributed to the decline in convention deliberation.

The mass media has contributed to the decline of convention deliberation in its own efforts to retain viewers in an increasingly competitive media market. Coverage is marginalized and minimized because there is less newsworthy material to broadcast as so many key decisions are made prior to the start of the convention. The mass media's response to this trend is to broadcast less of the actual convention while developing and producing news stories about actors, events, and issues that are less central to the core convention purpose. Party efforts to demonstrate strength, purpose, and worthiness of public support are negatively affected as the media focuses on less important though perhaps more exciting matters. Still, there is an inherent expectation that conventions provide the institutional mechanisms for formally nominating presidential and vice-presidential candidates; adopting platforms; mobilizing party support through speeches, presentations, and pageantry over a four-day period; and energizing the most committed party activists, whether they attend the convention or not, to continue their campaign work.

While these particular structural aspects remain, other changes central to the nominating process, including convention activities and the role of the mass media, have resulted in a less deliberative role for parties and party conventions in that process. Several reasons explaining why party conventions no longer enjoy a deliberative role in the nomination process have been put forward. These include the advent of the presidential preference primary, candidate-centered campaigning, and general party decline, all of which have impacted and have been impacted by the mass media. The mass media has also contributed to the decline in the deliberative capacity of conventions as the media exercises greater control over convention proceedings.

One key change is partisan ties. While the electorate presently shows weak party ties, in the early 1950s most Americans considered themselves either Democrats or Republicans.[48] It was not until the mid-1970s that the growth of independents increased at the expense of both major parties. Declining voter turnout in presidential and congressional elections indicates declining party loyalty.[49] Party decline is also found in increased ticket splitting.

Party organization activity also suggests weaker parties. Primaries have re-placed caucuses as the key means for nominating candidates and leave control over nominations to those who tend to be less committed to the parties than those participating in caucuses. Candidate-centered elections also weaken parties. Candidates themselves, in their efforts to secure votes from those with weakening loyalties, may soften their party stances to secure support from a growing proportion of weakly affiliated and independent voters. Candidates deemphasizing party labels also diminish parties and party identification as voter cues.[50]

Shifts in public media consumption have also contributed to weakened parties. The number of commercial and cable networks has increased expo-nentially over the last two decades. During that same period, there has been a precipitous decline in newspaper publication and circulation. Many cities that had sustained two daily newspapers now support one or none. Newspaper readership has declined. Coincident with these changes in newspaper reader-ship has been a substantial increase in the number of commercial and cable networks. Many of the newer cable networks are devoted to twenty-four-hour news and information. One important result of these changes is that informa-tion quality has declined simply through the sharp reduction in the amount of information contained in news stories. Newspaper articles tend to include more depth and detail than brief televised news items, and the availability of visual images on broadcast news influences how the public interprets the information that they are hearing. The result of the advent of televised news as the primary public information source is that candidates who are more visually appealing may enjoy greater success than they did in the past while less physically attractive candidates may fare worse. The mass media also gives candidates the opportunity to reach out directly to voters in ways that they could not before the advent of television. Coupled with the increasing number of primary contests, candidates may run their campaigns without party help only to secure the nomination by those same parties.

Party unity in government has also diminished. Party-based voting, where members of Congress vote with their own party, as well as the rate at which presidential party members in Congress vote with the president, is not strong during this period. Following the 1994 congressional election, several congres-sional Democrats actually switched parties and became Republicans. Such behaviors are highly unusual. Divided government has also contributed to de-teriorating party unity and loyalty among elected officials.

The two major parties function in a centralized manner during their conventions even though the origins of the American two-party system and the concentration of electoral activity occurring at the state and local levels encourages decentralization. At other times they are two major labels shared by fifty state parties. Parties may literally and figuratively develop consensus and unity with their conventions. They can act as singular parties rather than the "multiple parties with shared labels" approach that they often display. Parties endeavor to put forward a unified front even if opportunities for consensus building are quashed at their conventions.[51]

The key decisions taking place outside conventions might make them unnecessary in their current form despite the opportunities that conventions provide for developing party consensus. For example, at no time since 1952 has more than one vote been required to secure a nomination. There is no party division over the nomination because most of the frontrunner's serious opposition has dropped out long before the convention. Once those opponents drop out, they eventually endorse the frontrunner and encourage their supporters to do so. Because the presumed nominee is known so long before the convention begins, nominations become pro forma coronations.

The presidential nominee now selects his vice-presidential nominee rather than allow his party to do it for him, and his selection is more often known before the convention begins. The presumed nominee interviews potential vice-presidential candidates long before the convention begins; a big announcement of the choice serves as a prequel to the convention and builds public excitement. Previously, vice-presidential candidates were either not named before the convention or were not known until party leaders made their choice at the convention. Such situations seem impossible today as the vice-presidential nominee selection comes out of the hands of party leaders and into the hands of the presumed presidential nominee.

The party platform has also become a document that is largely unread and more often not followed by those who write and endorse it unless doing so is consistent with their own goals. Platforms do tend to reflect enduring party tenets and respond to traditional party constituencies.[52] Platform pledges that are followed are not necessarily adhered to because they are part of the platform. Actions consistent with platform planks would have been taken anyway, even without promises being articulated in the platform.

The advent of the southern regional primary in March (known as "Super Tuesday"), as well as California's 1996 decision to move its primary from the last primary day in June to March, also insures that most delegates are selected much earlier than in the past. The early concentration of primaries encourages financial front loading and heavy early campaign spending.[53] Candidates drop out earlier, leaving the frontrunner as the sole candidate standing by the end of March. In the contested Democratic nomination contest of 2004, all of John Kerry's serious contenders dropped out by early March, including former Vermont governor Howard Dean. Dean later endorsed Kerry. In 2000, despite their stark political differences, John McCain endorsed George W. Bush after McCain dropped out of the nomination race in early March.

Recent rule changes also mean that certain candidates now enjoy more and greater advantages than in the past.[54] While rule changes may impact various procedures and placate various factions, they have not affected overall convention outcomes.[55]

National nominating conventions provide one means for parties to foster American democracy through interest aggregation and interest articulation. Yet evidence of party decline has affected party conventions by making them less meaningful conduits for the parties to serve in their deliberative and democratization roles. The advent of the broadcast media has occurred coincident with this decline.

Party conventions still seek to define for the electorate what the party is and how it fits in with their preferences.[56] During the last fifty years, nominee choice was taken from party elites and placed with an increasingly personality and single-issue driven electorate.[57] This same electorate participates on a sporadic basis, is becoming less tied to political parties, and is less likely to vote.[58] Nonetheless, the same circumstances hold regarding party perception and how the nominee impacts its reputation. Parties can still suffer if their victorious nominee fails to please the public at key points in his presidency. Actual and potential future candidates lose favor based on their party association. (Gore assumed that his association with Clinton would hurt him in 2000; he discouraged Clinton from campaigning for him on his behalf.) Party organizations now suffer for decisions they did not make.

Party efforts to democratize the nominations process have created more participation opportunities for the public and candidates. One key consequence is that events, foci, and party convention agendas have changed dramatically. These changes demonstrate that efforts to democratize the system have resulted in diminishing the deliberative tradition that conventions previously enjoyed.

THE SOLUTION: PARTY RECONSTRUCTION

The picture painted here is mostly negative. It suggests that party organizations exert less control over their own activities despite efforts at democratization. It also suggests that the mass media has contributed to this loss of control in its own efforts to secure viewers in an increasingly competitive media market-place. Tenets suggesting that parties are instruments of democracy because they allow an otherwise amorphous electorate to cleave to political anchors still hold.

These concerns suggest that parties must reclaim deliberative qualities. Deliberative parties are better able to perform their interest aggregation and articulation roles, while democratic parties foster continued public support and participation based on the perception that they are open and their leaders are accessible rather than being seen as closed organizations with inaccessible leaders. The mass media can play an important, positive role in advancing party deliberation and democratization. Meaningful convention activities would be newsworthy once nomination-related decision making returns to the hands of party officials and activists. Coverage of these events would provide the public with critical and relevant information about the parties and their candidates, which would then make the parties appear more accessible to the mass public.

The means to achieve the combined party goals of democratization and deliberation are well articulated by Gerald Pomper in his critical work *Passions and Interests: Political Party Concepts of American Democracy.*[59] Pomper's proposed reforms would retain the democratic nature of the post-1968 reform era while returning to the parties key deliberative and procedural elements, including conventions. Pomper argues that structural change would restore strength and convention deliberation to the parties. A strong core of party leaders encourages the leadership accessibility that Pomper considers essential. Because conventions provide opportunities for interest aggregation and articulation, Pomper suggests reforms that would change the actual structure of conventions in a manner insuring that they enjoy a more meaningful and deliberative role within the party system necessary for democracy. It is important to reflect on the potential positive impact of the mass media in party reconstruction even though Pomper does not discuss their role when outlining his proposed reforms.

Pomper proposes two structural changes that would make conventions themselves, and the parties in which they function, more deliberative and accessible. His ideas give the party back to party organizations and reflect a means to offset the consequences of party decline and recent party reforms. Pomper's proposals would strengthen rather than weaken parties, would revitalize the electorate, and ultimately would advance democracy. "Reconstruction of the parties must be directed toward fuller realization of each of the democratic values, interest optimization, the exercise of control, and civic development."[60]

First, convention delegations would be elected officials. Conventions would nominate offices beyond the president and vice-president. One half of the delegates would be elected office-holders (members of Congress or state governors) or local party leaders. This would insure a deliberative impact on the nomination because the delegates would play a role in determining the pool of potential nominees. Party leaders and public officials would, then, be working together toward the common goal of nominating those candidates most likely to earn public support. The present nominations process includes public officials. Democrats formally integrated public officials when they created "superdelegate" (ex-officio delegate) positions. Republican office-holders usually hold delegate positions despite the absence of formal requirements such as those implemented by the Democrats. However, the primary-driven system has meant that all delegates, regardless of their public or party positions, have little say in who becomes their party's nominee.[61]

The coming together of elected and party officials in a manner that deliberates rather than ratifies would be a healthy discourse for the public to watch. One criticism of the mass media's convention role is that it focuses on marginalized matters because those concerns considered mainstream are not deemed newsworthy. After all, most of the important decisions are made before the convention. Should the parties create deliberative roles for delegates, the mass media's content emphasis may shift as convention-related delegate activities become more meaningful.

Pomper notes that the nominees would not be selected at this convention. Rather, the identified party leaders and office-holders would present one or more nominees who had received at least 20 percent of the convention vote to mass party members who had previously enrolled in the party at no cost. The winner of this mass-based process would constitute that party's slate of nominees. Such procedures would return a deliberative element to party leaders while at the same time retaining many of the democratic characteristics that primary-driven systems enjoy.

Pomper also suggests that platforms be written by party policy commissions during the year preceding the conventions. These commissions would include a substantial number of party office-holders who would seek public input on platform development through national hearings.[62] Such changes would encourage deliberation, public participation, and platforms reflecting promises that might more often be kept. Abiding by platform pledges would be democratically motivated. The public would provide input while party officials would actually frame the document that would be ratified at the convention. Furthermore, platforms would be written well before the nomination becomes official. This change would mean that public and party officials, who could potentially be held accountable for failing to follow the platform or for writing a platform that party adherents do not support, would have worked together on the platform before its adoption. Party and public officials' participation in platform writing is critical because they are positioned to implement it in their official capacities. They would also sense whether pledges are realistic and likely to be implemented.

Media coverage of these deliberations would not likely impact the direction that these hearings take. Yet coverage of a revitalized platform writing process might raise public awareness of the platform and what it might mean for party members working together in their role as public officials. Should the platform become more meaningful to party members positioned to implement it, the public's understanding of platforms might contribute to increased awareness and support for the parties in their governance roles. Put another way, Pomper's proposed changes would make the platform writing process worthy of greater media coverage, and the public would benefit from such increased attention.

Pomper's concerns are important because they tell us that a key theorist, considering what parties can and should do with their conventions and what actually transpires with the process, is advocating stronger rather than weaker parties at the mass and elite levels. He also advocates structural change in his approach to fostering stronger parties. Past reform efforts, while they have led to more openness in decision making, have also taken the deliberative capacity from party leaders' hands. Looking at the nominations and the platform writing processes tells us that the future will bring increasingly weak parties linked to an increasingly detached electorate, a circumstance exacerbated by the presence of an increasingly competitive mass media. Pomper's proposals to bring more strength to the parties indicates that moving forward requires looking back with a keen eye toward the benefits of the last fifty years. One means to achieve this goal is to recognize that changes in the U.S. political system warrant meaningful change in the nomination process. Once these changes take place, the role and impact of the mass media in party convention politics may shift focus, thereby benefiting how the parties are perceived by the public. The combined benefits would be stronger parties and a more engaged polity.

Maisel questions whether nominating conventions decide anything at all anymore, while Pomper tells us that they can. The timeliness of such suspicious hope can only reinforce Schattschneider's view that there is no democracy save for vibrant political parties.

NOTES

1. E. E. Schattschneider, *Party Government* (New York: Holt, Rinehart, and Winston, 1942).

2. Ibid.

3. E. E. Schattschneider, *The Semi-Sovereign People* (Hinsdale, IL: Dryden Press, 1960).

4. Marjorie Randon Hershey, *Party Politics in America,* 11th ed. (New York: Addison Wesley Longman, 2005).

5. Gerald Pomper, *Passions and Interests: Political Party Concepts of American Democracy* (Lawrence: University Press of Kansas, 1992).

6. William Kornhauser, *The Politics of Mass Society* (New York: Free Press, 1959).

7. M. Margaret Conway, Gertrude A. Steurnagel, and David W. Ahern, *Women and Political Participation: Cultural Change in the Political Arena,* 2d ed. (Washington, D.C.: Congressional Quarterly Press, 2005); John Rawls, *A Theory of Justice* (Cambridge: Harvard University Press, 1971).

8. Gabriel Almond and G. Bingham Powell, *Comparative Politics: a Developmental Approach* (Boston, MA: Little, Brown, 1966).

9. L. Sandy Maisel, *Parties and Elections in America: The Electoral Process,* 3d ed. (Lanham, MD: Rowman and Littlefield, 1999).

10. Henry Roberts, *Robert's Rules of Order* (New York: Berkley, 1989).

11. Howard L. Reiter, *Selecting the President: The Nominating Process in Transition* (Philadelphia: University of Pennsylvania Press, 1985).

12. Nelson Polsby, *Consequences of Party Reform* (New York: Oxford University Press, 1983).

13. Norman R. Luttbeg and Michael M. Gant, *American Electoral Behavior 1952–1992,* 2d ed. (Itasca, IL: F. E. Peacock, 1995).

14. Reiter, *Selecting the President.*

15. John E. Mueller, *War, Presidents and Public Opinion,* 2d ed. (New York: University Press of America, 1985), 54–55.

16. Maisel, *Parties and Elections,* 267.

17. Ibid., 268.

18. Hershey, *Party Politics,* 186.

19. Reiter, *Selecting the President;* Polsby, *Consequences;* Nelson Polsby and Aaron Wildavsky, *Presidential Elections: Strategies and Structures of American Politics,* 10th ed. (New York: Chatham House, 2000).

20. Some were nominated more than once by which time they held a different office.

21. Hershey, *Party Politics.*

22. Paul Allen Beck and Marjorie Randon Hershey, *Party Politics in America*, 9th ed. (New York: Addison Wesley Longman, 2000), 185.

23. Gerald Pomper, ed., *The Election of 1992: Reports and Interpretations* (Chatham, NJ: Chatham House, 1993), 81–82.

24. Polsby and Wildavsky, *Presidential Elections*.

25. Garry Wills, *Nixon Agonistes: The Crisis of the Self-Made Man* (New York: New American Library, 1970).

26. James David Barber, *The Presidential Character: Predicting Performance in the White House*, 3d ed. (Englewood Cliffs, NJ: Prentice-Hall, 1985), 316.

27. George Bush was pro-choice on the abortion issue until he was nominated for vice president in 1980.

28. Lucius Barker, Mack H. Jones, and Katherine Tate, *African-Americans and the American Political System*, 3d ed. (Upper Saddle River, NJ: Prentice-Hall, 1999), 225–27.

29. Nancy E. McGlen, Karen O'Connor, Laura van Assendelft, and Wendy Gunther-Canada, *Women, Politics, and American Society*, 4th ed. (New York: Longman, 2005), 52.

30. Gerald Pomper, *The Election of 1984: Reports and Interpretations* (Chatham, NJ: Chatham House, 1985), 103.

31. Barker, Jones, and Tate, *African-Americans and the American Political System*.

32. One key way that African American voters impact election outcomes is by combining monolithic voting practices with turnout. Democratic candidates are helped when African Americans exhibit high voter turnout. Democrats are hurt, vis-à-vis Republicans, when the turnout decline among African Americans means fewer overall Democratic votes. The risk of losing votes to Republicans should Democrats not support African-American issues is nil. (See Barker, Jones, and Tate, *African-Americans and the American Political System*, 240.)

33. Walter Benn Michaels, *Our America: Nativism, Modernism, and Pluralism* (Durham, NC: Duke University Press, 1997).

34. Kelly D. Patterson, *Political Parties and the Maintenance of Liberal Democracy* (New York: Columbia University Press, 1996).

35. Terri Susan Fine, "Interest Groups and the Framing of the 1988 Democratic and Republican Party Platforms," *Polity* 26, no. 3 (1994): 517–30.

36. Maisel, *Parties and Elections*.

37. Hershey, *Party Politics*.

38. Geoffrey C. Layman and Thomas M. Carsey, "Party Polarization and the 'Conflict Extension' in the American Electorate," *American Journal of Political Science* 46, no. 4 (2002): 786–802; Walter J. Stone, Ronald B. Rapoport, and Alan I. Abramowitz, "The Reagan Revolution and Party Polarization in the 1980s," in *The Parties Respond*, ed. L. Sandy Maisel (Boulder, CO: Westview, 1990).

39. Gerald Pomper with Susan Lederman, *Elections in America*, 2d ed. (New York: Longman, 1980).

40. Gary King, Michael Laver, Richard I. Hofferbert, Ian Budge, and Michael D. McDonald, "Party Platforms, Mandates, and Government Spending," *American Political Science Review* 87, no. 3 (1993): 744–50; Richard Hofferbert and Ian Budge, "The Party Mandate and the Westminster Model: Election Programmes and Government Spending in Britain, 1948–55," *British Journal of Political Science* 22 (1992): 151–82.

41. Barker, Jones, and Tate, *African-Americans and the American Political System*.

42. Republican National Committee, Republican Party Platform, 1940, www.presidency.ucsb .edu/showplatforms.php?platindex=R1940 (accessed April 2, 2006).

43. Maisel, *Parties and Elections.*

44. Terri Susan Fine, "Party Platforms as Tools of Presidential Agenda Setting," *White House Studies* 3, no. 2 (2003): 199–211.

45. In its 1984 platform, the Democrats refused to hold national or multistate conventions in those states that failed to ratify the ERA. In 1988, Atlanta, Georgia, hosted the Democratic National Convention. Georgia did not ratify the ERA. The Democrats likely chose Atlanta to host its 1988 convention in its efforts to retain regional support from southern Democrats.

46. Hershey, *Party Politics.*

47. Maisel, *Parties and Elections.*

48. Hershey, *Party Politics;* Harold W. Stanley and Richard Niemi, *Vital Statistics on American Politics,* 5th ed. (Washington, DC: CQ Press, 1995).

49. Stanley and Niemi, *Vital Statistics;* William H. Flanigan and Nancy H. Zingale, *Political Behavior of the American Electorate,* 10th ed. (Washington, DC: CQ Press, 2002), 51.

50. John Kenneth White and Daniel M. Shea, *New Party Politics: From Jefferson and Hamilton to the Information Age* (Boston, MA: Bedford/St. Martin's Press, 2000), 76–79.

51. Jo Freeman, "The Political Culture of the Democratic and Republican Parties," *Political Science Quarterly* 101, no. 3 (1986): 327–56; Terri Susan Fine, "Political Parties Trumpet Inclusion," *Orlando Sentinel,* September 26, 1996, G-1.

52. Pomper and Lederman, *Elections in America.*

53. Emmett H. Buell Jr., "The Invisible Primary," in William G. Mayer, ed., *In Pursuit of the White House: How We Choose Our Presidential Nominees,* (Chatham, NJ: Chatham House, 1996); Elaine C. Kamarck and Kenneth M. Goldstein, "The Rules Do Matter: Post-Reform Presidential Nominating Politics," in L. Sandy Maisel, ed., *The Parties Respond,* 2d ed. (Boulder, CO: Westview, 1994).

54. Hershey, *Party Politics.*

55. Maisel, *Parties and Elections.*

56. Michael Nelson, ed., *The Elections of 1996* (Washington, DC: Congressional Quarterly Press, 1997).

57. Scott Keeter and Cliff Zukin, *Uninformed Choice* (New York: Praeger, 1983).

58. Hershey, *Party Politics.*

59. Pomper, *Passions and Interests.*

60. Ibid.

61. Ibid.

62. Ibid., 147.

12

THE NEW ROLE OF THE CONVENTIONS
AS POLITICAL RITUALS

Gerald M. Pomper

THE PREVIOUS ESSAYS IN this volume have analyzed the great influence of the mass media on contemporary presidential nominations in the United States. Incorporating these analyses, this concluding chapter argues that conventions in the media age are now best understood as political rituals, different from their historical heritage. Once decisive in the choice of party leadership, conventions are now most prominent as political rites of passage. Still, they remain important and can be improved through deliberate reforms.

Once upon a time, party conventions made decisions. In one momentous meeting, Republicans in 1860 maneuvered frantically to nominate Abraham Lincoln:

> There was much to be done after midnight and before the convention assembled on Friday morning. There were hundreds of Pennsylvanians, Indianans and Illinoisans who never closed their eyes that night. . . . Henry S. Lane . . . had been operating to bring the Vermonters and Virginians to the point of deserting [New Yorker William] Seward. . . . This was finally done, the fatal break in Seward's strength . . . destroying at once, when it appeared, his power in the New England and the slave state delegations. . . . The [Pennsylvanian Simon] Cameron men, discovering there was absolutely no hope for their man, but that either Seward or Lincoln would be nominated, and being a calculating company, were persuaded to throw their strength for Lincoln at such a time as to have credit of his nomination.[1]

Compare the proceedings of the major party conventions of 2004:

> The presidential candidates were known long in advance of the conventions. Republican George Bush effectively gained his party's nod

when he entered the White House after the disputed presidential election four years earlier. Massachusetts senator John Kerry was assured of the Democratic Party's designation when he won a series of state primaries on March 12, twenty weeks before the party convention conducted its nominating roll call.

Both candidates in 2004 lacked opposition at the convention. All of the Republican delegates voted for Bush. Of the Democratic delegates' votes, Kerry won nearly all. Except for a few lost-cause votes, an observer would have no inkling that ten other men and women had once sought the party's leadership. Each state announced its typically unanimous support in declarations that emphasized tourist attractions, not political deliberation.

The vice-presidential candidates were determined by the presidential candidates, upon their own authority and after only restricted consultation with other politicians. No convention delegate voted against Bush's choice of Richard Cheney in 2000 and 2004; none verbally opposed Kerry's designation of John Edwards. Moreover, in the past decade, the designation of a running mate has been proclaimed by the presidential candidate even before the convention opens; Kerry's came weeks beforehand.

The conventions formally adopted platforms for their parties, presenting their cases to the electorate and providing cues of their future conduct in government. In 2004, as has been true for decades, however, the convention delegates had no effective role in determining their own program. The Republican manifesto was written in the White House, the Democratic program in a drafting committee dominated by Senator Kerry's designees. No dissent was voiced by those Republicans who wanted to ease the party's antiabortion position or those Democrats who wanted to express greater opposition to the U.S. war in Iraq.

Media representatives, numbered 15,000, triple the count of delegates, and used far more space than the combined Republicans' delegates and audience at Madison Square Garden in New York or the assembled Democrats at Fleet Center in Boston. The press stories, however, lacked the drama of the 1860 report quoted at the beginning of the chapter. In place of such exciting accounts, or the simple transmission of the convention itself, reports focused on hometown news, journalists' interpretations in place of politicians' activities, and commercials. Television, the dominant medium, downplayed the conventions. Instead of continuous coverage, commercial networks broadcast only two hours nightly and gave uninterrupted attention only to the presidential candidates' acceptance speeches.

The conventions now seem to serve media needs more than any public interest, notes a press analyst.[2] "'If you're remotely in the sphere of being a political reporter and you're not at the convention, that means, almost de facto, you're not really a political reporter,' says Vanity Fair columnist Michael Wolff. 'This is really a shared identity event which has nothing to do with news and everything to do with who you want to be.'" At the last Democratic convention in Los Angeles, he recalls, the buzz was about "Clinton walking down the hall, the Gore kiss, all this staged stuff you might as well have seen on TV."

THE LOSS OF FUNCTIONS

As these particulars evidence, conventions ain't what they used to be. Their changed character is evident in rereading the classic analysis of national conventions by scholars at the Brookings Institution.[3] Precisely at the time that they began to change, Paul David and his co-authors delineated four critical functions of the party conclaves. Compare the situation then and now.

Selection of Leadership. Choosing the presidential and vice-presidential candidates was the original purpose of conventions. A national and representative body provided legitimacy for the candidates and unity among party factions. For these reasons, Andrew Jackson promoted a Democratic party convention in 1832 to consolidate support for his vice-presidential preference, Martin Van Buren. The opposition Whigs called their first convention in 1840 to achieve a united front and an ultimate victory for their candidate William Henry Harrison.

The national convention became the central institution of American electoral politics because for many years it fit well with the political conditions of the nation. The Constitution required an absolute majority of electoral votes to win the presidency. Political practice altered the reality of the Electoral College, eliminating any possible deliberative role. Statewide victories in the popular vote became decisive, as the states came to adopt the practice of casting all of their electoral votes for the leading candidate. These developments meant that the key participants in presidential politics would be the state party organizations and that success would depend on achieving a coalition of these factions unified behind a consensual ticket. There were few independent or undecided voters, reflecting the partisan character of newspapers—the only "mass media" then available—and the extensive reach of campaign activists. Once a party had formed its unified coalition, election efforts would center on mobilization, bringing firmly partisan voters to the polls.

Today, as already stated, the convention has no effective role in the selection of the party leadership. The party bosses who once would bargain over the ticket are only fabled memories, their erstwhile power eliminated through the progressive reforms of primary elections and internal party democracy. The free-wheeling (and dealing) delegates are no longer available for negotiation because delegates are now chosen principally in primary elections, and almost all owe their selection to their declared fidelity to an announced presidential candidate.[4] Even the smoke-filled rooms where politicians once negotiated have been eliminated, first by air conditioning, then by the social ostracism of smokers.

The selections of the presidential candidates on the first nominating roll calls in 2004 replicated the actions of every major party convention since 1952, an invariant pattern over half a century. The same single ballot pattern describes the choice of the vice-presidential nominee, with the exception of an open contest at the Democratic conclave of 1956. In the past, great leaders had to work harder for their nominations: Lincoln required three ballots, Franklin D. Roosevelt four, Woodrow Wilson forty-six. But their successors, arguably less eminent—such as Goldwater, McGovern, Carter, and Dole—all won on the first ballot. Indeed, there has not been a meaningful number of roll-call votes for any candidate other than the triumphant winner since 1980.

The presidential nominee can now usually be predicted at the beginning of the election year, long before the convention meets, even before a single delegate has been selected. Incumbent first-term presidents are always renominated without opposition. When the choice is not foreclosed by an incumbent, William Mayer has shown that the winner is typically the candidate who holds the leading position in the first public opinion poll of the year and, of lesser importance, who has the most money.[5] That model did not correctly forecast Kerry's nomination at the beginning of 2004, as the muddled contest confused all observers.[6] Nevertheless, Kerry did quickly achieve party dominance, again leaving the convention no more than a symbolic role in the selection of the party leadership.

Program Development. As the largest party meeting and the only body that appears to represent the total membership, the national convention has a claim to be the authoritative voice of the party. Conventions have often been notable for their platforms and policy development, a function sometimes rivaling the selection of leadership. American history was significantly affected, for example, by platforms that proclaimed the Republicans' 1860 opposition to the extension of slavery, the Democrats' 1896 support of the free coinage of silver, the Democrats' 1948 endorsement of civil rights legislation, and the Republicans' 2000 support for major cuts in personal and corporate taxes.[7]

In developing platforms, however, the parties have always faced two inherent conflicts. First, the platforms reflect the constitutional separation of institutions: "Platforms are written for use in *presidential* campaigns, yet they consist mainly of proposals for legislation that will be meaningless unless there is *congressional action.*"[8] Second, the manifestos incorporate the tension between campaigning and governing. Winning votes is the primary purpose of a campaign, but promises that gain votes may not be feasible or desirable as actual public policy.

A common way to resolve these conflicts is for a convention simply to present platforms that will help its presidential candidate and disregard the likely sentiments of Congress or the likely results of its promises. Indeed, that is the standard and cynical view: "A platform is to run on, not to stand on." As stated in a classic condemnation, "The platform, which is supposed to be the party's profession of faith and its programme of action is only a farce—the biggest farce of all the acts of this great parliament of the party. The platform represents a long list of statements relating to politics, in which everybody can find something to suit him, but in which nothing is considered as of any consequence by the authors of the document, as well as by the whole convention."[9] Cynicism aside, however, the platforms are surely consequential because shrewd politicians, historically and contemporaneously, have devoted much time to their construction, and interest groups still devote much effort to win planks supporting their particular claims. They underline the differences in party philosophies and point to the differing policy consequences that will follow from each candidate's victory. In fact, much of the platforms are specific and significant, and large proportions of these pledges are actually redeemed by the winning candidate and party.[10]

Platforms continue to be significant today, and there is likely to be more discussion and even occasional debate on these manifestos than on the choice of party leadership. What is different is the autonomy of the convention. Although the platform is written by a committee of the convention, the dominance of the presidential candidate is clear in its proceedings, and this dominance is easier to assert because the candidate is known long before the convention itself meets. Negotiations will still occur, compromise language will still be crafted, but it will be done behind closed doors and under strong control of the known party leader.

Governing the Party. The national convention is the ultimate authority in the party's government, and that function continues to this day. It is the convention that decides on the allocation of delegates, the rules for its own proceedings, and the administration of the party between conventions. Conventions have—and have used—their power to mandate the racial and sexual composition of delegations, to allocate or to ignore representation among states by population, and even to scramble the alphabet in the nominating roll calls. The rules they establish for the party can even override state laws, free from judicial review.

But conventions also have the authority to diminish their own power. Such has been the effect of their changing the rules for the selection of party leadership, as the parties have done since 1968. Previously, conventions were sites for potential bargaining: many delegates were chosen in closed state party meetings, they were often uncommitted, and states often voted as unitary blocs. Now, primarily but not exclusively among the Democrats, the overwhelming proportion of delegates are chosen in state primaries open to contending candidates, prospective delegates must declare their candidate preferences, and state delegations are divided proportionally among the contenders.

In effect, these convention changes have altered the character of party government in the selection of leadership from a republican, or even an aristocratic, form to that of a mass democracy. The presidential candidate is not chosen indirectly through party leaders interpreting or anticipating the wishes of the electorate; he is chosen directly by "the people," or at least those who respond to opinion polls or the approximately 20 percent of citizens who vote in primaries. Perhaps significantly, this "democratic" trend is also evident in other nations, such as Britain and Israel, which have come to choose nominees by direct vote rather than by party conventions (although they confine the electorate to declared party members).

Campaign Rally. Emotions are basic to politics, as to all of life; conventions have always been vital in stimulating the passions of party members and ordinary voters, enlisting their support in the cause of the candidates and programs. American history records the vivid language of convention speeches: Bryan's challenge, "You shall not press down upon mankind a cross of gold"; FDR's promise, "I pledge you, I pledge myself to a New Deal for the American people"; Reagan's boast, "the Republican Party has a platform that is a banner of bold, unmistakable colors with no pale pastel shades."

Conventions attempt to rally two different audiences—the thousands of party leaders physically present at the conclave and the tens of millions of voters who will watch, hear, read about, and consider the rally's messages. Major addresses, such as the keynote address, may become launching pads for future presidential aspirants. For the immediate audience, the convention rally is intangible compensation for the hard work of politics. The party gatherings recognize, reward, and encourage the activists who get out the vote, the donors who contribute dollars, the younger campaigners who will provide the next generation of national candidates. Just like national meetings of the Knights of Columbus or the Girl Scouts, party conventioneers have fun, meet people who share their goals and loyalties, and return home with new methods and new enthusiasm.

The larger audience is the electorate. The convention provides each party with its best, and free (indeed government-subsidized) opportunity to make its case. For four days and nights, the political world becomes almost exclusively Democratic or Republican, with 15,000 reporters and almost every television station transmitting unchallenged claims of the virtues of its candidates and message. The presidential candidates' acceptance speeches highlight this coverage, drawing the largest audience of the election campaign other than that for the fall debates among the candidates, with the added advantage that neither the opposition nor the media interrupt.

The campaign rally, particularly the presidential candidate's acceptance speech, does affect the election results. For many voters it is the first time they see nonincumbent nominees as serious contestants for the presidency. Moreover, many voters make their election choice at the time of the conventions. The impact of the acceptance speeches is highlighted by media practice; by limiting other coverage, they give even more significance to the speeches, and they heighten this effect by framing the orations as the critical moments for candidates to "introduce themselves to the American people." This emphasis gives these speeches a significance akin to a president's State of the Union address. Almost always, this event brings the candidate a considerable "convention bounce," a rapid rise in the opinion polls. Even relatively flawed candidates have benefited from this effect: George H. W. Bush gained twenty-three points in 1988, Al Gore seventeen in 2000. But both saw the effect disappear quickly as the race tightened, with Bush eventually winning and Gore losing the White House.

The campaign rally, however, has built-in dilemmas for the parties (as Bryon Shafer analyzed insightfully).[11] If they play to their internal audience, they will want to emphasize the rallying calls of the party faithful, but these appeals may repel undecided and independent voters, who are likely to decide the election. Had George W. Bush used his acceptance speech in 2004 to demand a "right-to-life" constitutional amendment, as his partisans might have wished, he would probably have lost votes among the majority of Americans who support a woman's right to abortion. Had John Kerry used his acceptance speech to demand an immediate troop withdrawal from Iraq, as his partisans might have wished, he would probably have lost votes among the majority of Americans who support continued efforts to stabilize the Middle East. Both candidates chose to emphasize their wider campaigns, disappointing many of their party zealots.

A larger dilemma pertains to the conduct of the convention itself. It is no coincidence that the autonomy of the conventions began to decline concurrently with the spread of television across the nation. In emphasizing their campaign messages, the parties want to show a united front, to use their television opportunities to stay "on message," and to exploit the technical and commercial realities of the media. Speakers are carefully chosen to represent demographic variety, their speeches are scripted in advance, they are precisely scheduled to put the best speakers in "prime time," they end within twenty-eight minutes to allow time for commercial breaks on the hour and half-hour, and all express their unreserved devotion to the nominees.

Truly vibrant organizations, however, do not work this way. Instead, their members argue with one another, debating rather than nodding silent consent to their program. They let the subject matter, not the clock, determine when and how long they will argue. People speak because of their commitment, using their own words, not because they are the "right" sex or ethnic group, or can mouth the words prepared for them by campaign consultants.[12] Nominating conventions once were vibrant. The delegates argued, allied, divided, felt, and truly participated. Now, in their effort to put on a good show for the mass audience, conventions have become stage sets for the campaign rally, their delegates reduced to (literally) dumb claques who (literally) applaud on cue for the show's top banana.

THE NEW ROLE OF CONVENTIONS

The problem, however, is that the effort to put on a "good show" actually results in a bad show for television and other mass media. The media are attracted to stories that involve novelty, dramatic conflict, a visible battle of good and evil, with an uncertain or surprise ending.[13] Commonly skeptical toward politicians, the press favors stories of corruption and scandal; a touch of sex can also tantalize. By these criteria, contemporary party conventions are awful stories. Nothing happens that is not planned, announced, and scripted in advance. All possible conflicts are repressed, other than shadow combat with the unseen enemy. The climax of the story, the presidential nomination, has been known for months. The candidates are idealized and idolized and therefore of no interest to media in search of human faults. Even sex is so remote that a kiss between husband and wife (the Gores in 2000) becomes a major photo event. Finding nothing new, there is no "news" by media standards, and the media, particularly television, have therefore limited their coverage. Anchors such as Peter Jennings and Dan Rather have left the conventions early, the networks provide no more than an hour or two nightly, and much of that time is given over to commentators rather than the party politicians. Ironically, the parties' efforts to change their conventions to please television has been reciprocated by neglect and disdain.

Nearly fifty years ago, an insightful political scientist predicted this decline. By 1976, William Carleton foresaw, conventions would be held only to ratify previous decisions and "to stage a rally for the benefit of the national television audience."[14] Indeed, if they were not superb campaign rallies, parties might not need to hold conventions at all. They were essentially superfluous in half of the conventions since 1956—the nine which renominated incumbent presidents, and the four that chose the incumbent vice president.[15] These candidates also determined all other convention decisions, leaving the delegates with no real business at hand. Even in the remaining conventions of this period, the presidential nominee still dominated the proceedings.

Kerry carried this development to its logical conclusion, when he considered avoiding his formal nomination at the convention, in order to preserve his freedom to spend campaign funds outside of limitations on money provided by the government.[16] When he decided against this untraditional action, his website explanation implicitly showed how the campaign rally had become the major function of the convention: "John Kerry has decided to accept the nomination in Boston as planned, rejecting suggestions that he delay and raise primary funds for an additional five weeks. He wants nomination night to be a defining moment—one that propels us toward victory on November 2nd. And he believes our history-making grassroots campaign will overcome George Bush's five-week advantage."[17]

CONVENTIONS AS POLITICAL RITUALS

Yet the conventions remain, and remain important. They are no longer significant sites for political decisions. Rather, they are important as rituals, as political rites of passage.

The entire convention can be seen as a political ritual: "Ritual action has a formal quality to it. It follows highly structured, standardized sequences and is often enacted at certain places and times that are themselves endowed with special symbolic meaning. Ritual action is repetitive and, therefore, often redundant, but these very factors serve as important means of channeling emotion, guiding cognition, and organizing social groups."[18]

Much of the convention's events exemplify ritual. They are laden with symbols, such as the flag. The recall the history of the group, as in the invocation of past leaders and triumphs. Their sites are chosen for symbolic resonance—the Republicans in New York seeking to recall the events of September 11, 2001, the Democrats in Boston seeking to recall the birth of the American Revolution. They are staged events, using multimedia techniques to develop desired emotional responses, building to the dramatic climaxes of the presidential candidate's nomination and acceptance speech.

The convention itself is a ritualized form of representative democracy. In form, the delegates are making decisions on program, party government, and leadership. In reality, it resembles a village meeting in Tanzania described by Sally Falk Moore:

> For all the explicit verbal commitment to popular initiative, participation, and self-government, to welcoming suggestions from the citizenry, the autocratic and preemptory behavior of the Party officials running the meeting made the opposite quite clear. Only certain very limited proposals made by the rank and file would be welcomed. . . .
>
> The Kilimanjaro meeting was a form of political co-ceremoniality staged in such a way as to allow the interpretation that it was an outer sign of political agreement. But to allow this inference, all that was required were the common acts. Attendance, an appearance of political attention, applause when given the sign, some supporting speeches, and an absence of expressions of serious objection were needed. The leader-

ship could interpret these as a sign of success, as legitimation of its role, and as a carrying forward both of immediate practical tasks and long term political education.[19]

Within the overall convention ritual, there is special significance in what anthropologists have defined as a "rite of passage." The originator of the term explained, "The life of an individual in any society is a series of passages from one age to another and from one occupation to another. Wherever there are fine distinctions among age or occupational groups, progression from one group to the next is accompanied by special acts. . . . For every one of these events there are ceremonies whose essential purpose is to enable the individual to pass from one defined position to another which is equally well defined."[20]

Particularly relevant to our subject are "rituals of status elevation, in which the ritual subject or novice is being conveyed irreversibly from a lower to a higher position in an institutionalized system." Like birth, puberty, marriage, and death, these are "moments of transition which all societies ritualize and publicly mark with suitable observances to impress the significance of the individual and the group on living members of the community."[21]

As a rite of passage for the nominee, we can compare the conventions to nonpolitical rites in our society, such as a wedding ceremony or a bar mitzvah.[22] In these rites, the outcome is not in doubt. In both, the central drama involves the protagonist single-handedly overcoming a challenge of his leadership and his verbal abilities—for the bar mitzvah reading the Torah and prayers, for the candidate reading his acceptance speech. Although these persons are tested, they inevitably succeed. Nobody ever fails a bar mitzvah, and no presumptive candidate ever fails nowadays to receive the party nomination.[23]

The arrangements for both rites are similar. The central figures are isolated and then stirringly introduced to the audience before their climactic appearances. The impact of the ceremonies is enhanced by the witnessing attendance of large numbers of well-wishers, making the extravagant size of the conventions or the crowding of bar mitzvah celebrants desirable rather than clumsy. These occasions also bring financial gifts—federal campaign funds for candidates ($75 million in 2004) or the gifts of family and friends at a bar mitzvah (less, but still generous).

Although the outcome is fully known in advance and predictably choreographed, rites of passage gain even more impact by following prescribed routines that invoke emotive symbols of identification. They bring recognition, social support, and even power to the person who goes through the rites. The final result is a change in status for the celebrant, marking his maturation into a different role. "Today I am a man," according to the imagined cliché of the bar mitzvah; "Today I am (almost) President of the United States," the nominee might hopefully intone.

Like a bar mitzvah, a convention may have different impacts on the candidates who pass through this ritual. Some may accept "the cynical view," that the event "is just a performance, a time when a young person learns ancient skills of cantillation and gives a recital demonstrating competence." Or the candidate may come through the experience more like "adolescents [who] have wrestled with themselves and with God [and now] can enter adulthood, not with complacency but with the goal of striving for self-improvement and for *tikkun olam,* making the world a better place."[24]

Through its rites of passage, the convention invests its nominees with new authority as leader of the party and a possible president. As David Kertzer explains, "In order to invest a person with authority over others, there must be an effective means for changing the way other people view that person.... That the same person one moment has no such authority and at a subsequent moment acquires it must be represented through ritual performances."[25]

The final act of a convention is the presidential candidate's acceptance speech. The speech is significant as a policy statement and as a campaign tactic. But, viewed as a ritualized rite of passage, it is most important as a claim to authority:

> The political leader who wants to create the public impression that he is a champion of justice, equity, and the general good is far more likely to achieve a deeper and more lasting impression by staging a dramatic presentation of this image than he is by simply asserting it verbally. His appearance should be replete with appropriate symbols and managed by a team of supporting actors.... The drama not only constructs a certain view of the situation, but it also engenders an emotional response that associates notions of right and wrong with the elements in this view. It is, indeed, a moral drama, not just an instructional presentation.[26]

In this final ritual of the convention, as the crowd roars, the candidates are joined on the rostrum by scores of party officials, including defeated aspirants. It is a symbolic act of unity and deference to the new chief, resembling the toasts of "Long Live the King" at a royal coronation. As befits a democracy, there is no anointment oil, only balloons fall on the leader's head; there is no deferential kissing of hands, only egalitarian handshakes, hugs, and kisses. Yet, as Henry Jones Ford wrote of the presidency itself, the formal nomination of the candidate "has revived the oldest political institution of the race, the elective kingship. It is all there: the precognition of the notables and the tumultuous choice of the freemen, only conformed to modern conditions."[27]

RITUAL AND REFORM

Party conventions will endure, though perhaps only as political rituals. But their future role remains unclear and subject to change. One direction for reform would be to attempt to revive the conventions' power over the selection of party leadership. Political scientists continue to advocate greater "peer review" through fuller involvement by party and elected officials, who "understand what it takes to satisfy an electoral majority . . . are frequently well acquainted with the potential nominees and can share this experience and knowledge with the other delegates . . . [and] are in a position to broker a tumultuous conclave and smooth over conflict."[28]

An expanded role for professional politicians could come in two ways. One is to increase the number of elected officials chosen as delegates. For a time, particularly among Democrats in the 1970s, the conventions were becoming bereft of this leadership. More recently, the Democrats have given automatic seats to their leading officials such as members of Congress and the party national committee, and allowed them to be unpledged to any candidate, while Republicans have included these leaders in the state delegations. Despite their presence, however, they have not increased the autonomy of the conventions because these leaders too have eagerly joined the bandwagons of the leading presidential candidates.

A more radical proposal is to change the timing of the conventions to solve the basic problem in nominations, "the fact that the alternatives of choice must be discovered as part of the process. The choices must somehow be reduced to a manageable number; and in open nominating situations, even after a considerable amount of clarification has occurred, the number of genuine availables is seldom as few as two."[29] As the contemporary nominating process has developed, these alternatives are not well defined or are defined outside of the expertise of politicians. The presidential candidates are reviewed neither by their peers nor over an extended period but hastily by the media or unrepresentative electorates. The process prevents the deliberative consideration that was once potentially available through conventions.

Currently, potential candidates are first reviewed by media pundits, judging which candidates are "mentionable," often tending to disparage all of them as "the seven [or more or fewer] dwarfs," as they characterized the Democratic candidates of 2004 and the Republican aspirants in 1996. A great deal of attention is then paid to the first contests, the sparsely attended Iowa caucuses and the primary in highly atypical New Hampshire.[30] Because early victories are thought to create momentum for the winners in these states, others have moved their primaries earlier and earlier in the calendar year, "front-loading" the nomination process so that the contest is resolved very early in the election year.[31] In effect, the United States already has an unacknowledged national primary—the "Super Tuesday" of state primaries in March, but without the time for full consideration of the alternative candidates. Voters respond uneasily to the early results, trying to make choices with scant information, even before most of them have thought seriously about the presidential election.[32] By the time knowledgeable politicians are involved, the contest is effectively over, resulting in the possibility that the party will soon feel "buyer's remorse," but with no means to choose a more appropriate candidate.

One common proposal—a national presidential primary—would not resolve these problems; indeed it would worsen them. A national primary would effectively limit the presidential nomination race to the most well-funded, most prominent, and most telegenic aspirants. It would be conducted largely through the mass media, adding to the expense of campaigns while ruling out most new candidates, and would not provide the opportunity for voters' reconsideration of their initial preferences. The earlier cautionary conclusion of the Brookings scholars is still appropriate: "It thus seems unlikely that any form of national primary could be trusted to do as good a job as the conventions in finding and installing the popular choice of each party."[33]

A different, and potentially better, reform would be to hold the party conventions before rather than after the state presidential primaries.[34] Adopting the practice in a number of states, national party leaders could meet in a mini-convention to review the candidates and select a small number for ultimate decision by the voters in a national primary. This system would combine the expert peer knowledge of politicians with democratic participation by all interested voters. (Still more radically, the nominee could be chosen by enrolled party members in a combination of mail, telephone, and Internet polling.) Every Democrat or Republican participating in the national primary would then have equal weight, in contrast to the present system, which gives unjustifiable power to voters in early states and leaves the others impotent.

There are great practical problems in establishing such a system. Who would be the legitimate participants in the miniconvention and in the national primary? Wouldn't presidential aspirants conduct the same kind of campaigns for delegates to the miniconventions as they now do for delegates to the established national conventions? What rules would govern participation in a national primary? Would a second, run-off primary be needed if no candidate won an absolute majority? Would there be a second, mass convention to ratify the primary choice and conduct the opening campaign rally? Would federal legislation or even a constitutional amendment be necessary?

While all of these practical problems could likely be resolved, their complexities probably make such a course unfeasible. The major obstacle is ideological; this system can easily appear undemocratic, an attempt to return to the fabled "smoke-filled room." The American electorate does not take kindly to suggestions that it needs guidance from experts, and certainly not from politicians. And those candidates who were not favored by party officials would surely exploit this sentiment.

We are probably, then, stuck with something like the present system, and its appearance—dubious as it is—of openness to candidates and responsiveness to voters. Conventions are more likely than not to remain political rituals and campaign rallies. Yet, there may still be ways to reform the conventions, at least to make their campaign rallies more useful to reasonable electoral choice.

A change in the schedule of primaries can better the convention campaign rally, even as it might improve the selection process itself. In 2000, both parties considered a proposal to alter the schedule to have the states vote on a monthly basis from March to June. The contests would be grouped each month according to the population of the states, moving progressively from the smallest states (such as New Hampshire) to the largest (such as California). This arrangement would allow new candidates to emerge in the beginning through local canvassing and would facilitate extended consideration and peer review of the aspirants, give equal weight to every primary voter, and still accord the decisive voice to the largest, media-oriented states. The new system would build interest and suspense over an extended period and make the ultimate nominee a clear favorite among all of the party's voters. Greater legitimacy and fuller voter participation would make the convention's campaign rally more enthusiastic, more genuine, and more convincing to the viewing public.

Adoption of this plan faces many practical obstacles in implementation, particularly the need for changes in state election legislation, although party rules can override state law. The greatest obstacle, however, comes from the lack of political will by the parties themselves. Among Republicans, despite prestigious sponsorship, the plan was ditched in 2000 to avoid a convention fight that might disrupt the party's desired image of unity behind Bush.[35] Democrats gave even less attention to the proposal, instead opting to allow still more "front-loading" of primaries, in the belief that early resolution of the nomination would give their presidential candidate more time to win the general election.[36] These short-term considerations are likely regularly to prevail over the longer-term benefits of fuller representation and more extended consideration.

Even if it remains not fully representative and not at all deliberative, the convention could still be changed to improve its role as a ritual campaign rally. The following changes might be helpful.

The formal conventions could well be shorter. As it stands, there is insufficient business before the delegates to fill four days and nights; in fact many, perhaps most, delegates do not attend the first two days of speeches and parliamentary motions, unless a member of their own delegation is on the rostrum. In an abbreviated schedule, the parties could accomplish their organizational business on one day and nominate on the second, while hearing one or two especially moving presentations, and then cheer the nominees' acceptance speeches on the third day. Other national organizations (even the American Political Science Association!) are able to accomplish their tasks in shorter time; the parties might follow their example.

More concise and dramatic, shortened conventions would be likely to draw more extended television coverage and a larger overall audience, with more focus on the party's own message—the essentials of successful campaign rallies. There would still be plenty of off-the-floor time for interest group meetings, campaign workshops, cause rallies, and just plain fun before the convention formally convened, during its recesses, and after the final gavel. With a more concentrated schedule, the intensity of the convention would be greater and the televised spectacle more attractive.

Some of the functions of the convention could be shifted to their national committees. When presidential nominating conventions were first established, the national committees were only campaign organizations, disappearing after the election. Now, they are large, permanent, and professional institutions, central to the party cause.[37] Deferring to an incumbent president or prospective candidate, they already effectively write the party platform and establish its governing rules. If these realities were recognized in party statutes, the convention could concentrate on its remaining functions—acknowledging the rite of passage of the nominee and cheering this leader at its exuberant campaign rally.

Platforms particularly could be entrusted to the national committees. The conventions now do little more than ratify the programmatic statements developed through the central party organs—the White House and the national committees. Compared to the historical periods when they were actually constructed at the party conclaves, they are longer and more detailed, and reflect broader input through open public hearings. Disputes over the platform are rare because the party wants to avoid any open fights that would disrupt the known candidate's campaign. The platform would be even less threatening to election prospects if it were adopted after the convention (as is true in some states like New Jersey), when the presidential candidate is fully legitimated. Since actual implementation of the platform will depend on the election victory of the presidential candidate, party accountability would be enhanced if he and his party had to assume open responsibility for the manifesto. Resolving any policy disputes would also provide a good test of the candidate's leadership abilities.[38]

These proposals would not radically change the party conventions but rather would recognize the realities of their changed character. Party conventions, strange as they are, have sometimes succeeded brilliantly. As one analyst wrote, amazed, of Lincoln's nomination: "Midnight conferences of liquor-stimulated politicians, deals for jobs, local leaders pulling wires to save their state tickets, petty malice, and personal jealousies—a strange compound, and the man of destiny emerges."[39] In their new role, no new men (or women) of destiny will emerge from the convention hall, and delegates will be able to do little more than cheer lustily for their predetermined choice.

Yet politics also requires its rituals to enlist the labors and loyalties of democratic citizens. Convention delegates no longer choose the actors of our national election drama, but they still are vital participating audiences, helping to provide what American and all other politics always needs: theater, "that which is mystic in its claims; that which is occult in its mode of action; that which is brilliant to the eye; that which is seen vividly for a moment, and then is seen no more; that which is hidden and unhidden; that which is specious, and yet interesting, palpable in its seeming, and yet professing to be more than palpable in its results."[40] On with the show!

NOTES

1. Murat Halstead, *Three Against Lincoln*, ed. William Hesseltine (1860; reprint, Baton Rouge: Louisiana State University Press, 1960), 161–63.

2. Howard Kurtz, "In Boston and New York, Predictable Coverage for Predictable Conventions," *Washington Post*, May 31, 2004, C1.

3. Paul T. David, Ralph M. Goldman, and Richard C. Bain, *The Politics of National Party Conventions* (Washington: Brookings Institution, 1960); Paul T. David, ed., *Presidential Nominating Politics in 1952*, 5 vols. (Baltimore, MD: Johns Hopkins University Press, 1954)

4. The insistence on delegate loyalty was underlined among Republicans in 2004. A gay activist and council member was removed from the District of Columbia delegation after he said he would vote for Bush's renomination at the convention but would then oppose the president in the general election; see Vanessa Williams, "Catania Leaves D.C. GOP Over Convention Seat," *Washington Post*, May 28, 2004, B01.

5. William G. Mayer, *The Making of the Presidential Candidates 2004* (Lanham, MD: Rowman and Littlefield, 2004), chap. 3.

6. William G. Mayer, "Handicapping the 2004 Nomination Race: An Early Fall Prospectus," *Forum* 1 (2003); available at www.bepress.com (accessed June 10, 2004).

7. Donald Bruce Johnson, ed., *National Party Platforms* (Urbana: University of Illinois Press, 1978).

8. David, Goldman, and Bain, *Politics*, 498.

9. M. Ostorgorskii, *Democracy and the Organization of Political Parties*, 2 vols. (1902; reprint, Garden City, NY: Doubleday Anchor, 1964).

10. Gerald M. Pomper and Susan S. Lederman, *Elections in America*, 2d ed. (New York: Longman, 1980); Gerald M. Pomper, "Parliamentary Government in the United States: A New Regime for a New Century?" in John C Green and Rick Farmer, eds., *The State of the Parties*, 4th ed. (Lanham, MD: Rowman and Littlefield, 2003).

11. Bryon E. Shafer, *Bifurcated Politics: Evolution and Reform in the National Party Convention* (Cambridge, MA: Harvard University Press, 1988).

12. For analysis of the realities of participatory organizations, see Jane J. Mansbridge, *Beyond Adversary Democracy* (New York: Basic, 1980).

13. Timothy E. Cook, *Governing With the News* (Chicago: University of Chicago Press, 1998).

14. William G. Carleton, "The Revolution in the Presidential Nominating Convention," *Political Science Quarterly* 72 (June 1957): 224–40. Belatedly, I recant my early disagreement with Carleton's insightful predictions in chapter 9 of *Nominating the President* (Evansville, IL: Northwestern University Press, 1963).

15. We might even add a fifth convention to the list, the 1984 nomination of former vice president Walter Mondale. If he and Carter had been reelected in 1980, Mondale would have been a prohibitive favorite for the nomination, which he won anyway.

16. Nebra Pickler, "Kerry May Delay Acceptance of Nomination," *Washington Post,* May 21, 2004.

17. johnkerry.com, May 28, 2004 (accessed June 10, 2004).

18. David I. Kertzer, *Ritual, Politics, and Power* (New Haven, CT: Yale University Press, 1988).

19. Sally Falk Moore, "Political Meetings and the Simulation of Unanimity: Kilimanjaro 1973," in Moore Myerhoff and Barbara G. Myerhoff, eds., *Secular Ritual* (Amsterdam: Van Gorcum, Assen, 1977).

20. Arnold Van Geenep, *The Rites of Passage,* trans. Monika B. Vizedom and Gabrielle L. Caffee (1908; reprint, Chicago: University of Chicago Press, 1960).

21. Victor W. Turner, *The Ritual Process* (Chicago: Aldine, 1969), 167–68.

22. In this discussion, I refer only to males, although young Jewish women commonly now have a similar ceremony, a bat mitzvah. When a woman is nominated for president, as is likely soon, it would be appropriate to use both male and female gender terms.

23. The same certain result is true of wedding ceremonies. Although marriages often do not succeed, the wedding ceremony itself almost always comes to its predicted happy conclusion. Storied fears of brides being left at the altar (as in movies like *The Graduate* and *My Best Friend's Wedding*) are themselves part of the ritual of commitment.

24. Melvin L. Silberman and Shoshana R. Silberman, "From Bar/Bat Mitzvah Through the Teen Years," in Rela M. Geffen, ed., *Celebration & Renewal; Rites of Passage in Judaism* (Philadelphia: Jewish Publication Society, 1993), 62, 69.

25. Kertzer, *Ritual, Politics, and Power,* 40–41.

26. Ibid.

27. Henry Jones Ford, *The Rise and Growth of American Politics* (1898; reprint, New York: Da Capo, 1967).

28. Larry J. Sabato, *The Party's Just Begun* (Glenview, IL: Scott, Foresman, 1988).

29. David, Goldman, and Bain, *Politics.*

30. Gary R. Orren and Nelson W. Polsby, eds., *Media and Momentum: The New Hampshire Primary and Nomination Politics* (Chatham, NJ: Chatham House, 1987).

31. William G. Mayer and Andrew E. Busch, *The Front-Loading Problem in Presidential Nominations* (Washington, DC: Brookings Institution, 2004).

32. Larry M. Bartels, *Presidential Primaries and the Dynamics of Public Choice* (Princeton: Princeton University Press, 1988); Paul R. Abramson, John H. Aldrich, Phil Paolino, and David W. Rhode " 'Sophisticated' Voting in the 1988 Presidential Primaries," *American Political Science Review* 86 (March 1992): 55–69.

33. David, Goldman, and Bain, *Politics.*

34. This is not a new idea. A good case for this plan was presented twenty years ago by Thomas Cronin and Robert Loevy, "The Case for a National Pre-Primary Convention Plan," *Public Opinion* 6 (Dec.–Jan. 1983): 50–53.

35. Adam Clymer, "G.O.P. Panel Seeks to Alter Schedule of Primary Voting," *New York Times,* May 3, 2000, A1.

36. Democratic National Committee, *Beyond 2000* (Washington, DC: Democratic National Committee, 2000).

37. Leon Epstein, *Political Parties in the American Mold* (Madison: University of Wisconsin Press, 1986), chap. 7; John K. White and Daniel M. Shea, *New Party Politics*, rev. ed. (Belmont, CA: Thomson/Wadsworth, 2004), 105–11.

38. This proposed practice would be in keeping with current notions of party responsibility. See John C. Green and Paul Herrnson, *Responsible Partisanship? The Evolution of American Political Parties Since 1950* (Lawrence: University of Kansas Press, 2002).

39. Eugene H. Roseboom, *A History of Presidential Elections* (New York: Macmillan, 1959), 180.

40. Walter Bagehot, *The English Constitution* (1867; reprint, London: Oxford University Press, 1958), 7.

CONTRIBUTORS

John C. Berg is professor of Government and Director of Graduate Studies at Suffolk University. His publications include *Unequal Struggle: Class, Gender, Race and Power in the U.S. Congress* and *Teamsters and Turtles? U.S. Progressive Political Movements in the 21st Century.*

Michael Cornfield is a consultant at the Pew Internet and American Life Project. Cornfield studies campaign politics, public discourse, and the Internet, and is the author of *Politics Moves Online: Campaigning and the Internet* and *The Civic Web: Online Politics and Democratic Values,* co-edited with David M. Anderson. Cornfield writes a monthly column for *Campaigns and Elections,* the leading trade publication for professional politicians. Cornfield is also an adjunct professor at the Graduate School of Political Management (GSPM) of the George Washington University, where he has taught the core course on strategy and message development since 1994. Cornfield received his B.A. from Pomona College and his Ph.D. from Harvard University. He has previously taught at the University of Virginia and the College of William and Mary.

Terri Susan Fine is an associate professor of Political Science at the University of Central Florida. Her research interests include women and politics, public opinion and voting behavior, and political methodology.

Peter L. Francia is an assistant professor in the Department of Political Science at East Carolina University. He received his Ph.D. in 2000 from the Department of Government and Politics at the University of Maryland, College Park. He is author of *The Future of Organized Labor* and co-author of *The Financiers of Congressional Elections: Investors, Ideologues and Intimates.* His work has also appeared in *Social Science Quarterly, American Politics Research,* and *State Politics and Policy Quarterly.*

R. Sam Garrett is a Ph.D. candidate in the Department of Government at American University. He serves as an instructor in the Department of Government and is the assistant director for research at the Center for Congressional and Presidential Studies. Garrett has been affiliated with the center since 2000, contributing to a variety of projects on campaigns and elections, political consulting and congressional-presidential relations.

John C. Green is a professor of political science at the University of Akron and director of the Ray C. Bliss Institute of Applied Politics, a bipartisan research and teaching institute dedicated to the nuts and bolts of practical politics. Green has published widely in various research areas. He is the co-editor of *The State of the Parties: The Changing Role of Contemporary Party Politics,* now in its third edition, *Multiparty Politics in America,* and *The Politics of Ideas: Intellectual Challenges to the Major Parties.* He is the editor of *Vox Pop,* the newsletter of the Political Organizations and Parties Section of the American Political Science Association. Green is the editor of *Financing the 1996 Elections* and the author of numerous articles on campaign finance in scholarly journals and collections. He is also co-author of *The Bully Pulpit: The Politics of Protestant Clergy* and *Religion and the Culture Wars: Dispatches From the Front.*

Michael G. Hagen is a professor of political science at Temple University. He is co-author (with Richard Johnston and Kathleen Hall Jamieson) of *The Presidential Campaign of 2000 and the Foundations of Party Politics;* co-author (with Paul M. Sniderman) of *Race and Inequality: A Study in American Values;* and a contributor to *Reasoning and Choice: Explorations in Political Psychology,* winner of the American Political Science Association's Woodrow Wilson Foundation Award for 1991. Hagen was previously Associate Professor and Director of Undergraduate Studies in the Department of Government at Harvard University. He also has taught at the Annenberg School for Communication at the University of Pennsylvania, where he was a senior research fellow and co-director of the Annenberg 2000 Election Survey. He earned his B.A. from Stanford University and his M.A. and Ph.D. from the University of California, Berkeley. Hagen was most recently the director of the Center for Public Interest Polling (CPIP) at the Eagleton Institute of Politics at Rutgers University.

John S. Jackson III is a visiting professor of political science at Southern Illinois University at Carbondale.

Richard Johnston is a professor and head of the political science department at the University of British Columbia. He is author or co-author of *Public Opinion and Public Policy in Canada: Questions of Confidence; Letting the People Decide: Dynamics of a Canadian Election; The Challenge of Direct Democracy: The 1992 Canadian Referendum;* articles in *CJPS, AJPS, BJPolS, JOP, Electoral Studies,* and other journals; He has won four APSA organized-section best paper prizes. He was principal investigator of the 1988 and 1992–1993 Canadian Election Surveys and a consultant to the 1996 New Zealand Election Study. He was on the Planning Committee for the 1998 US National Election Study Pilot. He is co-investigator on the major collaborative research initiative, "Equality, Security, and Community," at UBC and on the 2000 National Annenberg Election Study at the University of Pennsylvania. His central preoccupation is with public opinion, elections, and representation, with special reference to campaign dynamics and the role of information. He is also interested in connections among social capital, civil society, and support for the welfare state. He received his Ph.D. from Stanford University.

Jonathan S. Morris is an assistant professor of political science at East Carolina University. His research focuses on political communication with particular emphasis on cable news, new media, and the role of entertainment in political news. He has published in journals such as *Political Communication, The Harvard International Journal of Press/Politics,* and *Legislative Studies Quarterly.*

Costas Panagopoulos is a postdoctoral research fellow at the Institution for Social and Policy Studies at Yale University. He is also a visiting assistant professor in the Department of Political Science at Fordham University, where he serves as director of the Elections and Campaign Management Program. He was previously an APSA Congressional Fellow (2004–2005) in Senator Hillary Rodham Clinton's office (D-NY). His articles have appeared in *Public Opinion Quarterly, PS: Political Science and Politics, Presidential Studies Quarterly, Social Science Computer Review, Women & Politics,* and the *Journal of Political Marketing.* He is contributing editor to *Campaigns & Elections* magazine and senior editor of the *Journal of Political Marketing.* He has provided extensive political analysis and commentary for various print and broadcast media outlets, including the *New York Times,* the *Los Angeles Times,* CNN, NBC Nightly News, Fox News, and BBC Television. He received his B.A. in government from Harvard University and his Ph.D. from New York University.

Gerald M. Pomper is Board of Governors Professor of Political Science at the Eagleton Institute of Politics of Rutgers University (Emeritus). A specialist in American elections and politics, he is the author or editor of nineteen books, including *Passions and Interests, Elections in America,* and *Voters' Choice.* His most recent is *The Election of 2000,* the seventh volume in an ongoing series on U.S. national elections. Dr. Pomper also has been a Fulbright or visiting professor at Tel-Aviv University, Oxford, and Australian National University, and held the first Tip O'Neill Chair in Public Life at Northeastern University. He has been honored for career achievement by the American Political Science Association and has served as an expert witness on campaign finance, reapportionment, and political party regulation. At Rutgers for over forty years, he was chairman of the University and Livingston College political science departments.

J. Mark Wrighton is assistant professor of political science at the University of New Hampshire. He served as an APSA Congressional Fellow in 2004–2005.